What Is It Then between Us?

What Is It Then between Us?

Traditions of Love
in American Poetry

ERIC MURPHY SELINGER

Cornell University Press

Ithaca and London

First published 1998 by Cornell University Press

Printed in the United States of America

Library of Congress Cataloging-in-Publication Data
Selinger, Eric Murphy.
    What is it then between us? : traditions of love in
American poetry / Eric Murphy Selinger.
      p.   cm.
    Includes bibliographical references (p.   ) and index.
    ISBN 0-8014-3262-6 (cloth : alk. paper)
    ISBN 0-8014-8466-9 (pb. : alk. paper)
    1. Love poetry, American—History and criticism.
I. Title.
PS310.L65S45   1997
811.009'3543—dc21   97-31041

To Rosalie Selinger Murphy

Nothing yields more pleasure and content to the soul than when it finds that which it may love fervently, for to love and live beloved is the soul's paradise, both here and in heaven.

—JOHN WINTHROP

Contents

Acknowledgments

In 1988 I promised Michael Colacurcio that I would write an essay on Emerson and love. After its many incarnations—as a set of essays, a sprawling dissertation, a much cut manuscript, and now a finished book—this volume makes good on that promise, however little it now mentions Emerson by name. Over the years a number of friends and colleagues have given me support, encouragement, and provocation. My thanks to Martha Banta, Calvin Bedient, Elisabeth Frost, Deborah Garfield, J. D. McClatchy, Barbara Packer, Karl Rosenquist, Maeera Shreiber, Mark Scroggins, and Stephen Yenser.

My thanks to Cornell University Press for its help in bringing this book to fruition, as well as to publication. Bernhard Kendler's early enthusiasm for the project was invaluable, as were his patience and help as I reworked the manuscript. Two anonymous readers provided me with keen, judicious insights. I thank them for their interest and attention to detail.

First and finally, however, I am grateful to my wife, Rosalie Murphy. My first notes on this topic date from our engagement, and she has helped me with it in more ways than she knows. At times when I agreed with the Preacher that "of the making of books there is no end," she was there to remind me of Gertrude Stein's more promising dictum: "In the midst of writing there is merriment." (And to suggest that I take out some quotations.) This book would never have been begun, let alone finished, without her.

A much expanded version of my Emerson discussion has been published as "'Too Pathetic, Too Pitiable': Emerson's Lessons in Love's Philosophy" in *ESQ: A Journal of the American Renaissance* 40 (1994): 139–82, copyright © 1994 by the Board of Regents of Washington State University. A shorter, ear-

lier version of the James Merrill chapter appeared as "James Merrill's Masks of
Eros, Masques of Love" in *Contemporary Literature 35* (Spring 1994): 30–65,
copyright © 1994 by the Board of Regents of the University of Wisconsin System. I thank the anonymous readers of these journals for their suggestions,
and the journals themselves for permission to reprint previously published
work. An extension of my Mina Loy discussion will appear in *Mina Loy: Person
and Poet* (Orono, Me.: National Poetry Foundation, 1997), edited by Keith
Tuma and Maeera Shreiber.

I am grateful for permission to quote the following material:

Lines from "The Crisis," "The Gift," "The Warning," "The Whip," "The
Rain," Something," and "The Hole" by Robert Creeley, from *Collected Poems of
Robert Creeley, 1945–1975*, copyright © 1983 by The Regents of the University
of California, are reprinted by permission of the University of California Press.
Excerpts from *Mabel: A Story*, © Robert Creeley 1972, 1976, 1984, are reprinted from *The Collected Prose of Robert Creeley*, by permission of Marion
Boyars Publishers, New York and London.

Excerpts from a letter by Emily Dickinson are reprinted by permission of
the publishers from *The Letters of Emily Dickinson*, edited by Thomas H. Johnson, Cambridge, Mass.: The Belknap Press of Harvard University Press, copyright © 1958, 1986 by the President and Fellows of Harvard College. Poems
and selections from poems by Emily Dickinson are reprinted by permission of
the publishers and the Trustees of Amherst College from *The Poems of Emily
Dickinson*, edited by Thomas H. Johnson, Cambridge, Mass.: The Belknap
Press of Harvard University Press, copyright © 1951, 1955, 1979, 1983 by the
President and Fellows of Harvard College; quotations from *The Complete
Poems of Emily Dickinson*, edited by T. H. Johnson, copyright 1929, 1935 by
Martha Dickinson Bianchi, copyright © renewed 1957, 1963 by Mary L.
Hampson, are reprinted by permission of Little, Brown and Company.

An excerpt from "Mermaid Emerging" from *The Dolphin* by Robert Lowell,
copyright © 1973 by Robert Lowell, is reprinted by permission of Farrar,
Straus & Giroux, Inc., and Faber and Faber, Ltd.

Excerpts from "Songs to Joannes" from *The Lost Lunar Baedeker* by Mina
Loy, edited by Roger L. Conover, copyright © 1996 by the Estate of Mina Loy,
are reprinted by permission of Farrar, Straus & Giroux, Inc., and Carcanet
Press Limited.

Material by Ezra Pound, Hilda Doolittle, and William Carlos Williams is
used by permission of New Directions Publishing Corporation: from *The Collected Early Poems of Ezra Pound*, copyright © 1934, 1968 by Ezra Pound; from
The Cantos, copyright © 1976 by the Trustees of the Ezra Pound Literary

ACKNOWLEDGMENTS

Property Trust. From *Hermetic Definition* by Hilda Doolitte, copyright © 1972 by Normon Holmes Pearson. From *Imaginations* by William Carlos Williams, copyright © 1970 by Florence H. Williams. From *The Collected Poems of William Carlos Williams: Volume I, 1909–1939* and *Volume II, 1939–1962*, copyright © 1986, 1988 by William Eric Williams and Paul H. Williams.

Selected excerpts from *The Fact of a Doorframe: Poems Selected and New, 1950–1984* by Adrienne Rich, copyright © 1984 by Adrienne Rich, copyright © 1975, 1978 by W. W. Norton & Company, Inc., copyright © 1981 by Adrienne Rich, are reprinted by permission of the author and W. W. Norton & Company, Inc.; selected excerpts from *Time's Power: Poems 1985–1988* by Adrienne Rich, copyright © 1989 by Adrienne Rich, are reprinted by permission of the author and W. W. Norton & Company, Inc.; selected excerpts from *Your Native Land, Your Life: Poems by Adrienne Rich*, copyright © 1986 by Adrienne Rich, are reprinted by permission of the author and W. W. Norton & Company, Inc.

The poem "Galant Chateau," from *Collected Poems* by Wallace Stevens, copyright 1936 by Wallace Stevens and renewed 1964 by Holly Stevens, is reprinted by permission of Alfred A. Knopf, Inc., and Faber & Faber Ltd.

Selected excerpts from the poem "Toward a Definition of Marriage," from *If It Be Not I*, by Mona Van Duyn, copyright © 1959 by Mona Van Duyn, are reprinted by permission of Alfred A. Knopf, Inc.

Quotations from the following works by James Merrill are also reprinted by permission of Alfred A. Knopf, Inc.: *From the First Nine: Poems 1946–1976*, copyright © 1981, 1982 by James Merrill; *A Scattering of Salts*, copyright © 1995 by James Merrill; *Selected Poems 1946–1985*, copyright © 1992 by James Merrill.

The DePaul University Research Council funded these permissions and other expenses in the preparation of this book. I am grateful for their support.

E.M.S.

What Is It Then between Us?

Introduction

"If ever two were one"

The American poet . . . has had as his abiding task the reconciliation of the
impulse to freedom with the impulse to community, as the use of language in
poetry may help bring it about.
— ROY HARVEY PEARCE

The real history of literature is the history of love.
— HAYDEN CARRUTH

Is there a tradition of American love poetry? If any, then many: that, at
least, debates over canon formation ought to have taught us. Indeed, in these
days of prismatic study one might well split the question into a set of distinct
spectral inquiries. A first might look at love in poetry by the poets of a single
cultural moment, teasing out their ideologies and consequent aesthetics; an-
other might focus on poems by men or by women, or on gay or lesbian verse,
and so on. Any less refractive, less fastidious approach appears conservative
at best—a restatement of studies such as Roy Harvey Pearce's *Continuity of
American Poetry* (1961) or *American Poets: Puritans to the Present* (1968) by Hyatt
Waggoner. At worst, it can blur the varied shades of American affection into
one dull stream of off-white light.

Still, one must start somewhere. And since no one before me has put to-
gether a book on American poetry of love, either a critical study or an anthol-
ogy, I have no monolith to undermine, no canon to shoot down. Instead I have
the more peaceable pleasure of illuminating, from a new perspective, a largely
familiar landscape, so that the once-discrete rises and wetlands of American
poetry take their place in a single erotic terrain. My guides to this prospect are
Walt Whitman, whose resonant question "What is it then between us?" I have
borrowed for my title, and Robert Creeley, whose claim that "it is the *me* and *you*
which have concerned us [poets in America]—the interstices of human rela-

tionships brought home, so to speak," has rallied me when the project seemed most scattered.[1] With an eye to both broad contours and local detail, I want to trace a second, long-overlooked "continuity of American poetry." In it, Pearce's "abiding task" of using poetic language to reconcile "the impulse to freedom with the impulse to community" plays out in a more intimate, less strenuously masculine key.[2]

From Anne Bradstreet to James Merrill and Adrienne Rich, American poets have implicated questions of poetics in questions of love. "What is it then between us?" they demand. What separates the American "me" and "you"? Can love or language close that gap, perhaps when a poem "fuses me into you now, and pours my meaning into you," as Whitman writes in "Crossing Brooklyn Ferry"?[3] Or is such fusion unattainable—and if so, what is to blame? (Flaws in the self and the love it can muster are the usual suspects, as is the way, for a poet, the words at hand compete with the person in mind.) If two can never be one, they wonder, what about some other, more chastened connection? Love's federal paradox of liberty and union has an enduring attraction for American poets, no doubt because of its political familiarity. Think of Emily Dickinson's pledge, in an early letter, that she and her Valentine "will be David and Jonathan, or Damon and Pythias, or what is better than either, the United States of America."[4] The mutual recognition between two still-sovereign lovers might write small the larger community so many of our poets dream of, an "America of love."[5] What, though, would such love look like as *art*? What blazons, idealizations, allusions, and other traditions of lyric must be sacrificed to capture its intersubjective dailiness, its dialogic tension? Is their loss, in the end, worth the gain?

These are not exclusively American concerns. Some of them date back to archaic Greece, where poets such as Sappho and Archilochos first defined the three-part structure of "lover, beloved, and that which comes between them."[6] Such love is essentially a mode of desire, in which the actual beloved is the occasion for and object of the lover's imagination. For all that it may dream of perfect union, this love demands a certain distance, dodging reciprocity. It flowers in the fine, frustrated romances of Petrarchism, where the Lady and her poet never squander their attraction in the duties of domestic life or the brief commotion of actual sex.[7] And, as Freud understood, it lives under the "law of ambivalence," in which "loved ones are on the one hand an inner possession, an ingredient of our personal ego, but on the other hand are partly strangers, even enemies," simply because of their continued exteriority.[8]

The writers I have chosen for this book are, by and large, uneasy with this first tradition of love. They may still use it. (Few traditions have a prouder pedigree.) But they are often drawn to a more recent, and contrasting, companionate ideal. This ideal may date back to ancient times as well.[9] It has flourished, however, both as theory and as art, mostly since the English Renaissance. English Protestant preachers mocked the Petrarchan structure of idealizing, ever-unacted desire. In its place they offered the delights and cares of marriage, where the lover joins "in conjugal fellowship a fit conversing soul."[10] So did poets such as Spenser, Jonson, Shakespeare, and above all Milton, whose hymns to wedded love in *Paradise Lost* have shaped, according to Anthony Low, "a substitute Petrarchism for our time."[11] Indeed, modern writers on love often insist that it is, properly speaking, a mode of *relationship* between two people, married or otherwise, and not a state of the lover's or poet's mind. The free play of the imagination must answer to the actual beloved in his or her fullest particularity. The "Other than self / O inconceivable" must become an "O believable" at last, and the "me" and "you" respond to each other with what Ortega y Gasset calls "warm corroboration."[12]

The split between these two traditions runs deep, and may be irreconcilable. Proponents of the second sort of love, from Milton to Simone de Beauvoir, see the first as idolatrous and inauthentic, a mask for narcissism. The partisans of Eros, for their part, see the first love as hardly worthy of the name. ("I'm talking about love, and you're talking about *marriage!*" a colleague once admonished me. And they say courtly love is dead.) For American poets, however, this tension between love's imagination and its enactment, its aesthetics and its ethics, has been quite productive, especially as the question of how to love bears on the question of how to write. Does a poem of companionate love require, for example, the presence of two voices, whether engaged in Miltonic "fit conversation" or mere bickering? May it be shapely and accomplished, or should it be loose, improvised, or serial in form? If the redeeming design of a poem wins aesthetic victory from an ethical or emotional defeat, is this a good thing, or an evasion? What about when a poet's allusive praise turns the merely human beloved into a less authentic, but perhaps more poetic, Master or Mantram or Muse?

Other writers on literature and love, including some of the best, have felt the need to choose sides between these two traditions.[13] To avoid this, while still availing myself of their insights, I turn also to philosopher Irving Singer. In his magisterial three-volume history *The Nature of Love*, Singer sifts accounts of love into two broad categories, appealing in their Jamesian openness.[14] On the one hand, he explains, there are writers and philosophers who think of love as the pursuit of perfect union or reunion. Singer calls this the *idealist* tradition; its great source-text is Plato's *Symposium.* Here Aristophanes sketches the

4

comic scene of our cartwheeling, self-sufficient progenitors, split by Zeus like halves of a fillet, longing for their lost completion. "Love is always trying to re-integrate our former nature," he argues, "to make two into one, and to bridge the gulf between one human being and another," yielding "an utter oneness with the beloved."[15] Whenever lovers aim at a mystical merger, an *absolute* satisfaction in which contingency and difference melt away, this tradition is at work, whether that merger is with another person or with the divine.

In the contrasting *realist* tradition, love is "an overlapping or wedding of interests rather than a merging of personalities" (Singer 2:6). The grand metaphysical claims of idealist lovers reveal, in a realist light, psychological facts; and realists from Ovid to Proust have sketched the failures, disappointments, and self-deceptions of a lover's push to oneness.[16] They have also proposed a number of disillusioned, but perhaps thereby more lasting, visions of romance. The "metaphysical isolation of man" does not just "teach us independence," Emerson pledges in "Manners." It also lets lovers "guard their strangeness"—indeed, it is "myrrh and rosemary to keep the other sweet."[17] More recent feminist thinkers propose that love need not aspire to sublime or idealist union because we aren't all that separate to begin with. We do not want, as a rule, "the impossible absolutes of 'oneness' and perfection," writes Jessica Benjamin. A dash of difference ensures that there is a world outside the self, delightful or recalcitrant, nourishing, real. "Things don't have to be perfect," Benjamin assures us; "in fact, it is better if they are not"—a paradox I return to throughout this book.[18]

As space permits, then, and insight requires, I read my poets in these broader contexts. In this introduction, for example, I show how Anne Bradstreet finds a compositional spur in Puritanism's careful balance of idealist and realist loves. Her allusive aesthetic of "seeming thine," despite theological strictures, will be a useful reference point as later poet-lovers negotiate between idealization and strict conscience. As the Puritan *ars amorica* evolves through Milton's hymns to marriage into the mix of sanctity and sentiment that Robert Polhemus calls "erotic faith," it breeds dissenters, including Ralph Waldo Emerson.[19] His undeceived philosophy of love recapitulates Puritan distinctions between idolatrous and duly weaned affections, while his vision of the "great and crescive self" proves more jealous than the God it is modeled on.[20] Emerson offers a number of escapes from solitude. He cannot write the poetry they suggest, but his wariness joins erotic faith in two poets who can: Walt Whitman and Emily Dickinson.

In Chapter 1, I show how Whitman replaces Emersonian anxieties with a poetic of "acceptation" and idealizing praise—an imaginative mix that Singer calls "bestowal." Through bestowal, Whitman trades the impossible idealist dream of merger for a realist rhythm of identification and withdrawal. He uses this rhythm to enact a love-cure of the reader, with the "I" of *Leaves of Grass* alternatively our therapist and an exemplary patient. We need his love to draw us out of melancholia, and he needs our bestowals to keep his verses from being merely *literature*, lyric poems whose words do not accomplish contact but rather take the place of those the poet loves.

Dickinson, too, offers an ideal of love as contact—but her poems do not ease anxiety so much as they tease it. Chapter 2 outlines her engagement with Puritan and sentimental topoi, especially of marriage. I read her poems of defiant devotion through lenses supplied by Simone de Beauvoir and Emerson, and show how the love she calls "Bondage as Play" allows her "great and crescive self" to be restrained, overmatched, and thereby *met*. This strategy is as visible in her poems of love for Susan Gilbert, I argue, as it is in those for any putative male Master. As "Susan's Idolator" adopts the role of suffering poet-lover, she lays claim to an inherited, largely male tradition of love poetry and sets the foundation for a modern poetics of "authentic" intersubjective love.[21]

By the early 1920s, Victorian erotic faith had been widely upbraided and debunked. Its old codes of romance were undermined by a corrosive realism that J. W. Krutch, at the end of the decade, deplored as "the modern temper."[22] In Chapter 3 I use Mina Loy's *Songs to Joannes* to unfold the aesthetic implications of this crisis in love's meaning and value, then explore two sets of responses. T. S. Eliot, Ezra Pound, and H.D. answer the modern temper by allusively resuscitating premodern ideals of erotic experience and meaning, which Pound names "the secret ways of love." Wallace Stevens and William Carlos Williams (and Gertrude Stein, among others) give a second, more secular response. Building on the realist dream of companionate affection, they find contrasting poetic means to enact what Jessica Benjamin calls the "decisive problem" of modern love: that of *"recognizing the other."*[23] Stevens meditates, in a despairing tone, on how the woman loved slips away into signs. Pledging himself to the Muse who remains, but owning up to his failure and loss, he turns romantic loss to reflective, conscientious, aesthetic gain. Williams, by contrast, trusts that a revitalization of both love and poetry will follow on moments of amatory crisis. The clash and reconciliation he seeks proves a couple's authentic encounter, and it supplies him with a model for a poem's—and a marriage's—redeeming, forgiving design.

These conflicting modes of modern love supply the context for Chapters 4, on Robert Creeley and Robert Lowell, and 5, on Adrienne Rich. Creeley's early sense of marriage as a "hammering at the final edge of contact," drawn from

6

Williams and D. H. Lawrence, underwrites the clenched poems of crisis, divorce, and remarriage in *For Love*.[24] His later dedication to "literal" language and serial composition, notably in *Words*, *Pieces*, and *A Day Book*, works to deconstruct his isolating male ego and make it capable of true relationship, with mixed aesthetic results. A second-generation poet of the "modern temper," Lowell joins Creeley in his pursuit of encounter with a resistant other. In the notebook poetics of his later sonnets, and in the chancy prosopopoeia of *The Dolphin*, where two women's voices confront and console him, Lowell, too, struggles to shrug off solitude and mastery. Again, the results are mixed, both as ethics and aesthetics—and in Chapter 5, I contrast them with the related efforts of Adrienne Rich. I trace Rich's long quarrel with ideals of solitude and amorous community from her poems of marriage in the 1960s into her vision of a lesbian-feminist (and Whitmanian) "America of love." Here, too, however, she finds solitude coming back to haunt her, and she returns to earlier women writers, notably Dickinson and Elizabeth Cady Stanton, to understand its place in her life and art. Where Creeley and Lowell struggle to break out of isolation into relation, Rich must imagine a love among women that will admit the impediments of difference: a love she gives the political name of "mutual recognition."

Creeley, Lowell, and Rich share a period ideal of companionate affection—and, as its proper aesthetics, a period suspicion of too polished an art. Since *Divine Comedies* (1976), James Merrill's work has offered a contrasting vision, in which the arts of love and poetry repair and echo (or "translate") each other. Both are "V-work," he tells us in *The Changing Light at Sandover*: V for *vie*, or life; V for victory, as of the shaping imagination over entropy or melancholy; and V for the number five, as in (among other numerologies) the five feet of a shapely pentameter line. But in his earlier books *Nights and Days* (1966), *The Fire Screen* (1969), and *Braving the Elements* (1972), Merrill approaches the anxieties of his contemporaries. Here he tests a series of myths and metaphors for the relationships between love and illusion, passion and imagination, contact and composition, and he finds them all wanting. Merrill does not aspire to forge an America of love, or to stage the dramas of mutual recognition so central to Emerson, Dickinson (one side of her, at least), Williams, Creeley, Lowell, and Rich. Instead he picks up a thread that links Bradstreet to Whitman, Dickinson (the other side), H.D., and Stevens: that is, a poetry that embraces the power of love's "as if" against theology and conscience and the crisis of the caustic modern temper. "Let the seeming take itself seriously," Julia Kristeva advises postmodern lovers; and indeed, by "turning the crisis into a *work in progress*" Merrill brings this book to an open-ended close.[25]

A word about inclusions and exclusions. This project grew out of an essay on Emerson, Whitman, and Hart Crane, which rapidly expanded forward to John Ashbery. As the study grew, so did the number of relevant poets. Even when I decided to keep contemporary writers out of the picture, I faced an embarrassment of talent. In the end, I decided against the encyclopedic approach. Without pretending to be comprehensive, I chose instead to cast a sort of multigenerational domestic drama, its characters linked by family resemblances, its plot determined, in Hugh Kenner's words, by "our needs and our sense of what is complexly coherent: what accords with the facts, and folds them into a shapely story."[26] Crane and Ashbery now appear only in brief, strategic cameos. Extended treatments of John Berryman's *Sonnets to Chris* and Gertrude Stein's *Lifting Belly* were trimmed. Millay, Zukofsky, Rukeyser, and Swenson show up only for crowd scenes. To Hayden Carruth's *Sleeping Beauty*, which I encountered too late for use in this book, I can offer only this quick admiring nod. I will return to some of these characters; more important, I hope those annoyed by my choices will build on this book and find its literary-historical framework helpful, if only as provocation. I mean no insult to the performances, many delightful or moving, that I have left on the cutting room floor.

Near the end of this book I briefly discuss *The Changing Light at Sandover*, James Merrill's Ouija board epic of devotion, loss, and aesthetic rebuilding. The Sandover ballroom is, among other things, a salon revision of Eden after the Fall, where an assortment of angels replay, with JM and DJ, a scene of instruction like the one that closes *Paradise Lost.* Since William Spengemann has recently proposed we read *Paradise Lost* as an "American" poem, and since the "Doctrine and Discipline of Divorce" is an epochal essay in the history of companionate love, I might in good conscience start with Milton.[27] Early in April 1630, however, some dozen years before Milton's "Doctrine," John Winthrop preached a visionary lay sermon, "A Modell of Christian Charity," to his fellow colonists on the Puritan flagship *Arbella.* (In his audience were Anne Bradstreet, then eighteen, and her husband, Simon, twenty-nine. They had been married two years.) Poised at the start of the Puritan errand, Winthrop's "Modell" has served three generations of American scholars as an almanac, a book of revelations.[28] And since it was "charity," or *caritas*, a variety of love, that Winthrop hoped would make his distant slip of England truly New, his sermon bears a close introductory look here, too.

Like most Puritan sermons, the "Modell" starts with a text: "God Almightie in his most holy and wise providence hath soe disposed of the Condicion of

mankinde, as in all times some must be rich some poore, some highe and emi-
nent in power and dignitie; others meane and in subieccion." Such difference
means incompleteness; incompleteness, need. Need draws us to one another
through the Old Law, by which we must love our neighbors as ourselves, and
through the New, by which we love one another as parts of the Church. Not that
the colonists can do either "duty of loue" on their own. When Adam "rent in
himselfe from his Creator," Winthrop explains, he "rent all his posterity allsoe
one from another, whence it comes that every man is borne with this principle
in him, to loue and seeke himselfe onely." The elect, however, can recognize
their "image and resemblance" in one another, because God recognizes and
loves Himself in them. Their self-love has been replaced by a "continual sup-
ply" of Christ: a complete and ongoing transfusion that allows them, or God
in them, to love "with a pure heart fervently." When Winthrop exhorts his
comrades to "delight in each other, make others' conditions our own, rejoice
together, mourn together, labour and suffer together," and so on, he asks them
to put this regenerate love into action. *E pluribus unum.* Difference falls away,
and the "scattered bones" of "perfect old man Adam" are reconnected and re-
vivified.[29]

Winthrop's city on a hill will thus be a community of lovers. It is the first—
a not-yet-lost—America of love. Like those envisioned by poets from Whit-
man to Rich, Winthrop's amatory ideal aims to cure both social faction and in-
dividual solitude. The social goal is easiest to see. By 1630 the English body
politic was split by class struggle and theological dissent, well on its way to
civil war. As an antidote Winthrop offers the classical trope of the body politic,
seasoned with a taste of what Freud calls *Einfühlung,* an empathic bond
achieved through shared identification with a loving, idealized Father. (*Leaves
of Grass* will make a similar gesture—though its One Man is Whitman, not
Christ.) To spot the threat of *personal* isolation behind the "Modell," how-
ever—a threat just as important for later American poets of love—it helps to
take the sermon on its own religious terms. For Winthrop's vision of union
counters a threat within his own theology: the isolation that Elizabeth Cady
Stanton would later call "our Protestant idea" of "the Solitude of Self."[30]

The "Modell" assumes that its listeners are regenerate, parts of the Body of
Christ. In strict theology, however, only God knows if I am one of the Calvinist
elect. And as Minister Hooper discovers in Hawthorne's story "The Minister's
Black Veil," this theology has the potential for devastating emotional conse-
quences. However plausible the clues, I am as excluded from sure knowledge of
your regeneracy as I am from your sense of yourself, your life as lived from the
inside. As far as certain knowledge of salvation is concerned, no man is *not* an

island, in the end. No wonder Winthrop urges that the colonists must be united in one metaphorical body, and no wonder he insists on God's "more near marriage" to the Puritans. If my connection to other people is always subject to scruples and doubts, how much more do I need the presence of another, indubitable Companion. Setting the stage for the more familiar solitary selves of Emerson, Dickinson, Stevens, and so on, Puritan theology turns the practical difficulty of knowing another person into a metaphysical impossibility.[31]

To ease their version of this solitude, explains Stanley Cavell, Romantic writers "proposed an idea of marriage, call it daily mutual devotedness, as the only path left us for walking away from [the] skeptical doubt of cosmic isolation." The Puritans, however, were wary of this "metaphysically desperate degree of private bonding."[32] Secure in their faith in a heavenly Companion, they did not rely on mutual devotedness to save them, however much they treasured it for its own limited pleasures. They thus opened a space for the sort of love Simone de Beauvoir will call "authentic": a love that does not "pretend to be a mode of salvation" but is instead merely "a human inter-relation."[33] Ask this love to save you, and you sin through idolatry. Scorn it, and you sin again. You miss the sanctioned, necessary cure for what Milton calls our "God-forbidden loneliness."[34]

Milton means that "forbidden" quite literally. God and Adam did not make a sufficient, happy pair. Quite the contrary: their solitude-à-deux is the first thing in creation God declares *not* to be good (Gen. 2:18).[35] The infusion of Christ that knits up the bones of "old man Adam" may salve individual believers. It may bind the community as a whole. But it cannot supply the "fit conversation" that Milton has in mind. For the love supplied by Christ derives from the idealist tradition, in which, as Singer explains, "people lose their individuality [through love], or revert to a profounder oneness that preceded it. They are caught up by, immersed in, something bigger and grander than themselves as separate entities, something that negates and even destroys the boundaries of routine existence."[36] When Winthrop describes the love "between the members of Christ," you can see one such negation of boundaries in a slippery set of pronouns. "When the soul, which is of a sociable nature, finds anything like to itself," Winthrop explains, "it is like Adam when Eue was brought to him, shee must haue it one with herselfe this is fleshe of my fleshe (saith shee) and bone of my bone."[37] The "shee" of Adam's soul takes over his sentences, transforming the scene so that distinctions of gender, and therefore of rank, may be overcome or undermined by love. (*Simil simile gaudet*, Winthrop says of love: "like goes to like." His America of love proves as homoerotic as those of Whitman or Rich.) In an actual Puritan marriage, of course, distinctions of gender and rank were not to be forgotten—a sign that such marriages draw on the more skeptical, realist tradition.

As part of the realist tradition, Milton's ideal of "fit conversation" implies "companionship, solace, mutual concern, and the friendly communication of feelings and ideas."[38] It does not entail merger. When the minor New England Puritan poet John Saffin dotes on the "mutuall Communication" and "mutuall Delights" of marriage, founded on "Oneness of Interest," he sounds the same realist note.[39] Thomas Thatcher echoes it when he courts Margaret Sheafe with a plea for "words":

> I want your words oft, Words convey the Mind.
> Words deeds interpret and do satisfie
> The heart wherein they credit due do find.
> Words raise, Words fell the heart, words amplifie
> The kind expressions of more Silent Signs.[40]

He may tell Sheafe he's "ravish'd with [her] love." But he does not aspire to perfect, ravishing, unmediated union. That was to be found elsewhere. "Look not for Perfection in your Relation" with a spouse, Thatcher advised his congregation. "God reserves that for another state where marriage is not needed."[41]

No less than Shakespeare's Troilus, then, the Puritans knew that there's a "monstruosity in love." Between human lovers "the will is infinite and the execution confined"; "the desire is boundless and the act a slave to limit."[42] Such realism might well grow corrosive. But for the Puritans it served as a reminder that God had set a bound to earthly loves. If they satisfy they do not last, and if they last they cannot satisfy. For the joys of *complete* surrender and *complete* satisfaction, one must turn from creation to its Creator, the one lover "commensurate with human desire."[43] Anne and Simon Bradstreet would have known, as they listened to Winthrop's "Modell," that to be exemplary Puritan lovers they could be neither simply realists or idealists. They were to strike a wary balance, rendering unto each what it was due.

This is, of course, fair advice for any couple—the formula would outlast the Bay Colony by centuries, and in various secular versions it has been revived ever since. But when we turn from love to poetry, the stakes of this model grow clear. How to capture its balance in form, and not simply describe it? How to find it as inspiring as the high noons and blackest nights of courtly love and Petrarchan passion? "Give me more love, or more disdain," begged Thomas Carew. "Either extreme, of love or hate, / Is sweeter than a calm estate." And, he might have added, a sharper spur to art.

Around the time of Carew's "Mediocrity in Love Rejected" and Milton's tract on divorce, Bradstreet took this emotional balancing act as a compositional challenge. In a suite of four poems she celebrates the escape from solitude, the reciprocal pleasures of loving and being loved, and the wrestling with idolatry that a successful Puritan marriage was to bring. Witty, self-assured, extravagant, these poems stake the power of "seeming thine" against the Puritan literary ideal of "Conscience rather than Elegance, fidelity rather than poetry."[44] They too reject "Mediocrity in Love."

"I may seem thine, who in effect am none"

Like many of her seventeenth-century British contemporaries, Anne Bradstreet has little patience for the emotional and rhetorical extremes of Petrarchan love and poetry.[45] Burning chills and other symptoms of ambivalence were foreign to the Puritan dream of emotional constancy. So were the all-or-nothing contrasts between passion and despondency typical of poems like Carew's "Mediocrity in Love Rejected" or Donne's "Lecture Upon the Shadow." In Bradstreet's work we therefore find *odi* and *amo* keeping their distance, warmth and cold unmixed. When she makes love seem a Petrarchan quest, heady with unfulfillment, it is only temporary: a version of the "dayly whetting" of love that Reformed preachers advised.[46]

Bradstreet's marriage poems form a suite of variations on the theme of conjugal union: "If ever two were one," they pledge, "then surely we."[47] What does such a declaration mean? "Husband and wife are one person in law," we read in Blackstone: "that is, the very being or legal existence of the woman is suspended during the marriage, or at least is incorporated and consolidated into that of the husband: under whose wing, protection, and cover, she performs every thing." [48] But this legal fiction seems far from Bradstreet's mind. Could her vision of union derive from the Platonism of love poetry she knew, poetry within the idealist tradition? Here, though, the union is a merger of souls and a shading of genders abhorrent to Puritan theology.[49] In Christ there may be no man nor woman, as we saw in the slithery pronouns of the "Modell." But marriage is a more quotidian and more hierarchical matter, not to be imagined in this way.

Bradstreet seems to have read Spenser, and known the work of her distant relative Sir Philip Sidney.[50] I'd like to think that she knew the idealist tradition well enough to consciously eschew it, at least as far as the marriage poems were concerned. For in her claims of two becoming one I hear a stubborn resistance to its paradoxical rhetoric of love as a fusion of opposites or a union of essences. There's nothing comparable to Edward Taylor's astonished meditation on union with God, "The Experience": "My Nature with thy Nature all Divine / Together joyn'd in Him that's Thou, and I. / Flesh of my Flesh, Bone of my bone. There's run / Thy Godhead and my Manhood in thy Son." Taylor uses the language of marital union to describe the soul's "marriage" to Christ. By saying "Flesh of my Flesh" he speaks as Adam; because every saint's soul is "feminine" to God, he's also Eve. "What hath thy Godhead, as not satisfide / Marri'de our Manhood, making it its Bride?" he asks elsewhere. [51] This marriage partakes in the union of finite and infinite, human and divine, flesh and spirit, accomplished in God's Son. It leaves the pleasures and pains and limited unions of earthly marriage behind.

Bradstreet's marriage poems have their own religious resonance, of course. When she insists that she and her husband share one body ("A Letter"), she implies that they as a couple form the body of Christ just as much as did the Puritan congregation addressed en masse on board the *Arbella*. But their "one body" is also defined by a Pauline description of marriage that Winthrop pointedly ignores in his "Modell." "Wives submit yourselves unto your own husbands, as unto the Lord," Paul tells the Ephesians. "For the husband is the wife's head, even as Christ is the head of the congregation, and the same is the saviour of the body. Therefore as the congregation is in subjection to Christ, likewise let the wives be in subjection to their husbands in all things" (Eph. 5:22–31). All saints are body to Christ's spirit, but regenerate wives are doubly physical. They are bodies in the communal Body *and* in regard to their Christlike husbands. Anne and Simon Bradstreet may have been one flesh, one bone. But together they were to God what Anne was to Simon on earth. Milton, somewhat later, put the hierarchy best. As far as emotional submission is concerned, rank follows gender: "He for God only, she for God in him."[52]

In an influential reflection on her predecessor, Adrienne Rich questions the impact these hierarchical gender relations had on Bradstreet's apparently transparent marriage poems. "To what extent," she wonders, is this work "an expression of individual feeling, and where does it echo the Puritan ideology of marriage, including married love as the 'duty' of every god-fearing couple?" Rich doubts that the poet's "individual feeling" would have embraced that ideology. "Where," she thus asks, "are the stress-marks of anger, the strains of self-division, in her work?"[53] When Ivy Schweitzer observes that the "witty and polished" love poems say nothing about how Bradstreet "*feels* about [her] fixed and constraining positions" in the Pauline world picture she follows Rich's lead.[54] Rather than read that silence as a sign of silencing, however, I want to stress the "fictive design" of Bradstreet's work: the public, dramatic, and finally orthodox quality of her personas.[55] Her formal devices, her use of echo and play, and even her explorations of gender hierarchy and marital union are, to my ear, less protective than performative. They signal a public self-fashioning, not an enforced disguise.

We can see this self-fashioning, and the poet's sense of play, in the opening conceit of "A Letter to Her Husband, Absent Upon Public Employment."

> My head, my heart, mine eyes, my life, nay, more,
>
> My joy, my magazine of earthly store,
>
> If two be one, as surely thou and I,
>
> How stayst thou there, whilst I at Ipswich lie?
>
> So many steps, head from the heart to sever,
>
> If but a neck, soon should we be together.[56]

At first glance the poem indeed seems shaped by Puritan ideology. Her husband is head to her heart and, later the Sun to her Earth. He is a "dearest guest" to be invited in her "welcome house"—a role that recalls Christ, the unexpected guest who must be welcomed at his second coming (Rev. 3:20). As Robert Daly explains, "earthly love is figured though the images and language of divine love," with all the hierarchies that follow. While "it is clear from the beginning that Simon is not God, not even her God," being instead her "magazine of earthly store," the love between them "becomes, in the powerful and central section of the poem, a similitude of the love between God and man." The poem explores "the essential univocity of love," our inability to talk about divine love without earthly tropes, and (for the Puritan) vice versa.[57]

Daly's reading is inarguable, but incomplete. For Bradstreet stands back a little from her metaphors and plays the univocity of love against its hierarchy. Consider the neck that sticks out from the last line I quoted above. It may be a narrow strip of land, one that "steps" could carry her across. It may stand as a stock allegorical figure for a "vigorous exercise of the grace of faith" that connects one "to Christ the head."[58] But the macabre, Dickinsonian humor of the image—a trod on, severed neck to be rejoined, as though it were "old man Adam's"—seems just as deliberate. Bradstreet toys with the literal image of two people forming one body and with the Pauline gender roles that underwrite her metaphors. When she mourns that head and heart have been cut off from one another, we have to remember that he's her head *and* heart, according to the first line. Later she will be both Earth and the overarching system of the Zodiac in which her husband's solar power is contained. If she associates her husband with Christ, Bradstreet also addresses him with words from the lover in Canticles (supposedly Solomon, an Old Testament type of the Messiah). "Return, return, O Shulamite, return that we may behold thee," the male lover-or-

14

Christ pleads in the Song of Songs. "Return, return, sweet Sol, from Capricorn," exclaims the female poet-or-Christ in Bradstreet's elegant, allusive verse.[59]

In "A Letter," Rosamund Rosenmeier explains, the usual gender divisions have been doubled and shuffled into a new, unexpected richness of association. "Counters have been conflated," she writes, "and the demarcations between opposites have been smudged, if not erased." By the time the speaker cries "Return, return," it is "as if the husband were the errant ecclesia, who at the end of time will be joined with the messiah."[60] It is tempting to interpret the poet's speech *in loco Christi* as an act of daring or rebellion. But that interpretation stands on a shaky and outdated notion of Puritanism. If in Canticles Christ speaks as a bridegroom, in the book of Proverbs he speaks in "the person of a Matrone, a Ladie, or Princess"—at least according to minister John Dod, who married Bradstreet's parents and wrote several books on both the Bible and marriage.[61] As long as Bradstreet's desires and claims are sponsored by the Bible, remarkable boldness may follow. She may dare God to count her sighs and teardrops (in "Another [phoebus make haste . . .]"), knowing that her words echo Genesis 22:17, or to chide her husband for a lack of sensual attention, knowing he will catch her references to the shared delights of God and the Church in Canticles. Through such "seeming," their merely human "mutual sweet content" may be restored.

In such lines Bradstreet reveals the poetic usefulness of Milton's otherwise limiting "she for God in him." The male love poet, if he is a Puritan, must shuttle between two different selves in his earthly and heavenly romances. To be a spouse to God he needs one set of tropes. He needs another, quite different, to love his spouse on earth. If he treats his love for his wife as salvific he's an idolator. His most passionate, extreme, delirious language and desire must play itself out on an upward trajectory. The Puritan woman poet, by contrast, can exploit the theological congruence between her love for the husband below and the Husband above. Duty-bound to love "above" herself, she risks only the confusion of tenor and vehicle in her metaphors. Even her most extreme expressions of love may be sponsored by a biblical pretext that saves them from the danger, or the charge, of idolatrous overvaluation. The realist love of a wife for her husband may be extravagantly expressed, as long as that expression relies on the perfect idealist love between God and the soul as figured in Scripture— and as long as the distinction between the two realms is, in the end, discernible. The art of Bradstreet's love poetry lies in how she allusively matches human to heavenly loves, how long she makes their meeting last, and how she will finesse their disengagement.

"To My Dear and Loving Husband"

All of this will seem rather impressionistic unless we ground it in a particular poem. Let me return to "To My Dear and Loving Husband" and show in some detail how Bradstreet orchestrates her personas, her flashes of humor, her flair with gender roles and biblical pretexts, and her supple juxtapositions of levels of love. Here is the poem in its entirety:

> If ever two were one, then surely we.
> If ever man were loved by wife, then thee;
> If ever wife was happy in a man,
> Compare with me, ye women, if you can.
> I prize thy love more than whole mines of gold
> Or all the riches that the East doth hold.
> My love is such that rivers cannot quench,
> Nor ought but love from thee, give recompense.
> Thy love is such I can no way repay,
> The heavens reward thee manifold, I pray.
> Then while we live, in love let's so persevere
> That when we live no more, we may live ever.[62]

Two lines shy of a sonnet, but shy in no other way, this poem must have been one of those "touching passages" that John Berryman allowed the subject of his *Homage*. But "To My Dear and Loving Husband" aspires to be a tour de force, not a "touching passage." If we push them a little, listen close, and set them in the context that her ideal reader, whether Simon or a Puritan posterity, would have understood, the lines will show themselves to be both virtuous and virtuosic.

Although the poem is written in heroic couplets, the first line is set off sharply from the rest. "If ever two were one, then surely we." No other line is a single sentence. In no other does Bradstreet feel the need to insist on her conclusion. I won't say that her insistence adds a note of uncertainty—that would go too far. But the couple's union, that "one" poised at the central stress of the line, is the start, not the end of their story. The focus of the poem opens from two-as-one ("we") to one loved by another (a man, a wife, a "thee"). In moments, that love becomes a matter of public knowledge and competitive display. As Bradstreet moves from private, intimate union to the distinctions involved in public identity, she refuses to claim that she and her husband enjoy the unlawful or extraordinary pleasures of idealist love. As we have seen in Taylor's meditations and Thomas Thatcher's sermon on the perfection that lies beyond marriage, God's love for his elect bears the idealist burden in the Puritan scheme.

But if Bradstreet will not make those claims, she will make ones that sound awfully close, drawing on licensed biblical pretexts. With the poem's first first-person singular—"Compare with me, ye women, if you can"—comes its first allusion. Stepping into her public role as "wife," Bradstreet plucks a chorus from thin air: the daughters of Jerusalem who challenge the beloved of Canticles with "How is your beloved better than another, O fairest of women?" (Cant. 5:9). Her boast preempts the question, steals the scene, and she starts the next full sentence with the poem's first "I." Rather than construct herself primarily through her private union with her husband, that is to say, Bradstreet portrays their relationship as public, dramatic, performative. After the "we" of the first line the couple separates, stepping into categories of man and wife, lover and spouse, that her biblical allusion underwrites.

Once the "I" is introduced, the poem's focus shifts. For the next three couplets we read a series of comparisons between Bradstreet's love for her husband and his for her. This bidding war shows off the poet's amorous and authorial abilities, to the "women" and to us. To begin, Bradstreet inverts the Renaissance conceit of woman as her master's treasure trove, the sort of thing we find in Donne's Elegy 19: "O my America, my new found land, / My kingdom, safliest when with one man manned, / My mine of precious stones, my empery."[63] "I prize thy love," she says, "more than whole mines of gold, / Or all the riches that the East doth hold." Her love is as fierce as death, its darts are darts of flame, at least implicitly— "rivers cannot quench" it, she writes, and we can look up the reasons why in Canticles 8:6–7. Only love from him, a love already compared to gold and riches, can "give recompense." But fires and riches are incommensurate images, as Bradstreet knows. Hence the awkward rhyme of "quench" and "recompense"; hence her pose of modesty, her protest that his love "is such I can no way repay." Payment is not the issue for a burning love like hers. "If a man offered all his wealth for love, he would be laughed to scorn," says the beloved in Solomon's song (Cant. 8:7). Surely a female Solomon, who has already dismissed the worth of her mines, would feel the same.

Heroic couplets can sag into rote symmetry. Heroic assertions of oneness do the same, as they drift into the doldrums of a marital "calm estate." Bradstreet's poem, by contrast, advances through a series of poised, propulsive asymmetries. "Compare with me," she demands in the fourth line—a flash of roundabout rhetoric, a way *not* to say simply, "I am happy in you." The comparisons she spells out between her husband and herself form a gymnastic pattern of uneven parallel loves. Were she able to "repay" his love, nothing more could be said on the subject. The poem would seem a bit self-satisfied, dull to her larger audience. Instead she sketches a projective distinction: his love, somehow, will recompense her own; and she pays him back—but indirectly, not out of any store or merit of her own. Her prayers reward him "manifold": many-fold, overmuch, with interest. Again, avoiding evenness, she keeps the verse alive.

By calling on heaven to reward her husband's love Bradstreet calls our attention to the theological roots of her allusive art. She also reminds us that the two-in-one marriage she has in mind is finally a realist, limited one. Adam and Eve's great error, at least according to Milton, lay in their "acting as if they were complete within their totality."[64] They rehearse this union and sufficiency in the moments before Adam eats:

> Within my heart I feel
> The bond of Nature draw me to my own,
> My own in thee, for what thou art is mine;
> Our State cannot be sever'd, we are one,
> One Flesh; to lose thee were to lose myself.
> So Adam, and thus Eve to him repli'd.
> O glorious trial of exceeding Love,
> Illustrious evidence, example high!
>
> . . .
>
> Adam, from whose dear side I boast me sprung,
> And gladly of our Union hear thee speak,
> One Heart, one Soul in both; whereof good proof
> This day affords, declaring thee resolv'd,
> Rather than Death or aught than Death more dread
> Shall separate us, linkt in Love so dear,
> To undergo with mee one Guilt, one Crime. . . .[65]

In all its attractive excess, *this* is idolatry. Adam and Eve love one another with no reference to the key third term in Puritan affections, their loving and jealous Creator. And though Puritan couples were warned that in Heaven there would be no marriage, Milton's Adam and Eve would rather disobey God than be separated by death, that bitter reminder of the limits of human love.[66] If death were to join them, one suspects, they would gladly eat and sing their *Liebestod* and die. But God is no Wagnerian. After the Fall they find their union both impeded by self-consciousness and opened to a chastened new form of affection. "Thou to me / Art all things *under Heav'n*," Eve says to Adam in Milton's final scene.[67]

Bradstreet's invocation of rewarding "heavens," like the closing couplet's ca-

18

veats about "while we live" and "when we live no more," performs the same careful, delimiting function. "Then while we live," the poem concludes, "in love let's so persevere / That when we live no more, we may live ever." Not may *love* ever. That would ask too much. Although Bradstreet does not express the longing, however, she clearly feels it, and leaves it in our minds by implication. We may know the only perseverance that counts is the Calvinist Perseverance of the Saints, and we may know that to the Puritans eternal life was never meted out as a reward for good behavior. But we are allowed to gloss over these difficulties. Using theological language to express what would be in Sidney's hands a commonplace about how the lovers' legends will survive, Bradstreet adds a dash of daring to her conclusion. She indulges the fantasy of union, even as her poem disentangles its initial two-as-one and weaves them, as separate threads, into the only lasting tapestry.

"I love my love because my love loves me"

In her marriage poems, then, Bradstreet draws on divine affections to enrich the marital world below. She uses allusion to "whet" the mundane world with a measured dose of transgression.[68] In their blithe, theatrical personas the poems have a poise and complexity unmatched by colonial and early nineteenth-century American poets. In fact, I hear nothing comparable until the essays of Emerson, which restate Puritan distinctions and Bradstreet's aesthetic of "seeming" in a philosophical key. For between Bradstreet and Emerson, in America and England, human love more and more successfully competes with its heavenly antitype, skewing the Puritans' balanced account of love.

I cannot, of course, tell the story of love's progress from the 1650s to the 1850s in this introduction. (It takes William C. Horne over three hundred pages to track British marriage poetry of the "long eighteenth century," 1650–1800.) It is clear, however, that some notion of love's idolatry troubles Americans well into the nineteenth century. "Daily you occupy a portion of my thoughts," Mary Holyoke Pearson wrote to Ephraim Abbot in 1812; "too large a share, I fear. Could I love my Creator in proportion to the creature, I should be happier." "I beg you, my dearest Mary," wrote Samuel Francis Smith in 1834, "see that you do not worship any image of clay—and pray that I may be kept from similar idolatry."[69] Well into the 1830s popular poet Martin Tupper could still warn husbands, "Take heed lest she love thee before God; that she be not an idolater." How seriously, however, can we take him? Elsewhere in the *Proverbial Philosophy* Tupper cheerfully defines love as "a sweet idolatry enslaving all the soul, / A mighty spiritual force, warring with the dullness of matter," with no worry at all about the contradiction. Admittedly, he's not much of a poet, and a British one at that.[70] But his awkwardness illuminates a major shift in Anglo-American romantic culture.

Through the eighteenth century, Horne observes of British poets, "marital companionship is celebrated more and more as a secularized heaven, perhaps as a substitute for the religiosity that this rational age was losing."[71] It takes no great leap of sentiment to see marital love as "quintessentially a heaven on earth": a domestic paradise that could model, or even compete with, heaven itself.[72] The same is true in American verse. Consider Richard Henry Dana Sr.'s "The Husband and Wife's Grave" (1827), one of the best pre-Romantic American love poems. The poet pauses at a grave, thinking of the companionate affection husband and wife once shared. "Domestic cares / Call ye not now together," he reflects. No longer can the couple wrestle disappointment or "speak of joy assured, and bliss / Full, certain, and possess'd." The poem moves towards consolation. But Dana's vision of love in heaven is much less compelling than the domestic scene where he began. For when he says the couple's "mutual love / ... *no longer* needs a speech / For full communion," he inadvertently implies that full communion *had been* achieved, through Miltonic "fit conversation," in life.[73] If so, what's left for heaven? The posthumous "union all mysterious" he promises is paradoxically *less* intimate than the care-worn human congress it replaces. Earthly marriage, it seems, is the right place for love. Even in heaven, it's not likely to go better.

To call a poem like "The Husband and Wife's Grave" sentimental isn't really an insult. It champions the force and value of sentiment against the chills of death and strict theology. But a more sweeping term is helpful for the grander claims that mark, say, Nathaniel Hawthorne's letters to Sophia. "Oh, my Dove," he confessed, "I have really thought sometimes, that God gave you to me to be the salvation of my soul."[74] In this "erotic faith," to use Polhemus's term, the soul's romance with God yields metaphors for human relations, and no longer the other way around.[75] This shift had a predictable impact on the companionate ideal. "Within the context of the nineteenth-century religion of romantic love," writes Lystra, "Milton's lines must be changed to reflect a different emotional logic: 'he for God in her, she for God in him.' "[76]

At its best, this mutual erotic faith allowed Victorian men and women to enjoy the same intensity and closeness others have observed in same-sex friendships and romances of the period. In diaries and love letters "men in the grip of romantic love swore that they shared a portion of their female partner's subjectivity and vice-versa," Lystra explains.[77] I will return to this vision of shared subjectivity in my reading of Walt Whitman, who extends it—at least metaphorically—to the relationship between author and reader. For now, though, let me point out its uglier side. The Puritans suspected that unchecked human love would shade into idolatry. By this they meant several things: a mutual self-satisfaction, so that the couple feels complete in itself, with no need for God; a refusal to be parted by death, that sign of the Fall; and, above all, a thinly masked narcissism, with self-love masked by overvaluation of the person adored. The writing of a minor mid-nineteenth-century poet such as Mary Elizabeth Hewitt is clotted with such alienated, circular affections: " 'That thou art weak,' he said, 'do I love thee, / And, sweet! I love my love because my love loves me.' "[78] (Verse like Hewett's sets the stage for Emily Dickinson's more searching and satirical poems of "bondage as play.")

Between the sentimental poets and Whitman and Dickinson, however, stand a few key figures, startling in their contrast. Some are women—Mary Moody Emerson and Margaret Fuller most memorably—who announce a feminist suspicion of romantic union. They suspect its idealizations: the way women overvalue the men they love; the way men etherealize women. They raise an eyebrow at erotic attraction, which leads to the entanglements of marriage and children and to a loss of self, a life lived solely through and for another. We can "live too much in relation," Fuller warns, falling "into distraction, or imbecility, from which [we] can only be cured by a time of isolation." Hence her praise of celibacy, of the "old bachelors and old maids" whose percentage of the population increased throughout the nineteenth century.[79] Hence also her bow to "a wise contemporary" who observed that "union is only possible to those who are units": a figure I suspect is Emerson.[80] More explicitly than Fuller, Emerson infuses a neo-Puritan strictness about love into his more obvious Platonic and Romantic philosophy. His work thus spans the "failure of continuity" critics have seen between the colonial and postromantic American imaginations and lays the groundwork for more recent disenchantments with and reaffirmations of love.[81]

"In youth we are mad for persons"

As I have shown, the first decades of the nineteenth century see Hewitt, Dana, and other sentimentalists championing human love. They call it worship, "full communion," and salvation: metaphors drawn from the soul's romance with God. When Emerson looked back on the same decades, however, he saw "a war between intellect and affection": a war that intellect won. "Instead of the social existence which all shared," he recalls, "was now separation. . . . The young men were born with knives in their brain," ready to cut all social ties and "driven to find all [their] resources, hopes, rewards, society and deity" within the self.[82] To these nonconformists from erotic faith the truest union had nothing to do with the "maudlin agglutinations" of sentimental marriage. In the first flush of "Initial Love" lovers might well "melt their sundered selves," but once melted, they "would be twain." And the later heights of "Celestial Love," on earth or in heaven, are just as brisk. "When each the other shall avoid," the poet writes, "Shall each by each be most enjoyed."[83]

Emerson was not always such a skeptic, of course. As he confessed in "The Oversoul," "in youth we are mad for persons," and he was no exception.[84] In December 1827, just before he met his young wife-to-be, Ellen Tucker, he preached a sermon flush with sentimental pieties. Throughout their short marriage, Robert Richardson reports, "the young minister, working on his journals, would break out in the middle of a thought, 'O Ellen I do dearly love you.'" They called each other pet names, wrote love poems to each other—hers often playful, his mostly high-flown—and were by all accounts "blissfully happy."[85] Even after her death he tried his best to avail himself of conventionally Christian, sentimental consolation.

In his unpublished elegies, however, Emerson mourns in a way that signals subsequent turns in his thought. He had thought of their marriage as an idealist merger. Ellen was "the spirit that dwelt in mine," he writes in one poem, "the spirit in which mine dwelt." She promised to "cleave to me forever" and be "present as my life." As the Puritans might have warned him, however, that presence was brought up short.[86] As for the hope of heavenly reunion, Emerson found it undermined by doubt. How can he *know*, he keeps asking, whether Ellen has become a watchful "angel wife," or whether he has been, instead, "forgotten by the dead"? "Does it [her soul] not know me now," he wonders mutely in another poem, unable to muster punctuation. "Does it not share my thought / Is it prisoned from Waldo's prayer / Is its glowing love forgot."[87]

By the end of the 1830s, then, the decade when, according to Lystra, "the personhood of the loved one" became "a powerful rival to God as the individual's central symbol of ultimate significance" in American romantic culture, Emerson had come to quite the opposite conclusion.[88] I may long for another to be as "present as my life" and "share my thought" in an interpersonal union, he concedes. But the only such merger my soul can *achieve* is with ideas or ideals, "a total infusion, impenetration of its own essence by the nature of justice, of truth." Strictly speaking, the soul "postpones persons, all persons, to this contemplation of the impersonal, the One." In Emerson's second marriage to Lydian and his difficult, passionate friendships with Anna Barker, Catherine

Sturgis, Margaret Fuller, Thoreau, and Carlyle, he repeatedly found that contact with the "personhood of the loved one" was temporary, partial, insufficient. It was, in the end, "supplementary to the primary teaching of the soul."[89]

Emerson thus reasserts, on platonic grounds, a familiar hierarchy of affections. The soul must move from the created to the uncreated, persons to the impersonal, to the world of the ideal. The soul may thus ride out loss and disappointment, and learn at last to distinguish the *feeling* of love from the *person* that seems to inspire it. Keep "Free as an Arab / Of thy beloved," the poet thus advises in "Give All to Love," since "Though thou loved her as thyself, / As a self of purer clay, / Though her parting dims the day, / Stealing grace from all alive; / Heartily know, / When half-gods go, / The gods arrive." And more than cold "gods" may be our reward. By "postpon[ing] persons," Emerson promises elsewhere, selves may yet gather into something like the community of love in Winthrop's "Modell of Christian Charity," with the Christian One Man replaced by an impersonal One Mind. As Winthrop's saints were members of the Body of Christ, in Emerson "the unity, the community of men" derives from a "strictly identical nature of which all the individuals are organs." "Persons themselves acquaint us with the impersonal," he puts it in "The Oversoul," because when we ask "What is it then between us?" the answer is a third term bridging the distance: "a common nature" that "is not social; it is impersonal; is God."[90]

To see the appeal and the limits of Emerson's impersonalism, it helps to look at a poem such as "To Eva."

> O fair and stately maid, whose eyes
> Were kindled in the upper skies
>   At the same torch that lighted mine;
> For so I *must* interpret still
> Thy sweet dominion o'er my will,
>   A sympathy divine.
>
> Ah! let me blameless gaze upon
> Features that seem at heart my own;
>   Nor fear those watchful sentinels,
> Who charm the more their glance forbids,
> Chaste-glowing, underneath their lids,
>   With fire that draws while it repels.

Eva may inspire a Petrarchan mix of attraction and repulsion in her lover, and she may exercise a "sweet dominion" over the poet who admires her. But Emerson "*must* interpret" these hierarchical, even idolatrous relations as "a sympathy divine" based on similarity, on a "common nature," and not on distinctions of rank and gender. Fear, blame, charm, erotic heat, possession: all snap as snugly and unconvincingly into place as Emerson's stiff verses. Possession by love turns into self-possession. "At heart," after all, her features seem "my own."[91]

As we see in "To Eva," Emerson's doctrine of the impersonal leaves something to be desired when it comes to love: namely, *other people*, in their threatening, enticing otherness. No wonder readers have winced at Emerson's accounts of love and friendship. They seem cold-hearted, alternately grim and rote expressions of platonic piety.[92] And, indeed, the writer felt this way about himself sometimes. He called himself a photometer, and not a stove; he saw that "his philosophy / Crouched like a cat sat watching close behind / And throttled all his passion." He even shares our misgivings about turning others into rungs on Plato's ladder. In the essay on "Love," for example, he tells a naively platonic story. "In the particular society of his mate," he writes, the lover "attains a clearer sight of any spot, any taint, which her beauty has contracted from this world, and is able to point it out, and this with mutual joy that they are now able, without offense, to indicate blemishes and hindrances in each other, and give to each all help and comfort in curing the same," bringing one another to perfection. Does he really believe this tale, which eerily predicts the tragic plot of Hawthorne's "The Birthmark"? By the final paragraphs of "Love" it is clear that he doesn't. "The soul which is in the soul of each, craving a perfect beatitude, detects incongruities, defects, and disproportion in the behaviour of the other," he says again. This time, though, what results is believably sour. Not "mutual joy," but "surprise, expostulation, and pain."[93]

Emerson was not happy with "Love." He sighed in his journals that he had had "much more experience than I have written there, more than I will, more than I can write."[94] We might take this, as critics have, as an invitation to biography. (When the essay says that "grief cleaves to names, and persons, and the partial interests of to-day and yesterday," we can fill in those names: his first wife, Ellen; his brothers, Edward and Charles. When it finds a "certain stain of error" discoloring every life, we can purse our lips and think, *survival guilt*.) Suppose we take the journal entry, though, as a hint to read "Love" and its companion essay "Friendship" against the later piece Emerson *called* "Experience." Here, after all, we find the hardest of Emerson's hard sayings about affection. In "Love" husband and wife faced being "shut up together for forty or fifty years" to learn the limits of companionate love; in "Experience" we find that "marriage (in what is called the spiritual world)" is, strictly speaking, "impos-

sible, because of the inequality between every subject with every object."
Poems like "Philosopher" and "To Eva" showed their author hemmed in by
self-consciousness. In "Experience" we learn that self-consciousness, "this dis-
covery we have made, that we exist," is "called the Fall of Man," and since this
Fall our dearest loves are mere "idolatries."[95]

The Fall of Man? Idolatry? As this mix of philosophical and theological
rhetoric suggests, Emerson relies on more than Plato and Plotinus to shake off
sentimental love. When Emerson decides to speak "strictly" or "in strictness,"
he shows a clear attachment to Puritan ideas, including a Protestant idea of our
spiritual solitude. "In strictness we ought to say, the soul seems to be insu-
lated," Emerson insists in "The Heart." "All persons, the very nearest and
dearest, underlie the same condition of an infinite remoteness." We long to say
that a beloved's selfhood is at least as real to us as our own. But this impulse
evaporates on close inspection. "In strict philosophy there is a quite infinite
distance between our knowledge of our own existence and the evidence we
have for the existence . . . of persons," he writes in the lecture on "Love." As
Emerson learned when mourning Ellen and his brothers, the love that makes
us think otherwise sets us up for sadness and shame. "The men are steel-
filings," he writes in "Nominalist and Realist," "yet we unjustly select a parti-
cle, and say, 'O steel-filing number one! what heart drawings I feel to thee! what
prodigious virtues are these of thine! how constitutional to thee, and incom-
municable.' Whilst we speak, the lodestone is withdrawn; down falls our filing
in a heap with the rest, and we continue our mummery to the wretched shav-
ing." Such "idolatry," with its "adulterate passion," leads only to "perpetual
disappointment."[96]

The "Real Marriage"

Emerson thus turns the distinctions of Puritan love-doctrine into an even
stricter philosophical system. He offers a vision of perfect union—but then
tells us that unless we "postpone persons," we cannot have it. The limits on our
knowledge of one another, ordained by subjectivity, that new "Fall of Man,"
take the place of the limits on love ordained by God after the biblical Fall. We
must again plot a course between solipsism and idolatry, guarding once more
against the temptation to love creation more than its creator. In this case, how-
ever, the creator is not God but the "great and crescive self," which "ruins the
kingdom of mortal friendship and love."[97]

This is, of course, the lonely Emersonian strain announced as "The Ameri-
can Religion" by Harold Bloom, denounced as male solipsism by progressive
critics, and mourned by Robert Creeley when he writes of "the isolation which

the American so often carries like a sore, marking him as lonely, lost, and a lit-tle pathetic." In it, as Creeley explains, "the *I* is worn as a merit in itself" so that "all forms break to it, and what hope of relationship to others there may once have been, is lost." But this doctrine is not entirely pessimistic. Quite the con-trary. Like the Puritans before him, Emerson too will display what Creeley calls "the attempt to move into form, again, with others," however tentatively.[98] Consider the essay on "Love," where the lovers finally "exchange the passion which once could not lose sight of its object for a cheerful, disengaged further-ance, whether present or absent, of each other's designs." Subtle puns suggest that more than prudery is at stake. If the couple leave *passion* behind they may now see love as an *action*: the action of renouncing dreams of merger, first of all. They may thus at last end their engagement (that is, become "disengaged") and enjoy the new relationship that Emerson calls "the real marriage."[99]

The philosophical underpinnings of Emerson's "real marriage" do not con-cern me here.[100] With an eye to how this ideal helps us read later poets, how-ever, I find that two of its elements bear comment. First, the ideal of "real mar-riage," asks the lovers each to leave off "clutching" at the other, demanding satisfactions that mere human love cannot supply. The marital bond will rely instead on the "municipal virtues" of "justice, punctuality, fidelity, and pity," which stand firm when the dream of shared subjectivity fails. This chastened connection yields the alluring mix of liberty and union described in "Sweden-borg," where "it is only when you leave and lose me, by casting yourself on a sentiment which is higher than the both of us, that I draw near." Emerson's "real marriage" thus looks at once back to the Puritan *ars amorica* and forward to the later love poetry of Adrienne Rich, for whom love will again be "a citizen before it is quite a cherub."[101]

But the "real marriage" is not just a matter of virtue. Rather, in its second crucial element, it counterpoints conscience with a quality we last saw in the poems of Bradstreet: an embrace of the power of seeming, the heart's "as if," the imagination. "True love transcends the unworthy object," Emerson writes at the close of "Friendship," because it treats objects as subjects equal to our own.[102] In the course of the "real marriage," that is to say, I may continue to make extravagant claims—but I do so as a deliberate, fictive, rhetorical gift. Just as Bradstreet deployed biblical allusions and personas against a strict the-ology, Emerson suggests we might play our impulse to ascribe or "bestow" vir-tues upon one another against a strict philosophy. Such love would remain too consciously performative to be idolatrous, really. And the poetry it sponsors would have both the force and the emotional appeal lacking in "To Eva" or "Give All to Love."

Emerson himself won't write this verse. Indeed, after the "Love" and "Friendship" essays his dictums grow more bitter, less confident that the pleasures of bestowal will suffice. ("Let us treat the men and women well: treat them as if they were real," he shrugs in "Experience": "perhaps they are.") Perhaps he was, in the end, simply too self-conscious, too quick to step back and sigh at the way "love attributes to the beloved person all which that person shares with his or her family, sex, age, or condition, nay, with the human mind itself," so that although "'tis these which the lover loves . . . Anna Matilda gets the credit of them."[103]

But if Emerson is unable to write poetry commensurate with his theory, others can and will. Here, for example, is Whitman's version of that "Anna Matilda" scene:

> O I could sing such grandeurs and glories about you!
> There is no endowment in man or woman that is not tallied in you,
> There is no virtue, no beauty in man or woman, but as good is in you,
> No pluck, no endurance in others, but as good is in you,
> No pleasure waiting for others, but an equal pleasure waits for you.
> I sing the songs of the glory of none, not God, sooner than I sing the songs
> of the glory of you.[104]

Whitman turns the bestowal of virtues we have seen in Emerson into a gracious bestowal of *value*: a small but poetically enabling shift of emphasis. He blurs the strict distinctions between human and heavenly loves that Emerson and the Puritans insist upon. And, in a gesture that still troubles critics, he cancels the distinction between love of others and love of self, trusting that the great divide between "me" and "you" may thus finally be crossed.

Whitman's generosity will make Emerson look wary, ungainly, a little stiff. But in the face of its more common alternative—the "metaphysically desperate degree of private bonding" of sentimentalism, in Cavell's words—the revival and revision of Puritan strictness we find in Emerson has a continuing appeal.[105] In a world where *never* two were one, the "municipal virtues" need to have their say. And while the exemplary couples of Emerson's most hopeful passages pursue the "real marriage" of a decorous "disengagement," they open a space for the more passionate ascriptions and encounters sketched by Bradstreet before them and by Dickinson and Merrill afterward. They may yet be, to quote Emerson's "Circles," "surprised out of [their] propriety" by the "flames and generosities of the heart."[106]

One

An Example to Lovers

Marriage (in what is called the spiritual world) is impossible,
because of the inequality between every subject and every object.
— R. W. EMERSON

Wherever the philosopher says *per impossibile* the poet shows the way.
— ALLEN GROSSMAN

When I began this book, I asked a poet for advice. Was there any-
thing, I wondered, distinctively *American* in American poetry of love. "We're
the nation," he replied at once, "where people write love poems to themselves."
This quip would have pleased Whitman, no doubt—except that he had asked
to be remembered as "the tenderest lover," not the patron saint of self-love. Any
protest by Whitman, though, would sound willfully naive. Is he no more self-
absorbed than, say, Rilke, a generation later? No more than Plato's Hippo-
thales, twenty centuries before? "I dote on myself," he announces, as they don't.
"There is that lot of me, and all so luscious."[1]

In the context we've explored so far, such lines come as a shock. The Puritan
God was allowed, indeed *obliged* to love Himself. But the rest of us, even two or
three centuries later, are expected to fix our gaze on Him or on each other, not
on our bodies or ourselves. When Leslie Fiedler calls Whitman's "Song of My-
self" "simultaneously a love song, a love affair (the poet's only successful one),
and a love child (the only real offspring of his passion)," you can hear the mild,
unmistakable chiding. Love affairs ought to be with people, not with poems;
love children should patter about on more-than-metrical feet. Even in recent
studies you'll hear of Whitman's "autoerotic isolation," his failed "marriage"
with the reader, and his "impotent potency"—charges that apparently also
apply to the *Calamus* sequence and the poems called "To You."[2]

Whitman has his partisans, of course. Some, like Michael Moon, praise him for undoing "the conventional moral distinction between masturbation and 'real,' mature sex."[3] Others read historically, and place him among the sex reformers of the early nineteenth century. They show how the poet tipped his hat to marital advice literature, wed phrenological notions of same-sex "adhesiveness" and heterosexual "amativeness" to his republican ideals, and joined other reformers in opposing "this tepid wash, this diluted deferential love" in which the body stayed out of sight.[4] Triangulating Whitman's poetics, his sexuality, and his social concerns, such readers spotlight the poet of erotic politics. They prove less helpful, I fear, in reading the more sentimental poet of love.

In the 1876 preface to *Leaves of Grass*, after all, Whitman describes his project in straightforward, almost embarrassing terms. "I would make a full confession," he declares. "I also sent out 'Leaves of Grass' to arouse and set flowing in men's and women's hearts, young and old, endless streams of living, pulsating love and friendship, from them to myself, now and ever."[5] On the evidence of later poets' work—Hart Crane, Allen Ginsberg, John Ashbery, and recently Alicia Ostriker—he succeeded. In this chapter, I want to look at *how*. How does Whitman teach his readers to love? What sort of love does he teach? Where do his declarations of love, for himself and for us, fit in his pedagogical poetic— and how do they ease the "solitude of self" that I have traced from the Puritans to Emerson? Whitman "permitted love," Ostriker writes; he was "myself in the slippery moment when I was able to fall in love with anything."[6] How does Whitman make this "impossible" marriage of self and other, subject and object, seem possible at last?

As I ask and answer these questions, I keep history in sight. Whitman's hope to "give an example to lovers" arises in part, after all, from his sense that his times "need[ed] satisfiers, joiners, lovers" to make them "compacted" and "whole."[7] But if we need to restore the poems' historical context, in a second gesture we must bring them close once more. For when Whitman addresses his "readers ages hence," his beloved "you, whoever you are," it is false to pretend he is not in some sense talking to *us*.[8] What he offers is nothing less than a love-cure for his audience. The speaker of his poems acts as both therapist and exemplary patient. We can always deconstruct or historicize his attentions; call him (as recent critics have) coercive, invasive, a seducer; shake his arm from our shoulder or waist. But the skeptical impulse to debunk him needs, itself, to be explored. It may depend on the same refusal of "satisfaction" and "acceptation," the same glum emotional wariness, that Whitman aims to cure. As Stanley Cavell asks, in a different context, "What do we gain ... by making ourselves unseducible, minions of Caesar? What petty Rome to administer will be our reward?"[9]

The Poet of Bestowal

Whitman is the first American poet to equate the amorous and the poetic imaginations, and to describe his poems as primarily acts of and searches for love. In the 1855 preface he is sweeping, magisterial. "The known universe has one complete lover and that is the greatest poet," he declares. "What balks or breaks others is fuel for his burning progress to contact and amorous joy. . . . His love above all love has leisure and expanse .... He is no irresolute or suspicious lover ... he is sure ... he scorns intervals." By 1876, as we have seen, Whitman has grown hushed and plaintive. While *Leaves of Grass* was meant to be "the Poem of average Identity (of yours, whoever you are, now reading these lines)," he now explains, it was also written to give voice to a "terrible, irrepressible yearning": a "never-satisfied appetite for sympathy" that the poet's "boundless offering of sympathy" would match and answer in an "old, yet evernew interchange of adhesiveness, so fitly emblematic of America." Where the lover of 1855 scorns intervals, the lover of 1876 wants to fill them, to "arouse and set flowing . . . endless streams of living, pulsating love and friendship, directly from [readers] to myself, now and ever."[10]

Yes, the sureness is gone. And yes, Walter Whitman the man was less than comfortable with the expressions of "living, pulsating love" he received from some of his admirers, especially when they were women.[11] But we can make too much of this irony, and of the difference between the prefaces. The bold claims of the first and the yearnings of the second, the poet's "leisure and expanse" and his "never-satisfied appetite for sympathy," may be more nearly matched than they seem.

To understand their connection, we need to begin with Whitman's equation of the lover and the poet. This is an old link in Western culture. You find it from Plato to the latest in Freudian theory.[12] But forging that link, as often as not, is a third term absent in Whitman: the madman. For Socrates the lover is mad, albeit with a heaven-sent madness that leads to the love of the Good. For Shakespeare's Theseus the similarity lies elsewhere:

> The lunatic, the lover, and the poet
> Are of imagination all compact.
> One sees more devils than vast hell can hold;
> That is the madman. The lover, all as frantic,
> Sees Helen's beauty in a brow of Egypt.
> The poet's eye, in a fine frenzy rolling,
> Doth glance from heaven to earth, from earth to heaven;

And as imagination bodies forth
The forms of things unknown, the poet's pen
Turns them to shapes and gives to airy nothing
A local habitation and a name.

Lover, poet, and madman are all essentially hallucinatory. But the undeceived Theseus sees that their "fine frenzies" *create*, at least in part, the objects that apparently cause their response. "Such tricks hath strong imagination," he sighs, "That, if it would but apprehend some joy, / It comprehends some bringer of that joy" (5.1. 18–20). Titania as she dotes on Bottom, Lysander and Demetrius as they "superpraise" poor Helena—for Theseus, such error is the very stuff of love.

Although he does not use the word, Theseus has given a thumbnail definition of idolatry: the problem that "balks or breaks" Emerson. With its magic potions and curative drops in the eyes, Shakespeare's play displays in comic form what Emerson knew more sadly: that love is prior to its objects; that we confuse the occasion of our happiness—brother Charles, first wife Ellen, second wife Lydian—with the efficient cause of it, which is Virtue or the God Within. We may long to delight in a beloved's full, unimpeachable presence, to experience "an union in partition / . . . / with two seeming bodies, but one heart" (3.2.200, 202). But something always comes between us, like the Wall in Bottom's play-within-the-play. We kiss the wall's hole, and not each other's lips; we love our perceptions, and not persons in themselves. In the end, as we have seen, Emerson's "great and crescive self, rooted in absolute nature," proves more jealous than the God it's modeled on. Untouched and untaught by attachments, it "ruins the kingdom of mortal friendship and love."[13]

As Emerson turns the Puritan doctrine of weaned affections into a strict philosophical system, he offers three ways out. "The one thing which we seek with insatiable desire is to forget ourselves," he writes at the end of "Circles": that is, among other things, to forget the demands of the great and crescive self. And since our isolation was to teach us stateliness, deference, and poise (that's the heart of the essay on "Manners"), when we forget ourselves we may be "surprised out of our propriety" by the "flames and generosities of the heart."[14] The poetry of this solution would be passionate, erotic, and inclined to the sublime, like Hart Crane's "Voyages." But Emerson is too self-ironic and New Englandly proper to write it himself.

In "Experience," the essayist suggests a less Dionysian solution. If the "evanescence and lubricity of all objects" turns out to be "the most unhandsome part of our condition," perhaps if we were less "manipular" in our attempts to reach one another, we would be more successful. With a little more restraint our condition might prove "handsome" indeed—that is to say *attractive*, drawing other people to us without the need to clutch at them and hold them fast.[15] I will take up this solution, with its attention to the "municipal virtues," in my chapter on Adrienne Rich.

As a path into Whitman, I want to trace Emerson's third escape route, his notion of bestowal. Like Bradstreet's aesthetic of allusion, bestowal enlists the power of "seeming" for love's use. The Puritan poet underwrote her extravagant affections with imagery from Canticles. She loved her husband *as if* he were Christ, and *as if* she were, and *as if* two could ever be one. In Emersonian bestowal, I love you *as if* you were as fully present to me as God or Virtue. Emerson's tone, however, couldn't be farther from Bradstreet's. Her *as ifs* are charged by pathos and transgression. His are grim. It's exciting to imagine ourselves on either side of Bradstreet's verse. But who wants to hear that we're shadows, needing help from Emerson's imagination to be lovable? What pleasure, at that, comes in the telling?

The flaw in Emerson's logic lies in his assumption that love ought to depend on what Irving Singer calls an *appraisal of value*.[16] He wants his love to be proportionate to the worth of the beloved. To know how much to love them, he needs to know whether the men and women he sees in the street are merely appearances or whether they are present and real. Even the vision of bestowal that we find in Emerson's "Friendship" bases love, in the end, on appraisals. We ascribe to one another the sovereign selfhood, the influx of God, which we then safely value and desire. That's a little circular—and a little perverse.

What Whitman offers, by contrast, is not some virtue deserving of value, which we then appraise. Rather, he bestows "value itself."[17] He may use the language of appraisal, may call us perfect, glorious, and the like. But these are, as Singer explains in another context, "honorific titles" that reiterate the lover's overflow of affection, rather than, as Emerson would have it, judgments passed on our fitness to receive it.[18] "He judges not as the judge judges," Whitman says of the poet in the 1855 preface, "but as the sun falling around a helpless thing," only to find that "his thoughts are the hymns of the praise of things."[19] No wonder, in the later "Song of Universals," he could speak of "Love like the light silently wrapping all."[20]

I don't mean to suggest that, for Singer or for Whitman, love is a matter of bestowal alone. The appraisal of virtues has its place in love, since "unless we appraised we could not bestow a value that goes beyond appraisal," as Singer explains, "and without bestowal there would be no love."[21] Yet while appraisals may be mistaken, as when I prize creation more than its Creator, or dream that my beloved is my God, the element of bestowal in love ensures that it "is not primarily a way of knowing," and cannot, therefore, be in error.[22] Rather, it is primarily a way of attending to the Other, an *appreciation*, that recognizes the value in and adds value to the beloved, out of affection's "sheer gratuity."[23] When Bradstreet posed the power of "seeming" against the strictures of Puritan realism, she was poised on the edge of this insight. Love does not merely enlist the poetic imagination. In Whitman, it *is* the imagination. The beloved it adores and adorns can be anything at all.[24]

Bestowal is the heart of Whitman's poetry, starting with his first notebook entry in the style of *Leaves of Grass*. "Of whatever I have I bestow upon you," he writes, "And first I bestow my love."[25] When he tells us that "the greatest poet hardly knows pettiness or triviality," he gives us a hint of how pervasive his bestowals will be. We find them in his acts of equation, when those appraised as lower in worth are defiantly embraced: "The wife—and she is not one jot less than the husband, / The daughter—and she is just as good as the son, / The mother—and she is every bit as much as the father."[26] When he disdains an auctioneer of slaves, it isn't because he dares to treat a human being as an object to be sold but because "the sloven does not half know his business." "Whatever the bids of the bidders they cannot be high enough for him," the poet says, and he turns the auctioneer's appraisive "examine these limbs" into an exposure of "wonders."[27]

In his hunger to bestow, Whitman unsettles more than just social appraisals. Jonathan Edwards taught that love should be proportional to the degree of *being* of the thing to be loved. An archangel, he decided, was surely farther from nonexistence than a worm. Such hierarchies, with God at their peak, collapse in Whitman's verse, where a "leaf of grass is no less than the journeywork of the stars."

> And the pismire is equally perfect, and a grain of sand, and the egg of
>> the wren,
> And the tree-toad is a chef-d'oeuvre for the highest,
> And the running blackberry would adorn the parlors of heaven,
> And the narrowest hinge in my hand puts to scorn all machinery,
> And the cow crunching with depressed head surpasses any statue,
> And a mouse is miracle enough to stagger sextillions of infidels,
> And I could come every afternoon of my life to look at the farmer's girl
>> boiling her iron tea-kettle and baking shortcake.[28]

Machinery and statues take their lumps—one thinks of Frank O'Hara's wonderful love poem "Having a Coke with You," where in the beloved's vital presence "it is hard to believe . . . that there can be anything as still / as solemn as unpleasantly definitive as statuary."[29] But they show up once more in the "iron tea-kettle" and the stillness of the final scene. Whitman does not articulate a simple preference for one realm over another, a re*appraisal* (that is to say) of the natural. Rather, he gives a supple, scale-juggling declaration of value as such. He lets us glimpse at the emotional and aesthetic pleasures of bestowal, in which the beloved "is, as we say, 'appreciated'—made more valuable through the special media and techniques in which love consists."[30] Whitman's poems aim, in a variety of ways, to teach those "media and techniques" to his readers.

Since bestowal is so pervasive in Whitman's work, it may be helpful to sort out its dominant forms. "I celebrate myself," the poet says. And indeed his first bestowals of value are reflexive, a matter of "adorning myself to bestow myself" somewhat later.[31] It's this love of self, more encompassing than mere autoeroticism, that even modern readers find a scandal. It is as though we still believed John Winthrop's equation of self-love and fallen selfishness. (When Adam "rent himself from his creator," you'll recall, he "rent all his posterity all so one from another; whence it comes that every man is born with this principle in him, to love and seek himself only.") Whitman's "Myself" confesses his own egotism with a relish that would be, indeed, off-putting, if not for two qualifications. First, he means his "I" to be a regenerate or never-fallen self: one of those who can love, as Winthrop commanded, "with a pure heart fervently," able to "delight in each other, make others' conditions our own, rejoice together, mourn together, labour and suffer together."[32] He offers a believable model, healthy, self-assured, proud that he is "capable of loving," and bluffly ready to "fetch you whoever you are flush with myself."[33]

With the ebullient narcissism of his "I," Whitman gives his readers words with which to name and value loving moods they have discounted or forgotten.[34] But Whitman has a second, broader goal as well. When he declares, in "Song of the Open Road," that he is "larger, better than I thought, / I did not know I held so much goodness," he forges a link between such high spirits and the broader claim that follows: "All seems beautiful to me."[35] Against the notion of self-love as selfishness, Whitman poses the more modern insight that a certain form of self-love is the basis for other affections. Love's twinborn foundations, writes Julia Kristeva, are *"narcissism* and *idealization,"* so that "the lover" is essentially "a narcissist with an *object."*[36] Whitman's bestowals of value on the self thus ease the tense distinction between selves and others, I's and objects, characteristic of Emerson. When the poet writes "I dote on myself . . . there is that lot of me, and all so luscious," his gently self-parodic "doting" introduces a tender, giddy cycle of bestowal, enjoyment, and wonder:

I dote on myself .... there is that lot of me, and all so luscious,
Each moment and whatever happens thrills me with joy.
I cannot tell how my ankles bend .... nor whence the cause of my faintest
    wish,
Nor the cause of the friendship I emit .... nor the cause of the friendship I
    take again.

To walk up the stoop is unaccountable .... I pause to consider if it really be,
That I eat and drink is spectacle enough for the great authors and schools,
A morning-glory at my window satisfies me more than the metaphysics of
    books.[37]

Linking ankles to wishes, the urges of friendship to a walk up the stoop, Whitman calls off the strict distinction between the me that enters into friendships and the not-me of everything else. Such Emersonian distinctions rely on the strict accounting of appraisal. The poet's bestowals declare both sides of the equation "unaccountable."

Pace John Winthrop, then, who found that self-love tore us all from one another, and *pace* Emerson, who found that the great and crescive self "ruined the kingdom of mortal friendship and love"—in Whitman to dote on oneself means to turn one's back on loneliness, and to turn back to the world. "We aren't very loving creatures, apparently, when we philosophize," notes Martha Nussbaum. We lack "passivity . . . trust . . . the acceptance of incompleteness."[38] In their bestowals on the self, and through these on the world, Whitman's poems invite us to indulge in passivity and acceptance, or as he puts it, "acceptation."[39] This "acceptation," and not Theseus's "madness," is for Whitman the bond between the lover and the poet. Either might be "the credulous man" who "sings unrestricted faith" in "Starting from Paumanok"; either might refuse to "see men and women as dreams or dots," the way philosophy threatened we might.[40]

A poet of bestowal, Whitman understands Emerson's skeptical "noble doubt" as Stanley Cavell understands skepticism more generally. He suspects that it "is motivated not by . . . intellectual scrupulousness but by a (displaced) denial, by a self-consuming disappointment that seeks world-consuming revenge."[41] Perhaps, after all, we already know as much and as well as we humanly could. What the skeptic needs isn't more knowledge but "the willingness to forgo knowing": the willingness to value what he or she knows already, to refuse disappointment and acknowledge our own enjoyment.[42] This is, indeed, Whitman's rhetorical move. When a personified "Speech" appears in "Song of Myself" it chides him, "Walt, you understand enough." And in "The

Terrible Doubt of Appearances," the poet confesses that he "cannot answer the question of appearances," despite his claims to possess "untold and untellable wisdom." "But I walk or sit indifferent," the poem ends; "I am satisfied." What solves the terrible doubt, then? In a line whose balanced hexameter and poised repetitions of sound give it a sense of repletion, Whitman names his answer: "He ahold of my hand has completely satisfied me."[43]

Whitman's claims of satisfaction mark a second common focus of bestowal: this time bestowals of value on "the known universe." That phrase recurs throughout the preface, as if in part to stress that the poet knows no more about the world than his readers—he just loves it more, or has the words to tell his love. The same proves true in the poems. The fifth section of "Song of Myself" may recount a rare initiatory moment. And the fruits of this union between self and soul may be knowledge: "the peace and knowledge that pass all the argument of the earth," to be precise. As he spells out what this knowledge entails, however, and at the moment he mentions love, Whitman pivots from mystical insights to home truths, and from high-toned religious diction to livelier, more commonplace detail.

> And I know that the hand of God is the promise of my own,
> And I know that the spirit of God is the brother of my own,
> And that all the men ever born are also my brothers, and the women my
> sisters and lovers,
> And that a kelson of the creation is love,
> And limitless are leaves stiff or drooping in the fields,
> And brown ants in the little wells beneath them,
> And mossy scabs of the worm fence, heap'd stones, elder, mullein, and
> poke-weed.[44]

The tender specificity of diction in the last three lines gives a sharp contrast to the declamatory generalities of the first three, and the pivot between them is a mention of love. This gesture eases any anxiety readers may feel over *not* knowing the hand or spirit of God as the poet does, and it revitalizes Whitman's verse. From the point of view of writing, as well as bestowal, the God we do not know may be no more important than the poke-weed that we do.

With his bestowals on "the known universe," Whitman refuses to join the Puritan-Emersonian tradition, which insists on the absolute privacy of some knowledge: God's knowledge of my election; my knowledge of myself. Indeed, he explicitly denies this privacy—in rhetorical gestures that often look like confessions of ignorance. In the passage just quoted, all the poet knows about the leaves, the ants, the poke-weed is that they are limitless (or "unaccountable"). When a child asks, "What is the grass?" Whitman can't say. "How could I answer the child?" he wonders, since, despite the moment of initiation a few lines before, "I do not know what it is any more than he." All he can do is "guess" that it is "the flag of my disposition," or "the handkerchief of the Lord," "itself a child," or "a uniform hieroglyphic," and to hazard that it "seems" to him "the beautiful uncut hair of graves." By the time he informs us decisively that "*This* is the grass," 260 lines have passed; and "this" now includes "the thoughts of all men in all ages and lands." If they're to be valued, it seems, thoughts themselves cannot be private. "If they are not yours as much as mine," the poet insists, "they are nothing."[45]

And if thoughts are to be shared, Whitman's poems ask, why not the soul? Throughout *Leaves of Grass*, but especially in poems like "I Sing the Body Electric," Whitman links the inaccessible soul to the public body, making the formerly private self available to love. "If the body were not the soul, what is the soul?" he demands near the start of "I Sing the Body Electric":

> The love of the body of man or woman balks account, the body itself balks
>   account,
> That of the male is perfect, and that of the female is perfect.
> The expressions of the face balks account,
> But the expression of a well-made man appears not only in his face,
> It is in his limbs and joints also, it is curiously in the joints of his hips and
>   wrists,
> It is in his walk, the carriage of his neck, the flex of his waist and knees,
>   dress does not hide him,
> The strong sweet quality he has strikes through the cotton and broadcloth,
> To see him pass conveys as much as the best poem, perhaps more,
> You linger to see his back, and the back of his neck and shoulder-side.[46]

Like Moses viewing only God's backside as he passes, Whitman slips past the risks of meeting a particular "face"—a gesture I'll return to in a moment. For now, let me note how his refusals simply to appraise or "account" turn to overflowing bestowals of value. "In bestowal," Singer explains, "we *attend* to the beloved."[47] Whitman's attentions dwell, delighted, on the *expressiveness* of the body brought to life by his attentions. Such a body can be read, like a poem. Such a body—like a poem, perhaps—can be both known and loved.

The Whitman who bonds body to soul in this way looks like a theological poet, or at least a mystical one. His claims are close cousins of Blake's remark, in *The Marriage of Heaven and Hell*, that the body is merely that portion of the soul visible to the five senses. Push them a step farther, and you reach the heady idealist claim that since bodies are souls, bodily union might in fact accomplish the spiritual merger that Emerson found "impossible." By the 1870s, sex reformers would make just that claim, and well into the 1920s husbands and wives were assured that soul union could be reached through properly executed sex.[48] I take up the poetry of their inevitable disappointment in my fourth chapter, in a reading of Mina Loy's *Songs to Joannes*. Here, though, let me suggest that Whitman's lines about body and soul might better be read in the purely secular, realist context of Jamesian psychology. Though we may all divide the world into the me and the not-me, William James writes, "between what a man calls me and what he simply calls mine the line is difficult to draw." Consider, he asks, "our fame, our children, the work of our hands." These may well be as "dear to us as our bodies are, and arouse the same feelings"; and as for those bodies: "are they simply ours, or are they *us*?"[49]

Worshiping "the spread of [his] body," then—a final common locus of bestowal—Whitman works to expand the borders of that confusion. The "root of washed sweet-flag, timorous pond-snipe, nest of guarded duplicate eggs" that make up his genitals and the "mixed tussled hay of head and beard" connect him to the world that feeds them, so that he may in good faith use its details to describe himself. Other people, at least in the form of the "hands I have taken, face I have kissed, mortal I have ever touched," also form part of his metaphorical "body." As he bestows value upon it, physical contact becomes a surrogate communion. Indeed, inasmuch as he lets the me include his body, "Disorderly fleshy and sensual .... eating drinking and breeding," he sets aside any claim to be a clean and proper and discrete incorporeal soul. What room is left for "solitude of self"? As Adrienne Rich will write in the "Twenty-One Love Poems," "A touch is enough to let us know / we're not alone in the universe."[50] At the same time, however, Whitman also frees himself from the flip side of that solitude: the idealist's ever-unsatisfied hunger for perfect union. Despite his reputation as a poet of "the merge," Whitman seems to me more a poet of motile, flickering psychological *identifications* than of metaphysical *fusion*. The difference will help us understand his claims to be "with us" in his poems. It will be also crucial to understanding Whitman's therapeutic project, his love-cure.

The Poet of "The Merge"?

Whitman's reputation as a poet of "the merge" was set by D. H. Lawrence. In *Studies in Classic American Literature*, he mocks the older poet's assertions that, as Lawrence puts it, "I am everything, and everything is me, and so we're all One in One Identity, like the Mundane Egg, which has been addled quite a while." More bitterly, he takes his precursor to task for extolling a series of mergings: first "the great merge, in to the womb," then "the merge of comrades: man-for-man love," and then, "almost immediately with this, death, the final merge of death."[51] His proof-text is "Scented Herbage of My Breast," the second *Calamus* poem, with its claims that love and death are "folded inseparably together"; his disappointment is born from Whitman's "mistake" in confusing "the mystery of Sympathy," in which souls remain separate, with the "old maddening bond of the love-compulsion," in which perfect, unmediated union is the goal.[52]

With his fierce rejection of merger, Lawrence marks himself as a poet of the modern period. As the historian Stephen Kern explains, "In the modern period the desire to fuse with a beloved did not disappear, but it was increasingly interpreted as an illusion, a failure, or a projection of oneself." Modernist authors often sketched characters "sickened by fusion," and they played down its "delusionary pleasure" in favor of "maintaining distance and danger in love."[53] I return to these questions in my chapter on modern love. For the moment, let me simply ask: how helpful are Lawrence's categories in understanding Whitman, rather than Lawrence himself? Are Whitman's poems really torn between dreams of merger and the more restrained, hands-off pleasures of sympathy?

Because of its placement in the *Calamus* sequence, "Scented Herbage of My Breast" seems to me a troublesome place to begin. Yes, the poet sings of love and death; yes, he wonders whether anything is "finally beautiful except death and love." In this, it would seem, he stakes his claim to a place in the Western tradition of *Liebestod* described by such theorists as Denis de Rougemont and George Bataille: the tradition, that is to say, of *passion*, where love is suffered, and is suffering. But having set those questions in our minds, hooking us with a song of love and death, the poet steps back with a smile. "I am not what you supposed," he warns us in the next poem, "but far different." When death appears in this poem, "Whoever You Are Holding Me Now in Hand," it is flat, unattractive, and *opposed* to love. On the one hand, "in libraries," the poet will "lie as one dumb, a gawk, or unborn, or dead." Once slipped out of the stacks and kissed by the reader, however, "with the comrade's long-dwelling kiss or the new husband's kiss," the poet comes to elusive, teasing life, slipping repeatedly out of our grasp.[54] For moments of merger, we need to look elsewhere.

The closest I find to merger in Whitman comes when the sense of touch undoes the poet's sense of being a distinct, neatly individuated person. "Is this then a touch?" the poet asks, "quivering me to a new identity, / Flames and ether making a rush for my veins, / . . . / My flesh and blood playing out lightning, to strike what is hardly different from myself." There, at last, is the shock and flutter that Bataille would lead us to expect from the erotic; and we hear it in "The Sleepers," too, where the dreaming poet will "become all the other dreamers," chanting "I am he" and "I am she," as Lawrence says he mustn't. Touch leaves the poet "flooded" by sensations, his "I" fluid, dissolved:

> Be careful, darkness .... already, what was it touched me?
> I thought my lover had gone .... else darkness and he are one,
> I hear the heart-beat .... I follow .... I fade away.

This fade-out marks a moment between mergers, since the poet flashes into focus once again, rendered self-consciously "hotcheeked and blushing" by his nakedness:

> O for pity's sake, no one must see me now! .... my clothes were stolen while I
> was abed,
> Now I am thrust forth, where shall I run?[55]

"Nakedness," writes George Bataille, "offers a contrast to self-possession, to discontinuous existence. . . . It is a state of communication revealing a quest for a possible continuance of being beyond the confines of the self."[56] "Thrust forth," the poet runs to a "pier" that mirrors his own erect state; but that pier shifts, in the space of two lines that show the poet calming down, to a metaphorical "bridge" that affords him a less drastic path to continuity, both between childhood and adult individuation, and between self and other:

> Pier out from the main, let me catch myself with you and stay .... I will not
> chafe you;
> I feel ashamed to go naked about the world,
> And am curious to know where my feet stand .... and what is this flooding
> me, childhood or manhood .... and the hunger that crosses the bridge
> between.[57]

Bataille insists on the "violence" incumbent on the search for continuity, and Lawrence on the voracious egotism masked by claims of merger. Whitman, though, is "curious," at ease. His curiosity keeps him at a distance from his shame, and his fondness for third terms, "bridges between," outweighs his hunger to eliminate distance, difference, or discontinuity.

When Whitman asks "Who need be afraid of the merge?" in "Song of Myself," his lack of fear suggests how rare "the merge" really is in his work. Does this make him, then, a poet of Lawrence's sympathy, that "feeling with" which allows the soul to "judg[e] for herself, and preserv[e] her own integrity"?[58] Not exactly. Like so many modernist poets of love, Lawrence is determined to be undeceived, and his sympathy touches base with appraisal at every turn. Whitman has no real interest in judging, except as the sun judges, "falling around a helpless thing," with "his thoughts . . . the hymns of the praise of things."[59] His bestowals thus offer a slightly different, equally realist alternative to the idealist dream of merger. In them, as in Lawrence's sympathy, self-awareness is not lost. We're not plucked out of separate selfhood and returned to a state of erotic discontinuity. Quite the contrary, as Jessica Benjamin explains, "by investing one's full attention in the object one allows it to emerge as real and whole, so that the self is not lost but heightened" through its enjoyment.[60] But as he invests his attention, bestowing value on what he sees, the poet need not insist on his "integrity." He is able to "loosen," not lose, his identity, caught up in the "embrace of love and resistance" that fleeting identifications entail:

> The wrestle of wrestlers, two apprentice-boys, quite grown, lusty, good-
> natured, native-born, out on the vacant lot at sundown after work,
> The coats and caps thrown down, the embrace of love and resistance,
> The upper-hold and under-hold, the hair rumpled over and blinding the
> eyes;
> The march of firemen in their own costumes, the play of masculine muscle
> through clean-setting trowsers and waist-straps,
> The slow return from the fire, the pause when the bell strikes suddenly
> again, and the listening on the alert,
> The natural, perfect, varied attitudes, the bent head, the curv'd neck and the
> counting;
> Such-like I love—I loosen myself, pass freely, am at the mother's breast with
> the little child,
> Swim with the swimmers, wrestle with the wrestlers, march in line with the
> firemen, and pause, listen, count.[61]

Idealization blurs into declarations of similitude, sight into contact. But idealist fusion is never really wanted or achieved. Even when he identifies with a child at the breast, Whitman doesn't yearn for a return to some putative lost state of symbiotic bliss. From the breast he is quickly drawn to the liminal world of water; from the water, back to land; and from there into a series of attractive, masculine roles, finally stepping back altogether to "pause, listen, count" once more. As he returns, however, Whitman takes no pains to distinguish this swimmer from that one, this fireman from another, to single one out from the group and look him or her in the face. Lawrence's sympathy demands such particular recognitions and discriminations; Whitman's love refuses to stand still and deliver them.

Is this refusal simply skittish, a flaw in Whitman's lessons of love? Camille Paglia thinks so. "A substitute for intimacy," she calls his work, "and a record of the swerve from it."[62] No doubt there is something to the charge. But Whitman wants to explore and record the experience of *loving*, rather than that of being in a *relationship*. As Theseus and Emerson insist, to love—to idealize, to bestow value—is a capacity of the psyche that lights on and illuminates a particular beloved, rather than being, strictly speaking, a *response* to him or her. This is a troubling thought. But when critics reproach Whitman for "diffusing the threatening qualities of sustained, individuated encounter," they miss his real claim on them.[63] For the one model of reciprocity Whitman does offer, and returns to again and again, is his announced love for *us*, which he invites us to return.

The Love-Cure

So far in this chapter I have used Jamesian psychology to explore Whitman's poetry of bestowal. The poet stands halfway, after all, between Emerson's lonely "great and crescive self" and those later psychologies and philosophies in which the "I" is unintelligible without some "thou," so that what was once supplementary to the self becomes constitutive.[64] James lets us see that as Whitman loves, he "loosens" himself by including more and more of the world in the metaphorical body of his "mine." These bonds will not attain the sublime extremity of fusion—but they don't require a *relationship*, either. When the poet declares, in "To a Stranger," "I ate with you and slept with you, your body has become not yours only nor left my body mine only, / You gave me the pleasure of your eyes, face, flesh, as we pass, you take of my beard, breast, hands, in return," you can't help but notice that this exchange takes place "as we pass."[65] To explore why Whitman's love so often seems a kiss before parting, and to understand the claims he makes for language as a means to connection with his truest, most lasting beloved, the reader, I need to shift my frames of psychological reference. From James I want to turn to Freud—or at least to the revisions of Freud in Kristeva's *Tales of Love*.

"In love," explains Kristeva, " 'I' has been an other." The risk this otherness runs in other contexts—say, of the loss of self into "raving hallucination"—is in love "accepted, normalized, made fully reassuring"; its impulse to "regression" counterpointed by "a certain amount of distance."[66] Whitman's sallies into otherness resemble the "transference love" described by the French psychoanalyst: the love of a patient for the analyst, which teaches him or her to avoid "the chaotic hyperconnectedness of fusion love as well as the death-dealing stabilization of love's absence." Still more, however, they recall the therapist's description of "countertransference love": the love of analyst for patient. Indeed, in *Tales of Love* Kristeva describes her role in surprisingly Whitmanian terms. Patients come to her suffering from "crises of love: let's admit it, lacks of love." She listens to them, bestows value on them, and in the process is able "to put myself in their place; looking, dreaming, suffering as if I were she, as if I were he. Fleeting moments of identification. Temporary and yet effective mergings. Fruitful sparks of understanding. Provided I move away."[67]

As they come into focus in "I Sing the Body Electric," "The Sleepers," and the *Children of Adam* and *Calamus* sequences, the patterns of Whitman's affection match Kristeva's "countertransference love" quite well. The fit should not surprise us. As many readers have noted, *Leaves of Grass* was meant from its earliest sketches to be a therapeutic book: one that would heal its readers, in part by causing them to love and identify with its "I." David Reynolds has described the "restorative" and reconstructive project of the 1855 *Leaves of Grass*, with its efforts to "resolve by fiat" the tensions that had brought the nation "near disunion," and to cure by sheer affirmation the "physical and psychological ills" that had left, in Whitman's words, the "public countenance . . . cadaverous as a corpse."[68] Just before the English Civil War, in "A Modell of Christian Charity," John Winthrop used his image of the One Man Christ to face down the perils of faction. In the years before his own country's Civil War, Whitman offered his poetic persona as a new One Man, and in the 1855 and 1860 editions of *Leaves of Grass*, he sketched an America of love for them to live in.[69] For his efforts to work, however, he needed readers who could recognize themselves in his community of "them that love as I myself am capable of loving."[70] If he did not find them, he would have to make them. Bestowals on the reader would be one tool; our theatrical identification with his all-bestowing "I" would be another.

Near the end of the Introduction, I juxtaposed a wry observation from Emerson's "Illusions" with a passage from Whitman's "To You." Love, says Emerson, "attributes to the beloved person all which that person shares with his or her family, sex, age, or condition, nay with the human mind itself. 'Tis these which the lover loves, and Anna Matilda gets the credit."[71] The shameless bestowals and attributions of Whitman stand that warning on its head. Being human, he insists, we get credit for every human glory. As for the fear of idolatry, Whitman slowly and deliberately flouts it in his praise. "I give nothing to anyone except I give the like carefully to you," he explains. Which means, as you might expect by now, "I sing the songs of the glory of none, not God, sooner than I sing the songs of the glory of you."[72]

Whitman's "songs of the glory of you" are designed to give his readers back a sense of their own power and lovableness. His gestures aren't always subtle, or even directly encouraging. "You there," he calls, "impotent, loose in the knees, open your scared chops till I blow grit within you." We are, he takes it, too abashed to accept his offer: too sickly, down for the count.

> Spread your palms and lift the flaps of your pockets,
> I am not to be denied .... I compel .... I have stores plenty and to spare,
> And any thing I have I bestow.

These bestowals are as irresistible as God's grace in the Protestant scheme. We "can do nothing and be nothing," they say, "but what [the poet] will infold [us]." Like Christ, he comes as a physician ("I am he bringing help for the sick as they pant on their backs"); and though he insists on visiting "strong upright men" as well, I find those visits as purely rhetorical as his questions to a too-self-satisfied reader: "Have you outstript the rest? Are you the President? / It is a trifle." More central to his project are these questions, from the "Song for Occupations":

> Why what have you thought of yourself?
> Is it you then that thought yourself less?
> Is it you that thought the President greater than you? or the rich better off
>   than you? or the educated wiser than you?
>
> Because you are greasy or pimpled—or that you was once drunk, or a thief,
>   or diseased, or rheumatic, or a prostitute—or are so now—or from
>   frivolity or impotence—or that you are no scholar, and never saw your
>   name in print .... do you give in that you are any less immortal?[73]

Such lines display the poet as Christ—not the Christ of Puritan theology, whose death provided only limited atonement, grace for the elect, but the one who gave his grace to prostitutes and tax collectors, too.

In a thoughtful rereading of the "poetry of praise" we find in *Leaves of Grass*, M. Wynn Thomas insists on the immediate social setting of these bestowals: the laborers and artisans whom Whitman identified with and saw as his audience. With poems such as the "Song for Occupations" and "To You," Thomas notes, the poet stoutly maintains that "personal value antedates social success and survives social failure; it inheres in the person himself and is inalienable." The poet's "extravagant impulse to praise the unsung qualities of the nondescript American," Thomas explains, "is based on the premise that the ordinary man presently lacks his full measure of self-respect." A reader may suffer guilt over "experiences the person has never previously dreamt could be opened to public sanction," including masturbation and homosexual eroticism. Struck glum by "social helplessness" in the face of economic turmoil, readers might be heartened by a poet's telling them that the political and economic world existed for them—and that the poem at hand was at their service, too.[74]

> The sum of all known value and respect I add up in you whoever you are;
> The President is up there in the White House for you .... it is not you who
>   are here for him,
> The Secretaries act in their bureaus for you .... not you here for them,
> The Congress convenes every December for you,
> Laws, courts, the forming of states, the charters of cities, the going and
>   coming of commerce and mails are all for you.
>
>   .   .   .
>
> All architecture is what you do to it when you look upon it;
> Did you think it was in the white or gray stone? or the lines of the arches
>   and cornices?
>
> All music is what awakens from you when you are reminded by the
>   instruments.[75]

Are all poems, then, what we do to them when we read them? Are they essentially what awakens from us when we are reminded by the words? Whitman suggests that his work lives only in a reader's response: a recurring theme of *Calamus* poems such as "Whoever You Are Holding Me Now in Hand," where what "awakens from us" and "what we do to" the lines when we read are both identified, albeit obliquely, as love.

Historicist readings identify both Whitman's immediate audience and their likely sources of self-doubt. With an eye to future readers, however, the poet casts his net more widely and more deeply than Thomas describes. He does not exclude the well-off, for example, from his treatments of self-doubt. Keeping his address in the third person, so that laborers could see that their afflictions were shared, Whitman's portraits of those who *should* be happy, in any appraisal of success, yield some of his most plangent passages. "Through the laughter, dancing, dining, supping, of people," he writes in "Song of the Open Road," "Inside of dresses and ornaments, inside of those wash'd and trimm'd faces / Behold a secret silent loathing and despair." It's that *silence* that grounds the hellish, Eliotic vision that follows:

No husband, no wife, no friend, trusted to hear the confession,
Another self, a duplicate of every one, skulking and hiding it goes,
Formless and wordless through the streets of the cities, polite and bland in
    the parlors,
In the cars of railroads, in steamboats, in the public assembly,
Home to the houses of men and women, at the table, in the bedroom,
    everywhere,
Smartly attired, countenance smiling, form upright, death under the
    breast-bones, hell under the skull-bones,
Under the broadcloth and gloves, under the ribbons and artificial flowers,
Keeping fair with the customs, speaking not a syllable of itself,
Speaking of any thing else but never itself.[76]

By refusing to name the source of all this loathing, silence, and despair, Whitman lets his readers project their own sources of guilt and alienation into the scene. But his reticence does something more.

In "Song of the Open Road," and elsewhere, in "To You," the poet clearly assumes that readers *have* unconfessed, unconfessable sadnesses and shames, and that at a hint, they will spring to mind. "What you have done returns already in mockeries," he remarks, and then asks, as an intimate aside, "(Your thrift, knowledge, prayers, if they do not return in mockeries, what is their return?)"[77] The poet bets that none would say his or her thrift, knowledge, and prayers have returned what was hoped. And even if they had, who would be satisfied with the results? As John Stuart Mill put it in a moment of despair in 1826, " 'Suppose that all your objects in life were realized . . . would this be a great joy and happiness to you?' And an irrepressible self-consciousness distinctly answered, 'No!' "[78] Where does this "no" come from? There is, Whitman seems to suspect, a loss before the losses of any adult life: an ur-dissatisfaction that Christianity knows as the Fall and Freudian theory describes as the loss of union with Mama. In both cases only love—that of God or that of, in Kristeva's terms, the pre-Oedipal "Ideal Father"—can reconcile us to and lift us out of the pain.[79]

In Kristeva's scheme, the Ideal Father is what Baby imagines Mama's *other* object of desire to be: an androgynous, radiant figure that becomes its initial constitutive metaphor, "I'm like that, or I will be." On the couch, her patient must learn to repeat this act of idealization and identification with the analyst, falling in transference love. And not only with the therapist. "We need manifold identifications," she writes: "plastic, polymorphic, polyphonic." When the traditional foundations for identification have come loose, "then two paths remain open to us: on the one hand, to read literature, and, on the other, to attempt love's reinvention."[80] Whitman's poems offer the reader a chance at both.

In a number of his poems Whitman invokes figures who resemble this ideal, imaginary father. In "As I Ebb'd with the Ocean of Life," the island Paumanok might be such a figure, one whose "kiss" enables the poet to make peace with the "fierce old mother," the sea. In "The Sleepers" we find the tender General Washington, "the father" who "holds his grown or ungrown son in his arms with measureless love," and the "red squaw" as well, at whom "my mother looked in delight and amazement."[81] And, of course, there is Whitman's Lincoln. Most often, however, the poet presents *himself* as this ambivalently gendered, healing figure. It is as such an ideal father, more than as "one of the roughs," that he has passed into American mythology. As Harold Bloom explains, "the most crucial fact about Whitman's psyche" was his need "to become the true father of all of his siblings, and perhaps of his mother also . . . even as he so beautifully became a surrogate father and mother for thousands of wounded and sick soldiers, Union and Confederate, white and black, in the hospitals of Washington, D.C., throughout the Civil War."[82] "The experience is a profound one, beyond all else," Whitman wrote to a friend in New York, "& touches me personally, egotisticaly, in unprecedented ways—I mean the way often the amputated, sick, sometimes dying soldiers cling & cleave to me. . . . It is delicious to be the object of so much love and reliance, & to do them good, soothe, & pacify torments of wounds etc—."[83] A delicious irony, if you look at it askance: he goes there to love and preach freedom, but he really wants to be the object of the soldiers' reliance and love. To which the bestowing spirit answers, *Honi soit qui mal y pense.*

In recent years, of course, *mal y pense* has become the critic's family crest. Whitman's bestowals on the reader are now eyed with even more suspicion than Lawrence gave his mentions of "the merge." Where readers of the 1950s and 60s approvingly described the poet as aiming to "assist at the poetic and godlike in every reader," that consensus has now begun to crack, to insist on the irony of ordering, as it's said, an Emersonian self-reliance.[84] Consider the bestowals of "To You." When the poet lays his hands on us to "make us his poem," we find ourselves at first in the not-unhappy position of receiving tender flattery, which we (and he) know is too general to be believed. "I whisper with my lips close to your ear," he says to us, "whoever you are." "I have loved many women and men, but I love none better than you." But what begins as a scene of seduction shifts registers, building from a whisper to an oratorical crescendo, so that the hands feel less like those of a lover and more like those of a man bestowing a blessing we may not, frankly, have asked for.

O I have been dilatory and dumb,
I should have made my way straight to you long ago,
I should have blabb'd nothing but you, I should have chanted nothing
but you.

I will leave all and come and make the hymns of you,
None has understood you, but I understand you,
None has done justice to you, you have not done justice to yourself,
None but has found you imperfect, I only find no imperfection in you,
None but would subordinate you, I only am he who will never consent to
subordinate you,
I only am he who places over you no master, owner, better, God, beyond
what waits intrinsically in yourself.
O I could sing such grandeurs and glories about you!
You have not known what you are, you have slumber'd upon yourself all
your life,
Your eyelids have been the same as closed most of the time,
What you have done returns already in mockeries.[85]

"Awakening the dormant will of the second person—the slumbering 'glory of
you'—" writes Kerry Larson of this poem, "amounts to paralyzing it," given
the poet's "crude and somewhat self-defeating" efforts, or "tactics."[86] As Terry
Nathanson observes, in the same debunking vein, "The passages that evoke
our liberation necessarily activate what balks desire and separates us from ful-
fillment."[87]

Critics like Larsen and Nathanson are equally skeptical when it comes to
Whitman's claims that written language makes him as intimately present in
his poems as he would be in person, speaking. "Whitman needs to remind us to
forget writing," Nathanson observes, "in order that the poet may speak, and
rise up and be revealed." His poems thus "elaborate the never-completed mo-
ment of a mystification": a mystification that Whitman himself could not sus-
tain through the 1860s, and that the critic of the 1990s must unmask.[88] This
challenge goes to the heart of Whitman's poetry of love. For if the poet offers
readers a model for what it looks and feels like to bestow value in love, and if he
gives heartening words to name those moods, or to confess to and forgive one
another, as our ideal father has forgiven us, behind both gestures lies an un-
abashed faith in the power of language. If Whitman seems at times to antici-
pate the Derridean assertion that all is text—"Human bodies are words, myr-
iads of words," he writes in the "Song of the Rolling Earth"—for him this
proposition underwrites literature, raising it in status rather than deconstruct-

ing what we thought was the rest of the world. To put it more bluntly, for Whitman, language *works*. It is a means to contact and intimacy, rather than something that leaves us, as Derrida writes, "dispossessed of the longed-for presence" in every "gesture of language by which we attempt to seize it."[89]

Like his bestowals of value on the body and the "known universe," Whitman's faith in language can be read as a swerve away from privacy of self in the direction of love. To refute the solipsist, as W. H. Auden observes, we need only open the *OED*.[90] As a young minister, even Emerson waxed lyrical about the way that language draws us together. "What were the state of minds that God had enclosed in unsocial bodies, with no language even of signs?" he demands in a sermon preached in 1829. "They are separated more effectually than if Oceans sundered them; the thought of one cannot penetrate to the thought of the other. They cannot cooperate—they cannot have affections—and the heart is oppressed by its pity for so forlorn a being." Speech is "this great bond of connexion between the seen and the unseen world, whereby the impenetrable darkness that covers the soul of man from man is taken away and I am made acquainted with the inaccessible soul of my brother."[91] Whitman's claim is that the same will prove true of writing, or at least of poetry. At the climax of "Crossing Brooklyn Ferry," for example, when he demands, "What is it then between us?" his question is rhetorical—but also crucial, pertinent, answerable. The *poem* lies between us, robs the "scores or hundreds of years" of their force, and "fuses me into you now, and pours my meaning into you." Haven't we readers accepted the poet's proposal, he asks, acting out if not saying our "I do"? "We understand then do we not?" he demands. "What I promised without mentioning, have you not accepted? / What the study could not teach—what the preaching could not accomplish, is accomplish'd, is it not?"[92] For the space of this poem, he promises, so long as you peruse it, my thoughts will be in your mind, my words in your mouth. The "innavigable sea" that Emerson saw between subject and object is transformed into the "eternal float of solution" Whitman mentions elsewhere in the poem (sections 5 and 9)—that is, into language, which refuses to be private, to let us be cut off from one another; and which undermines the strict distinction between me and not-me with its wash of semiosis.

"Words, words," a critic might say, turning away unconvinced. And, indeed, by the 1860s Whitman himself had come to despair of the slipperiness and circularity of writing, as opposed to speech.[93] You can see his hesitation in two of the "Sea-Drift" poems, "Out of the Cradle, Endlessly Rocking" and "As I Ebb'd With the Ocean of Life," which turn their backs on the hopes of his earlier work. In the first we see a boy-poet, like the one of "There Was a Child Went Forth," learn new and sadder lessons in the origins of poetry. He hears two songs, or "arias," sung by a male bird to, and then in longing for, his mate. The first song celebrates a union worthy of the happiest moments in "Calamus" or "Song of Myself": *"Singing all time, minding no time, / While we two keep together."* After the mate is lost, however, he sings a much longer and more elaborate elegy, a series of *"Carols of lonesome love!"* sung *"uselessly, uselessly all the night,"* which will prove the source for this boy-poet's later art. This is, we might say, a lyric moment: one in which language acts to take the place of an absent beloved.[94] So much so, in fact, that it threatens to displace the Other altogether. "Is it indeed toward your mate you sing," the boy wonders, "or is it really to me," closing a circle of language and loss? "O you singer solitary, singer by yourself, projecting me," comes his response, "O solitary me listening, never more shall I cease perpetuating you."[95]

Like "Out of the Cradle," "As I Ebb'd" stages a confrontation between the poet's earlier hopes and his later disappointment. "My arrogant poems," he calls his previous work, and in the course of "As I Ebb'd," they reappear as "the lines underfoot," "a few sands and dead leaves," and other forms of "debris."[96] None has sufficed to end the privacy and solitude of his inexpressible "real Me." "Amid all that blab whose echoes recoil upon me I have not once had the least idea who or what I am," the poet laments, since

> before all my arrogant poems the real Me stands yet untouch'd, untold,
>   altogether unreach'd,
> Withdrawn far, mocking me with mock-congratulatory signs and bows,
> With peals of distant ironical laughter at every word I have written,
> Pointing in silence to these songs, and then to the sand beneath.[97]

The "arrogance" of the previous poems lies in the way they pretended to solve the poet's solitude. His words have not embodied or expressed him, nor have they brought him into contact with a reader. Throughout "As I Ebb'd" the poet's "we" refers to the poet and his poems, or the "me and mine," or the poet's "dead lips" and the "exuding ooze" and "little corpses" into which he has died. Like the kingdoms of the world before Jesus, Whitman's poems are "spread out before" his readers, for them to accept or reject. The readers, in turn, are "up there" above the poet and not, as in the *Calamus* poems, holding him in hand.

In "Crossing Brooklyn Ferry" Whitman dreamed of written language as speech, perfectly connective. So long as he could envision readers bestowing value on his words, he could see "speech and love" as "parallel and equivalent acts of presence."[98] When the tide turns, when the poems turn back on their maker, language and love become equally conflicted. Roland Barthes's *A Lover's Discourse* gives a sadder but wiser passage to describe this turn. "To know that one does not write for the other," Barthes muses, "to know that these things I am going to write will never cause me to be loved by the one I love . . . to know that writing compensates for nothing, sublimates nothing, that it is precisely *there where you are not*"—this is, he concludes, "the beginning of writing."[99]

"Be it as if I were with you"

The "beginning of writing" described by Barthes could undermine Whitman's love-cure. In the context of *Leaves of Grass* as a whole, however, Whitman puts his moments of desolation to a more hopeful use. In effect, he asks readers to *rescue* him from this grim "beginning," to rise to the occasion of love and return his favors, bestowing value on him and on his words in a way the categories and appraisals of literary criticism tend to forbid.[100] "No one will get at my verses who insists upon viewing them as a literary performance," the poet warns in "A Backward Glance O'er Travel'd Roads." The loss would be as much his as his readers', the evidence of dejection odes like "As I Ebb'd" and "Out of the Cradle" suggests. Hence Whitman's repeated efforts to remind readers of their power, of how much he and his poems depend on them. Nervous, he gives them instructions: "Publish my name and hang up my picture as that of the tenderest lover" ("Recorders Ages Hence"). He puts a glad greeting in their mouths: "O take my hand Walt Whitman! / Such gliding wonders! such sights and sounds!" ("Salut au Monde!"). He confesses, near the start of "Crossing Brooklyn Ferry," that "you that shall cross from shore to shore years hence are more to me, and more in my meditations, than you suppose," and one tends to believe him. There is an element of danger in his poetics, after all, a chance that the reader will not "sign himself a candidate for my affections," and therefore that the "signs" of the tendered poem will be refused ("Whoever You Are," "Among the Multitude").[101]

In the *Calamus* poems, Whitman uses initiatory warnings, allurements, and withdrawals to get us to "sign ourselves" up as lovers and "élèves." When the poet speaks from his "secluded spot" at the start of the sequence, able for once to "respond as [he] would not dare elsewhere" to his pleasure in "manly attachment," he hints that we, too, are meant to respond as we have not previously dared. The poet dares us to join his "novitiate." "The way is suspicious, the result uncertain, perhaps destructive," he promises, sketching an adven-

ture in which "all conformity to the lives around you would have to be aban-
don'd." Just reading the poem is risky enough: "These leaves conning you con
at peril," he writes, with the chiasmus of the phrase insinuating that the poem
may be "conning," or tricking us as we read, or "con," it.[102] He addresses us re-
peatedly in cautionary tones:

> Whoever you are holding me now in hand,
> Without one thing all will be useless,
> I give you fair warning before you attempt me further,
> I am not what you supposed, but far different.
>
> ("Whoever You Are...")

> Are you the new person drawn toward me?
> To begin with take warning, I am surely far different from what you
>   suppose;
> Do you suppose you will find in me your ideal?
> Do you think it so easy to have me become your lover?
> Do you think the friendship of me would be unalloy'd satisfaction?
> Do you think I am trusty and faithful?
> Do you see no further than this façade, this smooth and tolerant manner
>   of me?
>
> ("Are You the New Person...")

Lines like these, or others in which the poet boasts of his protean elusiveness,
invite readers to feel they know him in a way that at least *seems* complex, and
even forgiving. Part of us no doubt stands off, aloof, noting the literary perfor-
mance played out before us. Part of us jots a reminder to slip "Are You the New
Person" under a door or in with a bouquet. But we may also join in the fiction of
the poem, assured that we have thereby defied the poet's admonition, "There-
fore release me and depart on your way." As such we are not merely "holding
[him] now in hand," as an early poem in the sequence names us. We are cer-
tainly not standing above him, ready to judge. Rather we find ourselves in the
figure who "sits a long while holding me *by* the hand." And thus, at least by im-
plication, in the friend whose "arm lay lightly around my breast—and that
night I was happy."[103]

The question of happiness returns in the final, most moving poem of *Cala-
mus*, "Full of Life Now." The present tense of the title marks both the "now" of
the writing and the "now" of our imagined acceptance of the poet's "wistful
and brave" offer of love.[104] Each stanza sketches half of that two-part "now,"

and if we are willing to pretend that we can "realize" the poet in *our* time, seeking him out in his words, then we can imagine him seeking and loving us in *his*. Our reward? A whispered companionship:

> Full of life now, compact, visible,
> I, forty years old the eighty-third year of the States,
> To one a century hence or any number of centuries hence,
> To you yet unborn these, seeking you.
>
> When you read these I that was visible am become invisible,
> Now it is you compact, visible, realizing my poems, seeking me,
> Fancying how happy you were if I could be with you and become your
>   comrade;
> Be it as if I were with you. (Be not too certain but I am now with you.)

The powerful figure who radiates bestowals "as the sun falling around a helpless thing" is also the artist whose work lives only in us, who needs not only our help, but our happiness.[105] Hence his urge to lift us from our passive, receptive status, to cure our inability to bestow. Once cured, we can use bestowal's grand, appreciative *as if* to "realize" the promise he's tucked in parentheses.

Whitman's love-cure, then, is built on a foundation of exposure, self-exposure, and reciprocal reassurance. The poet makes confessions of weakness on our behalf, inviting us to admit our weakness or unhappiness, our need of him. His bestowals of value—on himself and his body, on the "known world," and on us—make him seem a model of health and well-being, at times a coy seducer, but more often a radiant Ideal Father, whose words we take in and with whom we can identify.[106] As we read, however, we also find implicit and explicit confessions of weakness on the poet's part. Whether or not we see ourselves in his "you"—often we don't, but observe the "I" and "you" like characters in a play, or try on their roles by turns—passages like these invite us to cheer their author up, not least by bestowing value on him in return. When we do, we know ourselves to be cured, or at least capable of love.[107]

To read the love poems of *Leaves of Grass* as moments in a love-cure is to read them as, in some sense, *epistolary* verse. As Maeera Shreiber explains, the epistolary love poem has long stood as a "feminine" alternative to the tradition of the lyric: an alternative that strives to bring about that impossible literary ideal, mutual presence. Where the lyric thrives on absence and unreturned love, even usurping the beloved as the poet's object of desire and satisfaction, the epistolary poem can act as a bridge between self and other: an enabling moment in the love life, and not an alternative to it. If the lyric primarily lives in being *written*, with its author constructing himself through the metaphors of the verse, the letter-poem has always lived in being *read*, as a metonym for the body of its author.[108] Nineteenth-century American correspondents were familiar with this epistolary *as if*. "To get a letter, sealed and private," Lystra quotes one representative letter, is like "finding ourselves alone and taking each other in arms and hugging and kissing to our hearts' content."[109]

Perhaps he should have deconstructed her missive, or she his ardent response—in later chapters I will take up an impulse called "the modern temper," which casts just such a cold eye on love. I like to keep such exchanges in mind, though, when I read claims like the one that closes *Leaves of Grass* in "So Long!":

> My songs cease, I abandon them,
> From behind the screen where I hid I advance personally solely to you.
>
> Camerado, this is no book,
> Who touches this touches a man,
> (Is it night? are we here together alone?)
> It is I you hold and who holds you,
> I spring from the pages into your arms—decease calls me forth.[110]

It is precisely the epistolary *as if*, with its "credulous" naiveté, its bestowals of value on the word at hand, and its performative assertion of presence, that makes this rebirth possible.

The claim of presence is one that we can always deny. We may, after all, be embarrassed by the poet's claim on us, by his profligate bestowals, or the role we're asked to play. "We do not quite forgive a giver," Emerson remarks. "We can receive anything from love, for that is a way of receiving it from ourselves; but not from any one who assumes to bestow."[111] And yet, once we sign ourselves as the candidate for the poet's affections, the bestowals indeed come "from ourselves," and the role seems even alluring:

> O how your fingers drowse me,
> Your breath falls around me like dew, your pulse lulls the tympans of my
>   ears,
> I feel immerged from head to foot,
> Delicious, enough.

That "enough" probably means something like "satisfied and satisfying"—but there is something of *basta* in it as well. A disentangling gesture, it recalls Whitman's commitment to the two-steps-forward, three-steps-back of therapeutic love. Reminding us of the distance inherent to romantic realism, it is nevertheless a little disappointing: so much is promised, such pleasures half-begun. As a critic I'm tempted to add that the awkwardness of "tympans" and the neologizing of "immerged" break the spell rather earlier than the poet intends. But as a reader my response is closer to the complaint voiced in "No Way of Knowing," John Ashbery's poem about love, knowledge, and Whitmanian "camaraderie": "Why must you go? Why can't you / Spend the night, here in my bed, with my arms wrapped tightly around you?"[112] Ashbery vies with his precursor for the title of handsomest, tenderest lover: one more at home with Barthes's "beginning of writing," perhaps, but familiar with epistolary enticements, too.

In his recent essay " 'As If I Were With You'—The Performance of Whitman's Poetry," Stephen Railton smiles indulgently at Whitman's claims of presence. "Most readers probably decline to play the part of imaginary love that Whitman writes for them," he writes. "They remain readers holding a book, mystified and—if they think about it seriously—uncomfortable with the idea of suddenly finding a strange man in their arms."[113] Perhaps poets or would-be poets, of whatever sexual preference, are less mystified and more readily charmed. As my epigraph from Ostriker and those lines from Ashbery suggest, Whitman proves a continuing model for lovers and love poets: both those who openly declare their debt, like Hart Crane, Allen Ginsberg, and C. K. Williams, and those like Gertrude Stein, who suggest the comparison as they test the links between poetic language and intimacy. I return to Whitman when we reach Adrienne Rich, who wrestles with her precursor less over language than over the older poet's insistence that the poet is always finally a "single, solitary soul," albeit one able to forge the bonds of bestowal.[114] Is this limitation true, she wonders, of women as well?

Between Rich and Whitman lies, of course, another model for love and poetry: the example of Emily Dickinson. In the spring of 1850, just before the last of Whitman's pre–*Leaves of Grass* verses appeared in print, Dickinson composed the first of her 1775 poems. She was nineteen. It is a valentine:

> Oh the Earth was *made* for lovers, for damsel, and hopeless swain,
> For sighing, and gentle whispering, and *unity* made of *twain.*
> All things do go a courting, in earth, or sea, or air,
> God hath made nothing single but *thee* in His world so fair!
> . . .

Thine eyes are sadly blinded, but yet thou mayest see
Six true, and comely maidens sitting upon the tree;
Approach that tree with caution, then up it boldly climb,
And seize the one thou lovest, nor care for *space*, or *time!*[115]

Compare with me, ye women, if you dare. The brio of the verse is glorious, yet overmatched by a still more inventive prose valentine she sent the same season:

> Magnum bonum, "harum scarum," zounds et zounds, et war alarum, man reformam, life perfectum, mundum changum, all things flarum?
>
> Sir, I desire an interview; meet me at sunrise, or sunset, or the moon—the place is immaterial. . . . With soul, or spirit, or body, they are all alike to me. With host or alone, in sunshine or storm, in heaven or earth, some how or no how—I propose, sir, to see you.
>
> And not to see merely, but a chat, sir, or a tete-a-tete, a confab, a mingling of opposite minds is what I propose to have. I feel sir that we shall agree. We will be David and Jonathan, or Damon and Pythias, or what is better than either, the United States of America.[116]

Flaring from the charm and nonsense here we glimpse the concerns that Whitman would expound when he returned to print in five years' time. "Soul, or spirit, or body" are "alike" to the poet. Lovers ought by rights to resemble that greatest of romantic partners, the United States. Yet the bravura tone of these pieces, their command of language and their reader, and the intellectual reach that is hidden in the otherwise unlikely imprecation to "seize the one thou lovest, nor care for *space*, or *time!*" already suggest that Dickinson will not settle for Whitman's kiss-and-promise, all-bestowing, therapeutic role. "I am Judith the heroine of the Apocrypha," she declares in the prose valentine; "That's what they call a metaphor in our country. Don't be afraid of it, sir, it won't bite." Like Whitman, she takes part in the nineteenth-century transvaluation of sacred and secular unions. But she does so with supreme self-consciousness, teasing religious tropes and philosophical arguments to bring out their transgressive, theatrical, and erotic potential. She is our most demanding, most bracing poet of love.

Two

"Bondage as Play"

What Thou dost — is Delight —
Bondage as Play — be sweet —
Imprisonment — Content —
And Sentence — Sacrament —
Just We two — meet —
— EMILY DICKINSON, POEM 725

Who was Emily Dickinson's "Thou"? The question has nagged at readers since her death. The poet's brother Austin mutilated her manuscripts in an effort to disguise, excise, or render chaste her most passionate expressions of affection—especially, although not exclusively, those composed for Susan Gilbert Dickinson, his wife.[1] Susan's daughter, Martha Dickinson Bianchi, also took pains to obscure the eroticism of this relationship. She claimed on her mother's authority that Dickinson's one true love was a married man whom she'd been forced to renounce, perhaps the Reverend Charles Wadsworth.[2] The tale was quickly seconded by Austin's mistress, Mabel Loomis Todd, who passed it down to future readers. We "know for a fact" that "after some years of romance by correspondence, her friend made it clear that he could not or would not marry her," declares the Peter Pauper Press edition of Todd's revisions of Dickinson's *Love Poems,* a slim white volume that haunts the shelves of mall bookstores. The poems themselves "tell how she suppressed her inner loss and hurt," although "outwardly she grew only a bit more odd, more devoted, more sentimental—as might be expected of a sensitive maiden lady with big emotions and strange words to express them in."[3]

Such pronouncements don't just insult Dickinson the lover, whether of men or of women. As Lavinia Dickinson recognized in 1894, the itch to identify a "love disaster" in her sister's life remains the greatest obstacle to recognizing her "power of language."[4] We dare not underestimate the literariness of Dickinson's affections, the degree to which the roles of lover and beloved appealed to her *as roles.*[5] "Candor — my tepid friend — ," she warns, "Come not to play with me" (P 1537). And yet, as in my previous chapter, the question of *who* shades into a more helpful, more literary question: *how* did Dickinson love? What traditions of love underwrite her youthful valentines, with their mix, as Adrienne Rich puts it, of "sensual and metaphysical adventures"?[6] What sponsors such later poems as "As the Starved Maelstrom laps the Navies," with their passionate investigations of meeting, eating, and the appetites for power that may lie beneath them both?[7]

In American poetry of love, Dickinson is both peak and pivot, a crucial transitional figure. The Puritan distinction between human and heavenly loves, nineteenth-century erotic faith, Emersonian isolation, Whitman's tease of the reader's response—all inform her work. But she is also the first great American poet for whom difference is central to love: sexual difference, with its roles and power games; and the difference between any two persons, including lovers who are, in gender, "the same." Dickinson is, in some sense, the American Rilke, for she, too, imagines a love in which "two solitudes protect and border and greet each other."[8] Except, of course, that Dickinson's meetings and greetings are far *sexier* than this, sparked by the pleasures and dangers of what poem 725 calls "bondage as play."

In this chapter, I start by tracing Dickinson's debts to Puritan notions of love and, more important, to the novelized "erotic faith" of her own time.[9] This faith suffuses her poems of defiant devotion, in which love proves "the sweetest heresy" (P 387). It does not, however, quite explain the flair for self-abasement indulged by her otherwise grandly assertive "I." I look at some reasons why she might use masochism as a means to meeting, or to intersubjective encounter—and then, for a crucial test case, turn to the poems and letters for Susan Gilbert, where feminist critics have found a different, more egalitarian affection.[10] After that I explore to Dickinson's poems of "teasing the want." Here the poet subjects herself to the discipline of difference, refusing to name or assuage our desire to know what the alternative to separateness might be. As her poems enact the "Mutual Risk" and "Mutual Gain" of realist encounter, they anticipate the concerns of my next three chapters. Amy Lowell claimed that twentieth-century poetry began with Dickinson.[11] The same could be said of the modern poetics of love.

"The Love a Life can Show — Below"

Dickinson has long been read as an inheritor of New England Puritanism, if not also as its decadent, aestheticizing triumph. Indeed, a Nathaniel Dickinson was on board the *Arbella* for the 1630 Puritan exodus. Like Bradstreet he would have heard John Winthrop preach on social distinction, the selfishness of fallen love, and our need to be "knit together" through regenerate Christian charity. Two centuries later, however, Dickinson's Puritanism often seems mostly a matter of tone: an elitist "inwardness" of spirit that presumably contrasts with the soft, sentimentalized faith of her neighbors.[12] "Like Melville," writes Cynthia Griffin Wolff, "Dickinson was an anachronism," determined to confront a God and drama of redemption that her culture was steadily abandoning.[13] She was just as determined to wrestle the Puritan vision of love.

As I showed in the Introduction, some elements of that Puritan vision survived the American Revolution and the turn of centuries. On the one hand, there was a limited but valued realist love we are enjoined to enjoy here below; on the other, an unlimited, idealist union promised after death, a union not with each other but with the divine. Our usual mistake, the Puritans saw, is to ask heavenly satisfaction from a human mate. Death, distance, and mutability, those fruits of the Fall, hasten to put us back on course. They warn us off the self-love that infects all our affections, and they remind us of our inclination to idolatry.

Now, Dickinson rejects the charge of original sin on which so much of Puritan love-theology is based.[14] Nor does she take much comfort in the notion of a heaven where "they neither woo nor are given in wooing," as she put it rather coyly to Judge Lord. (Jesus said there would be no *marriage*.) "What an imperfect place!" she concludes, but her smiling dismissal is quite serious (L 751). As Richard Henry Dana Sr. feared in "The Husband and Wife's Grave," an eternity stripped of gallant and companionable affection is cold comfort indeed.[15] But to banish or dismiss a heaven above is one thing, and to claim its satisfactions below, quite another. In a note to Susan Gilbert, a believing Christian, Dickinson enclosed a poem (P 673) that slips a heavenly sublimity of union into a more secular, and more erotic setting:

> The Love a Life can Show — Below
> Is but a filament, I know,
> Of that diviner thing
> That faints upon the face of Noon —

And smites the Tinder in the Sun —
And hinders Gabriel's Wing —

'Tis this — in Music — hints and sways —
And far abroad on Summer days —
Distills uncertain pain —
'Tis this enamors in the East —
And tints the Transit in the West
With harrowing Iodine—

'Tis this — invites — appalls — endows —
Flits — glimmers — proves — dissolves —
Returns — suggests — convicts — enchants —
Then — flings in Paradise —

The range of reference in the first stanza is variously biblical and Miltonic, and in it the Love Above does holy, eschatological things. By the second stanza, however, the poem has left the sacred behind. Instead, Dickinson invokes sublime *art*, with its mixture of pleasure and pain. Like Nietzsche a decade later, she dwells on music, which hints at pleasures that it does not satisfy. Music lulls and lures us, reminding us that "at the very climax of joy there sounds a cry . . . of yearning lamentation for an irretrievable loss": the loss that marks our individuation, which sets the boundaries of self that love longs to cross.[16] The love we dream of, in this poem, is so overwhelming it is linked in our minds with violence and wounds (hence "Iodine"). We are invited, appalled, endowed by it. The boundary line between loves above and below flits and glimmers, luring us on to "prove" or test it, then dissolving as we approach. Finally it "flings in Paradise," an exuberant injection of the "diviner" realm into ours that flings us into its. This union does not come at the safe center of the poem, as in Bradstreet. Rather, it comes at the close, as if to suggest that when we reach what George Bataille calls "the sovereign moment at the farthest point of being," there is no discontinuity, no selfhood, no language left.[17]

Poem 673 marks Dickinson, not Whitman, as the American poet of "the merge." Its finally wordless push to "erotic continuity," as Bataille calls it, suggests that full and lasting satisfaction demands the obliteration of self and other in a *Liebestod*. (Wagner and Dickinson are contemporaries, more or less.) But its vision of ecstatic union is a rare extreme in Dickinson's work. More common, and more telling, are poems that settle the shaky ground between loves above and below, drawing on the Puritan topoi of marriage and idolatry.

60

I am less concerned with those poems in which Dickinson envisions the patri-
archal *fact* of marriage, especially as a burden to the women involved, than with
those in which the *fantasy* of marriage bears a telling thrill of transgression.
Where Emerson saw marriage as, at best, a mature and chastened alternative
to the objectifying, idolatrous impulse of passion, Dickinson imagines it as
(again at best) the relationship where sublime too-muchness gets a social habi-
tation and a name. In this, she takes her cues not from the Puritans but from the
blend of sentiment, passion, and kitsch that Robert Polhemus calls erotic faith.

The "Sweetest Heresy"

The roots of Victorian erotic faith, as we have seen, lie in the Protestant exalta-
tion of human marriage. The Puritans were careful to distinguish between
such earthly unions and the trope of marriage to the divine. When Bradstreet
used the language of Canticles to license her most extravagant claims of union
with her husband, she kept her allusions safely in the realm of compliments.
Reacting against the slippery slope of sentimental love, Emerson used the
promise of union with the impersonal to mock our impulse to pair off in search
of paradise.[18] Dickinson knows these traditions of Protestant and platonic
love, and she gives them a characteristically satirical twist. Consider her poem
on the elaborate, circular scheme in which God's Word, the Bible, informs us
that the Word that was God became flesh out of love so that we might love the
One we know through biblical words. In poem 357 she turns this plot into a sly,
outrageous, romance:

> God is a distant — stately Lover —
> Woos, as He states us — by His Son —
> Verily, a Vicarious Courtship —
> "Miles," and "Priscilla", were such an One —
>
> But, lest the Soul — like fair "Priscilla"
> Choose the Envoy — and spurn the Groom —
> Vouches, with hyperbolic archness —
> "Miles," and "John Alden" were Synonym —

The way "states" rings in "stately" reminds us how purely verbal a courtship
this is, while the speaker's Elizabethan "verily," drawn as easily from Shake-
speare as from the King James Bible, hints at how dated this wordiness has
grown. By the second stanza God himself adopts the poet's "hyperbolic arch-
ness" — a nice bit of geometric wordplay, since a hyperbola is itself an arch of
infinite extension, as well as a buried allusion to Longfellow's "archly" smiling

Priscilla. New words are now at work beside the Word, and new texts give her tropes for love.

In "God is a distant — stately Lover," the Christian tradition of metaphorical love meets a variety of secular languages, most obviously that of Longfellow's verse romance. *The Courtship of Miles Standish* displays a similarly blithe miscegenation. References to "Worshipping Astaroth blindly, and impious idols of Baal" and "the marriage-ring of the great espousal hereafter" sit comfortably alongside allusions to the wars and betrayal of Caesar, the Norse legend of Bertha, the spinner, and other nonbiblical imagery. All serve a secular tale of "Love immortal and young in the endless succession of lovers" — or more accurately, they serve the poet's deeper erotic faith.[19] M. M. Bakhtin attests that the late eighteenth and early nineteenth centuries saw the "novelization" of other arts and literary genres.[20] If this "meant in practice . . . a kind of eroticization," as Polhemus suggests, both Dickinson's poem and Longfellow's show the sway these trends might have over a Puritan inheritance. In Dickinson's verse the loved one's rivalry with God reflects the "raging heresy" of the Victorian love novel, where "redemption, if it is possible, lies in personal desire, imaginative power, and love" and not in the divine.[21]

Such novels underwrite Dickinson's frequent representation of love as the "Sweetest Heresy" (P 387). Whether love is a "joyful little Deity" (P 1771) or a more scathing Calvary, the passion that drives it scorns the limits the Puritan God had imposed by the grave—and it won't be satisfied by sentimentalism's new domestic heaven either. Love and death conspire to make the speaker of poem 718 an operatic, Heathcliffean exile; while in the proud calculus of "Till Death — is narrow Loving," the speaker finds that any boundary set on love below renders it "narrow," unworthy of the name. The poem that follows this in fascicle 40, " 'Tis Sunrise — Little Maid," takes this logic to its *Liebestod* conclusion. "Had'st thou broached / Thy little Plan to Die — ," this speaker murmurs, "Dissuade thee, if I could not, Sweet, / I might have aided — thee — " (P 908).

Now, love and death embraced in Whitman too. But they did so chastely, sweetly, sadly. In Dickinson their kiss brings a grin and a shiver, a tingle that reminds us of desire's extremity. Let us turn, again, to Bataille and de Rougemont. "If the union of two lovers comes about through love," announces the first, "it involves the idea of death, murder, or suicide." The erotic is a matter of "assenting to life up to the point of death," a "challenge to death through indifference to death" which prepares us for the "unknowable and incomprehensible continuity" we saw in Dickinson's flung-in Paradise.[22] De Rougemont, the theorist of "love and death, a fatal love," will claim that "what passion really *wants*—its true object" is not mutual presence but absence, or "*obstruction.*" His typic lovers, Tristan and Isolde, "behave as if aware that whatever obstructs love must ensure and consolidate it . . . and intensify it infinitely in the moment they reach the absolute obstacle, which is death." All each needs of the other is the fact of their love, an internalized "passionate dream."[23]

"The earliest passionate lovers whose story has reached us are Abélard and Héloïse," the French moralist continues.[24] Is it only a coincidence that Orlando Wight's *Romance of Abelard and Heloise* was, in fact, a widely read text in Dickinson's youth? Tales of separated lovers were a staple of popular culture in Victorian America, and such tales also no doubt played a part in the poet's sentimental education.[25] I return to the question of renunciation at the end of this chapter, for it forms a romantic subtext to Dickinson's poems of cognitive privacy. For now I simply note that if the test of an infinite love is the willingness, not to kill or to die, but to wait in passionate anguish, such tales posed a powerful counterweight to the New Testament's master narrative. (Christ died for us, poem 456 reminds its "you," but he did not love us well enough to "live without.")

The Puritans held no brief for passion, love-and-death, or erotic renunciation. All, they suspected, were masks for pride. But in the nineteenth-century's erotic faith, arrogant devotion no longer seems a sin. No wonder Dickinson loved *Wuthering Heights*, that Bible of sweetly heretical love by the "gigantic Emily Brontë" (L 742). "If he loved with all the powers of his puny being," cries Heathcliff of the languid Edgar Linton, "he couldn't love as much in eighty years as I could in a day." Dickinson's poem 528 rings with the same "gigantic" Brontëan tone, although this time the echo is rather of Catherine's equally proud declaration: "That is not *my* Heathcliff. I shall love mine yet; and take him with me—he's in my soul."[26] In love, runs this Song of Songs, my beloved is *mine.*

> Mine — by the Right of the White Election!
> Mine — by the Royal Seal!
> Mine — by the Sign in the Scarlet prison—
> Bars — cannot conceal!
>
> Mine — here — in Vision — and in Veto!
> Mine — by the Grave's Repeal —
> Titled — Confirmed —
> Delirious Charter!
> Mine — long as Ages steal!
>   (P 528)

The hammering anaphora hymns a self that cannot be contained by flesh (the bars of that blushing "scarlet prison") and that reserves the right to call another "here" in "Vision" or cancel him or her in "Veto." "Mine — by the Right of the White Election" has been read as both a love poem and a verse that exults in the poetic vocation. The choices involved draw on similar resources of "Domingo," as Dickinson sometimes named imaginative power.

In some of her most passionate poems, Dickinson exults in the power of declaring someone (or herself) "Mine." But the poet who loves choosing also rejoices in being *chosen*, and often blurs the distinction between them. To be chosen, after all, at least by a man, was to have a trump card to throw down against the niggling, exhausting demands placed on single women of the nineteenth century. To be chosen by a man who wasn't there was even better, at least as far as freedom was concerned.[27] In "How sick — to wait — in any place — but thine — ," for example, the speaker faces a well-meaning, insinuating comforter who tries to "twine" her as she waits for her absent beloved. He finds himself coldly rebuked, though not in the name of an Emersonian self-reliance. Though the speaker may look like a lonely woman, she sees herself as a wandering "Brig," "tossing" with her lover "wild through the sea" as she waits: at once a haughtier and a more socially acceptable prospect. "I turned — ducal — ," Dickinson writes, and the panting phrases of the first stanza's long lines slow into an imperious staccato: "*That* right — was thine — / *One port* — suffices — for a Brig — like *mine* — " (P 473).

Just as the Victorian novel supports the capitalist thrill of making someone *mine*, then, it makes the "defiant devotion" of being loved a form of wealth and power as well.[28] This alienated form of self-reliance is particularly open to women. Simone de Beauvoir identifies the temptation involved: "The woman in love," she explains, "feels endowed with a high and undeniable value," for "she is at last allowed to idolize herself through the love she inspires."[29] Romantic election is its own dowry, as the speaker of poem 473 learns, moving from the shame of her state as "a Dowerless Girl" to the commanding status of a "Bride." The verse builds to a climax on the command to "Bring Me my best Pride," a line that implies an assortment of prides already hanging in the closet, a previously hidden or neglected dowry. But there are dangers to this roundabout majesty. The speakers of "I am ashamed," "He put the Belt around my Life," and "How sick — to wait — in any place — but thine" all begin in states of self-abnegation. Each finds her recourse in the fact of being owned by another. In being his, she can be *him*, or at least partake of his independence. They have no other evident route to a "ducal" sovereignty of self.[30]

In Dickinson, then, marriage may be the site of novelistic heresies, may authorize the social heresy of renunciation, and may even let the spirit put on its "best Pride," all admirable ends. But it demands that women live out their own selfhood through a godlike master: a requirement that the poet seems at times, embarrassingly, to enjoy. "Forever at His side to walk — / The smaller of the two!" (P 246). "He touched me, so I live to know / That such a day, permitted so, / I groped upon his breast — " (P 506). What are we to make of such breathless verse, or of the so-called Master letters? "Except to comment upon their biographical significance," writes Gary Stonum, "Dickinson's best critics often pass over these poems in embarrassed silence, for they are difficult to reconcile with the more attractive, equally frequent poems in which images of noble, fiercely independent selfhood predominate."[31] The sweet heresy of human love seems to include a masochistic streak—one that is itself heretical, but this time to Dickinson's faith in herself.

"Imprisonment—Content"

What are the roots of this new heresy? As we have seen, Victorian American lovers commonly felt that their affection for one another was somehow salvific: a sentimental and erotic faith that competed with the older economy of salvation. Indeed, part of the pleasure of Dickinson's "Heaven — but not / The Heaven God bestow — " lies in its illicit sweetness, and its threat of punishment. The intrusive "They" of poem 474, "They put Us far apart," take away the lovers' eyes, thwart them with guns, put them in dungeons, and crucify them, making the verse a Grand Guignol "Annabell Lee." In other poems the "marauding Hand" is more explicitly identified as that of another, eternal, absolute lover. "You constituted Time / I deemed Eternity / A Revelation of Yourself," the poet writes her merely human beloved; "'Twas therefore Deity / / The Absolute — removed / The Relative away — / That I unto Himself adjust / My slow idolatry" (P 765).

As a woman of nineteenth-century New England, Dickinson would have had other reasons to dabble in idolatry. "A woman growing up in Dickinson's historical and literary context," writes Margaret Homans, "would have learned that men say I and that women do not": a disparate articulation we can see in the balkings and indirections forced at times upon such ambitious women as Margaret Fuller and Harriet Beecher Stowe.[32] A "feminine" speaker's self-abasement thus conceals a desire to gain access to the powerful selfhood of that "living God," the "ideal omnipotent other" who is her master.[33] The pleasures of this masochistic relation include those of abandoning oneself to the Other's mastery and of thereby being discovered and recognized, "owned of Thee," as poem 1028 has it. The corresponding sadistic impulse, which Camille Paglia has so gleefully traced in Dickinson, bears within it the urge to find a resilient Other who can survive one's most aggressive and destructive desires.[34] As Benjamin explains, "The masochist's wish to be reached, penetrated, found, released—a wish that can be expressed in the metaphor of violence as well as in metaphors of redemption—is the other side of the sadist's wish to discover the other." Each plays a part in an eroticized drama of "destruction and survival."[35]

The only problem with this feminist reading, at least to my mind, is that it sits poorly with the solitary and confident self we find elsewhere in Dickinson. Why should the love poems be so different? (The poet was weaker when it came to love? As Susan Howe puts it, not *my* Emily Dickinson.) A hint may be found in poem 765, where by glossing "Deity" as "The Absolute" and a human beloved as "The Relative," Dickinson reminds us that her vision of idolatry is as Emersonian as it is novelized and Victorian. "The longest love or aversion has a speedy term," we learned in "Experience," since "the great and crescive self, rooted in absolute nature, supplants all relative existence, and ruins the kingdom of mortal friendship and love." Idolatry ascribes an absolute nature to the merely phenomenal other, challenging the sovereignty of that soul whose "Superior instants," as Dickinson attests, "Occur to her — alone" (P 306). A chilly, ascetic doctrine, to be sure. No wonder in Emerson "all the muses" join "love and religion" in hating "these developments." For if we must live the "cold and so far mournful" life of truth in order not to be "the slave of tears, contritions, and perturbations," if "we must hold fast to this poverty" to "possess our axis more firmly" and avoid ascriptive illusions, then a warmer, more impulsive temperament might well decide that idolatry was worth the risk.[36] The soul's *inferior* moments, self-imposed, might let one please the muses, and trade poverty for debt. In one of those remarkable early valentines, Dickinson poses this insight as a brash romantic credo: "Mortality is fatal — / Gentility is fine, / Rascality, heroic, / Insolvency, sublime!" (P 3).[37]

From an Emersonian point of view, the poet's embrace of idolatry seems a way to *humble* that great and crescive self, to subject it to an explicitly and deliberately overvalued beloved. More erotic than Emerson's ideal of "the real marriage," such dominant/submissive relations constitute both a "strategy for escaping aloneness" and a "search for aloneness *with* the other."[38] Their rewards are twofold. First, they give unlimited credit to the amorous imagination, allowing it to run up the most exuberant and extravagant accounts of the other it serves without fear of bankrupting our inalienable "poverty." Second, they place power not within self or other, but between them. Inedible, ineffable, the other remains undevoured, a "Berry of Domingo"(P 872) that calls up "Hopes so juicy ripening — / You almost bathed your Tongue" (P 507).

These power games are, perhaps, a little perverse. Like her contemporaries Wilde and Baudelaire, Dickinson generally prefers anticipation to fulfillment, and suspects that desire and disappointment, not desire and fulfillment, mark our real options. But decadence is not her only motive. The oral gusto of those juicy hopes and tongue remind us that the Emersonian self is both unbodied and *unlovable*, as unwilling or unable to receive adoration as it is to give it. Insolvent and aroused, the self in Dickinson may meet its match. "The epistemological drama of a subject/object relation" is thus transformed into an eroticized "contest for supremacy between two subjectivities": one that, however "licked" and "lost," the poet cannot lose.[39]

To speak of Dickinson's masochism, then, in existential terms—to call it a desire to "see herself as a thing, to play at being a thing"—we must stress the element of *play* to such an extent that the rest of the definition begins to tremble.[40] "We dream — it is good we are dreaming — " the poet writes; "It would hurt us — were we awake — / But since it is playing — kill us, / And we are playing — shriek — " (P 531). In her inner theater Dickinson plays all roles, switching between submissive and dominant positions from poem to poem, and at times within a single verse. The zest of each position is increased by our knowing how thoroughly chosen and provisional it is.[41] The tsking, girlish speaker of poem 107 delights in identifying herself with both the "greedy, greedy wave" and the "little craft" that is "lost." In the anti-aubade "He was weak, and I was strong — then — " (P 190), the poet's desire to know "nought," to lose herself in another and so be "Home," involves a play between weakness and strength, but these are not parceled out by gender. Indeed, once the roles of strength and weakness have been switched, and once both lovers have been brought to "nought"—he in silence, she in knowledge—the poet introduces a third term against which *both* can wrestle: the conventional intruder "Day," stronger than the both of them. As they struggle with delicious unsuccess to play out their aubade and part, they bear out Paglia's observation that for Dickinson "affect is dependent on hierarchical distance," whether between two lovers or between them and someone else.[42]

Do I overestimate the theatrical lightness of these poems? Paula Bennet calls "He was weak, and I was strong — then — " a "chillingly fleshless exercise," in part *because* it articulates love as a contest for power: the very aspect of the poem that I saw as invigorating.[43] Am I just reading my own male taste for "dying in drama" into these poems, that is to say, ascribing to their author a taste for power games that more properly belongs to their *reader*? I am painfully aware of Karl Keller's observation that as "a man trying to write well about Emily Dickinson ... you must come off looking right, you are self-conscious, you dissemble. It is show biz."[44]

To test these scruples, let me now turn to texts where feminist readers have found an alternative vision of love: Dickinson's poems and letters for Susan Gilbert. If sadomasochism allowed one sort of intersubjective meeting, since the early 1980s the poet's relationship with her sister-in-law has been seen as the scene of a more appealing encounter, one where equal affections and an easy intersubjective exchange hold sway. In lesbian affection, writes de Beauvoir, "separateness is abolished, there is no struggle, no victory, no defeat; in exact reciprocity each is at once subject and object, sovereign and slave; duality becomes mutuality."[45] What space remains, then, for the dramas of meeting that underwrite Dickinson's poems of bondage as play? If none, what takes their place?

Susan's Idolater

In her influential essay " 'The Love of Thee — a Prism Be': Men and Women in the Love Poetry of Emily Dickinson," Adelaide Morris distinguishes between two groups of work: the letters and poems that address a male Master and the poems, letters, and fragments to Susan Gilbert. While "both sets of material are self-consciously idolatrous," employing similar rhetoric and imagery, such similarities mask a deeper difference in tone and structure. "The Master letters and poems offer the spectacle of a self willing itself to be an inessential other," Morris writes. "The poems and letters to Sue," by contrast, "though they participate in the rhetoric of exaltation and abasement, suggest a fundamentally different struggle: the asking and giving, accusing and apologizing of autonomous beings." "What the Master letters and poems take seriously," the critic concludes, "this material pokes fun at": specifically, the impulse to amorous hierarchy.[46]

This distinction between hierarchical heterosexual romance and lesbian egalitarianism has proved a powerful critical model. In *Emily Dickinson: Woman Poet*, for example, Paula Bennett holds that "the hierarchical conception of love ... did nothing for the poet." At best, it generated "some of the most disturbing and at the same time archetypically 'feminine' poetry that Dickinson wrote": verse that is both "painful" and "absorbing" to read as it "demonstrates all too effectively how Western sexual arrangements and the discourse in which they are embodied have helped mold women psychologically to embrace and identify with weakness, lack, and pain." The contrast with Dickinson's love poems for women is striking, since these emphasize "smallness, mutuality, and nurturance" in a relationship based on "sameness rather than difference," and eschew the emotional extremes of election and despair in favor of what poem 159 calls "a brief Campaign of sting and sweet."[47]

It is true that Dickinson's few poems of happy love have in mind a female beloved, and that when questions of power arise in such verse, they are frequently answered in a sanguine outcome, not a bloody one. An unmatched, uncontested power is bestowed by praise from the "Sweet" of poem 659. She "said that I was strong, / And could be mighty, if I liked"—a very different dynamic of praise and esteem from that of poem 738, "You said that I was 'Great' — one Day," where the speaker struggles to assert her power by trying on a dizzying, ironic series of personas: Great, Small, Stag, Wren, Queen, Page, Rhinoceros, and Mouse.

The playful richness of this imagery, however, casts quite a shadow over the more subdued egalitarian mode of poem 659. This difference leads Margaret Homans into a provocative critique of Morris's argument. In "'Oh, Vision of Language!': Dickinson's Poems of Love and Death," published alongside the Morris essay in the 1983 collection *Feminist Critics Read Emily Dickinson*, Homans finds that the hierarchical structures of heterosexual romance spurred the poet into more "daringly imaginative" verse than the "nonhierarchical structure of exact equality." In poem 458, "Like Eyes that Looked on Wastes," she sees lovers who experience themselves and each other as both subject and object, but their mutual gaze is like a hall of mirrors, reflecting only an empty hopelessness. "The two are both queens, and that is exactly what is terrifying," Homans comments. "It is precisely the lack of differentiation between them, the fact that they are equally queens, that causes them to be hopeless and to perish." If this poem does not end in the "violent stalemate" of other verses she describes, it points toward the "insufficiency of terms," the "lack of language" that makes the lovers of poem 1529, "'Tis Seasons since the Dimpled War," too much alike for comfort. The poetry of same-sex love, she argues, lacks invigorating difference. Its reliance on the language of contiguity, rather than on the gaps and sparks of metaphor, cannot "prevent what seems . . . the wholly undesirable collapse of one identity into the other." "It is the overcoming of hierarchy," Homans concludes, and "not the absence of it, that is conducive to poetry."[48]

There is something strained about Homans's readings. They seem to assume that gay or lesbian love blots out every other difference between me and not-me, simply because the two selves are of the same sex.[49] As Morris points out, the terrifying wastes of poem 458 have more to do with the fact that these women are trapped in a world where one king beats a pair of queens than they do with anguish over similarity. [50] The poem " 'Tis Seasons since the Dimpled War" likewise seems ill used, both by Homans, who understates the linguistic inventiveness of the opening and closing lines, and by the overly cheery Bennett, who is quick to downplay Dickinson's martial metaphor. Outside the formulas of heterosexual hierarchy, writes Bennett, the lovers "become a defended *and* secure place to each other (a sort of fortified *hortus conclusus* or barricaded garden of love)."[51] Fair enough. But the lovers' "Pink Redoubts" are also defended and secured *against* one another. There's a war on, if a dimpled one.

More than what Betsy Erkkila calls a "feminist and politically correct model of loving sisterhood" is at stake in this debate.[52] All of these critics start with the assumption that the poet's love for another woman meant first and foremost a relationship founded on *sameness*. This assumption encourages a variety of interpretive overstatements. And it sits poorly with the rhetoric of idolatry that Dickinson employs as readily with Susan Gilbert as with any masculine figure, in letters and poems from the early 1850s on. Read the letters and you find brash equations of Susan with Christ (L 77 and 88) and a predictable fear that the poet will be punished for her idolatrous desire (L 85). (It is not always clear whether God or Susan will do the punishing.) "Susan's Idolater keeps a Shrine for Susan," Dickinson reminds her in the late 1860s (L 325); at a word from this "Only Woman in the World" she declares that she "would forfeit Righteousness — " (L 447 and 554). In loving Susan, one letter even suggests, the poet is God the Daughter to Gilbert's God the Mother: "The World hath not known her, but *I* have known her, was the sweet Boast of Jesus — " (L 1024).

As Richard Sewall observes of this correspondence, "hyperbole is the rule, and images of uniqueness, size, power, totality abound."[53] Such hyperbole signals a poet reveling in bestowal, in the imaginative and amorous expansion to be had as she magnifies, glorifies, lauds, and exalts her beloved. But as it transforms the actual woman Susan Gilbert Dickinson into a romantic fiction, it sits poorly with the critical ideal of their egalitarian affections. The poet craves "a momentous, impossible competency," Farr notes, asking her beloved "to become a vast and magical mother, always at home for her to run to." The verse *clutches*, as Emerson would say. And, indeed, "I'll clutch — and clutch—," a speaker tells her "Diamonds" in poem 427, one of several in fascicle 19 that address love's avaricious imagination. "Count — Hoard — then lose — / And doubt that you are mine — / To have the joy of feeling it — again — ."

This rhetoric of possession reminds us of the ringing "mine, mine, mine" that we saw in the nineteenth-century novel's erotic faith. But if the poet relishes the "Bliss" of "own[ing] a Susan of [her] own" (P 1401), she also declares that the "one Glory" she longs to be remembered for is that "I was owned of Thee" (P 1028)—a phrase that would apply as well to the Master poems and letters as to the group for Susan. Such metaphors of ownership are hardly innocent, given the class difference between Dickinson and her sister-in-law. The poet's claim that Gilbert possessed "a different Wealth," whose loss "beggars," the poet reverses and thus highlights the actual class relationship.[54] In "Your Riches — taught me — Poverty," which Dickinson sent as a note in 1862, Susan is a pearl that has slipped the poet's grasp, or a diamond. Now she can only imagine the pleasures of gazing on her. "I'm sure it is Golconda — " she writes; "To have a smile for Mine — each Day, / Beyond my power to deem — " (L 258). Golconda? In an issue of *Harper's* three years before, as Farr explains, the magazine "described the Indian mines of Raolconda, five days' journey from the fortress of Golconda," a fortress-prison where, to quote the magazine, miners are "held in a slavery of the most abject kind, their lives being entirely at the mercy of their masters."[55] That "smile for Mine" thus figures extremes of wealth and deprivation, not equal exchange and reward.

One cannot, therefore, simply ascribe Dickinson's self-professed idolatry of Susan (as Morris does) to a "conventional romantic rhetoric" that signals "an intensity rather than a [dominant / submissive] structure."[56] Indeed, I find the lively spirit of "Bondage as Play" more common in poems for a male "you" than in the lesbian verse. When she muses on Gilbert the play is piercingly earnest, the danger more pressing, more real. The poems for Susan Gilbert show a wider range of emotional extremes than early feminist critics proposed, and they are intimately expressed by the work's rhetoric of worship and distance, not produced by it against the poet's will. If the *who* of Dickinson's love rendered it socially impossible, the *how* of it dwelled on and transformed that impossibility. It recreated Susan as an eternally retreating and alluring *domna*: a cunning strategy. By idolizing Susan, Dickinson joins the male pantheon of masochistic but triumphant poet-lovers, the tradition of Dante, Swift, and Mirabeau (L 393)[57] — and, as a second note implies, the tradition of Shakespeare's Antony. "Egypt — thou knew'st," she writes to Susan on a slip of paper in 1874 (L 430). In Susan's Shakespeare the full passage is scored in the margin, in what seems to be Dickinson's hand:

> Egypt, thou knew'st too well
> My heart was to thy rudder tied by th' strings,
> And thou should'st tow me after. O'er my spirit
> Thy full supremacy thou knew'st, and that

> Thy beck might from the bidding of the gods
> Command me.
>
> (3.11.56–61)

Farr tells us that "Dickinson means . . . that Sue has revealed to her the same depth of selfishness, the same craze for power, that Antony discovers in the queen" (172). I find this passage reveals primarily the appetitive delights of being mastered: the way the other does not meet us but draws us onward, past any boundary she might have set to be beloved. The second passage marked in Susan's copy reiterates this stress:

> Age cannot wither her, nor custom stale
> Her infinite variety. Other women
> Cloy the appetites they feed; but she makes hungry
> Where she most satisfies.
>
> (2.2. 236–239)

Like Antony, Dickinson is only as powerful as she is willing to be defeated, only as satisfied as she is willing to give up satisfaction for the luxury of heightened and reflective consciousness.[58] Dickinson's idolatry may help keep the two apart, as at least one letter indicates. ("I must wait a few Days before seeing you — You are too momentous. But remember it is idolatry, not indifference" [L 581].) But the high tension of an encounter between two sovereign subjects may *require* a certain distance and mediation—one for which, as we shall see, the presence-in-absence of language is an essential sign.

"Teasing the want"

Near the close of the last chapter we enjoyed a brief epistolary tryst with Whitman. "It is I you hold and who holds you," he promised, encouraging us to love him and thus bring his verse to more than literary life. Dickinson never addresses her readers this way. When she does address us at all, she takes pains to remind us how exterior we are to her concerns. We play the eavesdropper to her ongoing lyric drama, drawn to the poems in part by this very voyeurism, a tantalizing all-but-exclusion from the knowledge and contact they imply. Antony to Susan's Cleopatra, she is Cleopatra to us: grand, demanding, and mercurial. In this teasing exclusion, which models other ways that we are "lost" to each other, I find a final key to Dickinson's hierarchical but still intersubjective vision.

"The Way I read a Letter's — this," she tells us, her new confidants:

'Tis first — I lock the Door —
And push it with my
fingers — next —
For transport it be sure —

The close-up on those pushing fingers triggers the promise of erotic "transport" that we've learned from Whitman to expect from reading in privacy. (To push the door after locking it suggests that the bolt or mechanism only then clicks into place: an audible, tactile thrill.) But as the poem goes on, the speaker slips away from our eager, prying eyes:

And then I go the furthest off
To counteract a Knock —
Then draw my little Letter forth
And slowly pick the lock —

The textual variants for "slowly" are "slily" and "softly." They render the speaker a trespasser, one who relishes picking locks as much as locking them. The reader is both confidant and the mouse that threatens her privacy as she begins to read.

Then — glancing narrow, at the Wall —
And narrow at the floor
For firm Conviction of a Mouse
Not Exorcised before —

Peruse how infinite I am
To No One that You — know —
And Sigh for lack of Heaven —
but not
The Heaven God bestow —
    (P 636)

Drawn into the scene as we follow her glances, we find ourselves shut out just at the moment when an "infinite" bestowal has been awarded. Part of the speaker's infinitude surely comes from its contrast to the narrow confines in which we are forced to remain, conscious of a newfound "lack" all our own. Like God, in fact, we are superfluous, and our jealousy mirrors His own.

But what is it we want from her? A name? I don't think so. ("Peruse how infinite I am / To Susan Gilbert"? No.) If we can weave our way into the scene in the final lines—"Ah yes," we nod and wink, "*that* heaven," the erotically faithful one — such knowledge will not suffice. "The power of the Tease," Karl Keller calls this reticence. But if the reader is left, as Keller says, "a satisfied voyeur of unfulfilled desire, uncompleted desire," doesn't that suggest that the speaker, too, has gotten what she needs?[59] She's sighing not from longing, but from satisfaction? Is what we want not to fill the lack but to *feel* it?

"A loss of something ever felt I," Dickinson famously observes in poem 959. The need to maintain that productive sense of a "missing All" shapes much of her love poetry. It has often been understood biographically, most recently by Cynthia Griffin Wolff. If the poet "viewed all of human existence as essentially wounded," Wolff writes, this wound begins in "that intimate, unvoiced communion" that her mother "had failed to provide." Reading Dickinson's family history through D. W. Winnicott's theories of child development, Wolff notes that when the " 'magic time' of mother-infant intimacy, when silent dialogue is possible, has never properly occurred . . . the movement from silent, eye/face dialogue to verbal communication . . . may ever after be construed as a 'Fall into Language,' " with language "seeming a second-best alternative to some other, loosely defined, transcendent intimacy." When it comes to love and poetry, however, this may end up a fortunate fall. "The wound of separation makes love poetry possible," she concludes, since "if the lovers could be together, there would be no need for poetry: they would possess the unrestrained, wordless capacity 'to see.' Because they are parted, words become necessary, and the need for poetry is born."[60]

This tale of loss and language ought to sound familiar. We encountered a version of it in Whitman's "There Was a Child Went Forth," "Out of the Cradle, Endlessly Rocking," and "As I Ebb'd With the Ocean of Life"—this last, coincidentally, a poem that Dickinson might herself have read. We find it in Wordsworth's *Prelude*, where the infant babe "Drinks in the feelings of his Mother's eye" and holds "mute [Wolff: "silent"] dialogues" with his mother's heart until a mysterious and threatening "trouble . . . From unknown causes" intervenes.[61] In Kristeva's lively version of this tale, the troubling cause is a split, a scission, an inaugural rejection that constitutes subject and object. And, scandalously, there is an "acute pleasure" involved.[62]

Dickinson's poems of love and loss keep our eye on that scandalous rejection. Oral pleasure, that link between infantile suckling and the poet's honeyed words, might counteract its impulse to spit out, split and differentiate. But such pleasures appear in Dickinson's work mostly as unsatisfied hunger, the savors supplied by distance. We are proved "Sovereign" when we "own" and "touch" our "Crumb," not when we eat it (P 791). Only such frustrations keep hunger alive, and with it, a world outside the self, of things significant and lost. If we have "ever" felt a "loss of something," Dickinson hazards, it is because such absence forms the foundation of the self. It goes back as far as we do. No wonder the poet says, sadly, "We must meet apart" (P 640). Idealist fusion is impossible, because what we seek is not another but an irrecoverable part of ourselves.

And yet, whenever Dickinson seems about to pull up a chair next to Kristeva at Lacan's seminar on "The Subject and the Other: Alienation," she turns away with a sardonic smile. She has no patience with anyone's itch to give a name to the union that's been lost: "the Mother" in Wordsworth and psychology; "Eden" in theology, and so on. In "A loss of something ever felt I" (P 959), the speaker's images for that "something" grow from "a Dominion" from which she is "the only Prince cast out" to a set of "Delinquent Palaces"—that is to say, palaces that should have come to her already but haven't, a slightly different retrospection. Then, as "a Suspicion, like a Finger / Touches [her] Forehead now and then," it occurs to her that she has been looking in the wrong *direction*: "looking oppositely," as she puts it, "For the site of the Kingdom of Heaven." That quizzical-comical pose and the rhythmic bathos of the final stanza, with its sudden collapse into anapests, suggest that any such kingdom is nothing but a compensatory projection, cobbled out of other equally received images.[63] We may feel, in Cavell's words, "as though we have, or have lost some picture of what knowing another, or being known by another, would really come to — a harmony, a concord, a union, a transparence, a governance, a power."[64] But the name we give to this dominion says more about our education in cultural ideals than about the lost, delinquent harmony itself.

If what we crave in love is to know and be known, then, we also crave the bracing wind of an encounter with that which excludes us, keeps us guessing, holds us at bay. "In Dickinson's re-writing of central experience between persons," Grossman explains, "there is no possibility of honoring that experience if the *impossibility* of knowing other selves is not deeply inscribed."[65] The inquisitive, acquisitive self finds itself at once aroused and brought up short by an other who is "within its reach, though yet ungrasped," and who is going to remain so (P 1430). In a late letter to Susan, Dickinson adapted the two last stanzas of a poem on the sublime and constant otherness of nature, with "Susan" put in nature's place (P 1400, L 530):

> But Susan is a Stranger yet —
> The Ones who cite her most
> Have never scaled her Haunted House
> Nor compromised her Ghost —
>
> To pity those who know her not
> Is helped by the regret

That those who know her know her less
The nearer her they get —
                Emily —

Marked by pity, regret, and a sense of having trespassed, these lines suggest that American love poetry after Dickinson will be more concerned with the ethics of the imagination than any we have seen so far. We are on the cusp, in fact, of the modernist ideal of amatory *authenticity*, which will "haunt" the next two chapters as surely as Susan's ghost haunted her abashed Idolator.

In 1862, the year that Dickinson began to correspond with T. W. Higginson, the British poet George Meredith finished and published a sequence of sixteen-line "sonnets" on the guttering out of his marriage four years before. *Modern Love*, Meredith implies in his title, is defined by crisis, by infidelity, and by an awkward fit between the lover's imagination and the "poor twisting worm, so queenly beautiful" of its imperiously independent object (poem 8). Marriage promised the union through love of an "ever-diverse pair." It proves, instead, a "snare" in which two "rapid falcons" of subjectivity are "Condemned to do the flitting of the bat" (poem 50). Meredith links the failure of the marriage to a quest for certainty in a context ("this our life") that cannot give it. Too much "deep questioning" leads the couple only to "endless dole."

In the years after Dickinson's death, a "deep questioning" of the nature of love led to an even broader disillusionment than Meredith's verse records. Spotlighting the biological and cultural dynamics of love was a "modern temper" that gave little credit to the amatory imagination. As a foretaste of the concerns of these next poets, and a final touch of contrast, let me close this chapter with Dickinson's poem 580, "I gave myself to Him." At first glance it seems a critique of marriage, not unlike the exposés by Adams and Engels and others that would soon follow, with "gave myself" a euphemism for "sold." "I gave myself to Him," the speaker confesses, "And took Himself, for Pay." But the economy described is more imaginative than simply sexual. Each partner faces the threat of disappointment, not just in the other's "Wealth" but in his or her own, as "The Daily Own — of Love" begins to "Depreciate" the enticing "Vision" of desire. And out of that threat, and *only* out of it, comes a happier thought. Because "to own" may mean "to acknowledge or recognize" as well as "to have or possess," the "Daily Own" may mean a turn from the unlimited imaginative play of desire to the "Mutual Risk" of an actual engagement with the other, one extended past night's possibility and into, or through, time. "Till the Merchant buy," the speaker muses,

Still Fable in the Isles of Spice —
The subtle Cargoes — lie —

At least — 'tis Mutual — Risk —
Some — found it — Mutual Gain —
Sweet Debt of Life — Each Night to owe —
Insolvent — Every noon —

The risk behind this odd economy is not that one's investment will not be re-
covered. That would be laboring for the "restitution of idolatry"—a faithless
admission of "penury," like the one in poem 1219, "Now I knew I lost her." The
risk is rather that the investment will not be *reciprocated*, and that the other will
refuse to enter into this revolving, mutual erotic debt. As each vision is ex-
changed for the "subtle Cargo" of the actual, disappointments must provoke
compensatory bestowals. Only then can the rather stiff "solemn contract" of
the start of the poem turn into the eroticized insolvency of its close.

In the next chapter I take up a number of modern American poets just as
committed to love's rhythms of separateness and charged encounter as Dickin-
son had been. But in the cold light cast by the "modern temper," both solitude
and meeting look quite different. The selves in question are not great and cres-
cive but skittish and self-doubting, often too wary to idolize or bestow. They
may pursue "authentic" love, and test new aesthetics of allusion and antisym-
bolic "literal" language to capture it. But with a few exceptions, notably H.D.,
they will not risk the high drama of Dickinson's "bondage as play." Rather, they
will build on the more muted, more nuanced, more domestic and careworn ro-
mance of the "Daily Own."

Three

Liberation and Its Discontents

The rose is obsolete.

— WILLIAM CARLOS WILLIAMS

Forty-two years after Dickinson's death, in 1928, the essayist and drama critic J. W. Krutch published *The Modern Temper,* a "study and confession" of the spirit of his age. At its heart lies a grim chapter that illuminates the shift between the broad cultural contexts of my introduction and first two chapters (Puritan love theology, sentimentalism and its Emersonian reaction, and Victorian "erotic faith") to those of my final three. "Love," he calls it, "—Or the Life and Death of a Value."

The life of love, writes Krutch, was one of beneficent illusion. A "superstructure of poetry" built on the foundation of a mere "biological urge," love seemed through the Victorian age "the most *significant* of human experiences." It made whatever it touched a sign of something greater, something with "transcendental value." Indeed, love "stood between man and any ultimate pessimism," since "so long as love was possible" life "could not be either meaningless or not worth the living." Because it was too important to be "burdened with irrational proscriptions," British and American reformers struggled to remove them. "Not to cheapen or tarnish [love], but merely to free it," radicals, sexologists, and poets set about illuminating the Eros tucked within their parents' (and their own) erotic faith.[1]

A noble struggle. Yet, as wide-eyed Psyche will attest, love and lamplight make an awkward match. Reformers such as Margaret Sanger, Emma Goldman, and D. H. Lawrence may have preached a needed liberation. Their work may have allowed a new "language of sensual desire and joy" to flesh out late Victorian pronouncements on love and lovers' unions. But when they suggested that love was *reducible* to sex—"its origin, underpinning and essential ingredient," as the historian Steven Seidman puts it—they began to undermine their own success.[2] They conspired, however inadvertently, with a harsh, sardonic realist tradition in which love was never anything more than a ruse, a feminine or sentimental facade plastered over brute biological "truth." Unmasked, it soon collapsed from the sublime to the banal. Love's "superstructure of poetry," writes Krutch, was left to dangle, unsupported, in the wind.

Rumors of love's death are always somewhat exaggerated. What Krutch calls "the nastiness of, let us say, James Joyce's *Ulysses*" no longer seems so ominous.[3] Among the French moderns, whom Krutch does not mention, the most revolutionary notions of free love expressed an unabashed erotic faith. (Think of Apollinaire's "Poems for Lou," Breton's "Union Libre," the surrealist novel *L'Amour ou La Mort* by Robert Desnos, and any number of pieces by Paul Eluard.) Even in English, one finds more counterexamples than I can cite in this chapter, including works by e. e. cummings, Hart Crane, and Muriel Rukeyser. But Krutch's tale of "the modern temper" bears repeating, for two reasons.

First, Krutch intones a now-familiar litany of warning. In their search for sexual freedom and insight into relationships, runs this cautionary tale, modern lovers let something slip though their grasp: a fineness of passion and expression, a grace and weight and poignancy and force to their desires.[4] Like Maud Bailey and Roland Mitchell, the wary academics of A. S. Byatt's novel *Possession* (1990), they have grown too *knowing* for their own good. How can Byatt's protagonists muster the passion of her Victorian poets, Randolf Henry Ash and Christabel La Motte? "I was thinking last night," Maud tells Roland, as their modern romance hesitantly buds,

> —about what you said about our generation and sex. We see it everywhere. As you say. We are very knowing. We know all sorts of other things, too— about how there isn't a unitary ego—how we're all made up of conflicting, interacting systems of things—and I suppose we *believe* that? We know we are driven by desire, but we can't see it as they did, can we? We never say the word Love, do we—we know it's a suspect ideological construct—especially Romantic Love—so we have to make a real effort of imagination to know what it felt like to be them, here, believing in those things—Love—themselves—that what they did mattered.[5]

Hot for insight into love, desire, and the self, modern lovers have undermined all three. Lost with them is a faith that what we do, in our love lives and elsewhere, can matter.[6] As Julia Kristeva observes in *Tales of Love*, the "guidepost that assured our ascent toward the good have been proven questionable," ex posed as repressive or simply illusory. The result? "We suffer crises of love. Let's admit it: lacks of love."[7]

The "modern temper" named by Krutch writes large, then, as a cultural collapse, the malaise Kristeva spots in her patients. In this match, I find a second reason to cite *The Modern Temper*. Kristeva's "melancholia," Krutch's "death of a value," and Maud Bailey's sense that "we are very knowing" all leave their sufferers unable to see meaning and beauty in the "suspect ideological construct" of love. Why shouldn't they share a cure? Why shouldn't all three be healed by some restoration of those old codes of romance—or by their replacement with some new, thoroughly modern "order of perfection"?[8] And, indeed, in response to this collapse American poets have repeatedly summoned up that cure, through what Maud calls "a real effort of the imagination." Whether out of nostalgia for the Victorian boudoir or in a search for the new, they have made modern love a modern art.

I take my cue in this chapter, then, from the cultural historian Stephen Kern. It may well be, Kern admits, that we "have lost some of the Victorians' delicacy and poignancy, perhaps even some of their heroism." Perhaps, though, we thereby also "became more reflective," more authentic, *eigentlich*, able to own (*eigen*) or own up to our words and acts of love.[9] I start with a more detailed sketch of the "modern temper," looking briefly at Edna St. Vincent Millay, whose sonnets profit from its impulse to frisky demystification, and then in more depth at the *Songs to Joannes* of Mina Loy.[10] Loy's *Songs* illustrate the dangers described by Krutch, and they illuminate the reconstructive efforts other poets undertake. Some poets, such as Eliot, Pound, and H.D., answer the "modern temper" by resuscitating older structures of erotic experience and meaning. Others, notably Stevens and Williams, raise an eyebrow at the exaltations and idealizations incumbent on these "secret ways of love."[11] With their vision of love as an intersubjective encounter—or, if that fails, of the poem as an authentic "owning" of the failure—they look back to the poems of Dickinson I discussed a few pages ago, and forward to the issues of my next two chapters. They also remind us that, in Greek myth, Psyche's investigations of Eros led in the end to the birth of a daughter called Pleasure. Disenchantment has its own rewards.

Love in the Time of Melancholia

The modern temper has its roots, as even its critics concur, in a dream of liberation. For women, especially, this dream promised freedom: freedom from economic and sexual constraint; freedom from the secret sorrows and watery love-deaths that flood women poets' work from the 1880s through the early 1910s.[12] Edna St. Vincent Millay's arch sonneteers show that promise bearing tart, appealing fruit. The speaker of "I, being born a woman and distressed," for example, no longer confuses "a certain zest" with anything remotely transcendent, despite the way that "notions" taught to women have habitually linked these "needs." "Let me make it plain," she smirks at the close: "I find this frenzy insufficient reason / For conversation when we meet again."[13] In the witty carpe diem sonnet "I shall forget you presently, my dear" (1922), Millay's "unflappable flapper" persona is more appealing but just as aggressive.[14] "Make the most of this, your little day, / Your little month, your little half a year," she tells her lover, confident that he will listen close enough to hear his time grow longer line by line. This sexual confidence breeds literary bravado. By the end of the first quatrain she appropriates (and flattens) Shakespeare's "Where yellow leaves, or none, or few do hang" into the offhanded "Ere I forget, or die, or move away." The sonnet's tradition of poetic entreaty, protest and vows is hers to claim precisely because, Krutch writes, she recognizes how its "superstructure of poetry" was always founded on a "biological urge."[15] She gets the pleasure of both, now, each for its own sake.

As the closing poem of *A Few Figs from Thistles*, this sonnet is meant to be a little outrageous, a little risqué. But its appeal to nature has its price. Listen closely to the clinching couplet: "Whether or not we find what we are seeking / Is idle, biologically speaking." The repeated long *i* of "*i*dle, biologically" has less to do with Millay's willful, feminist "I" than she might like. I belongs to a Nature straight out of Schopenhauer: an impersonal, determinist force that uses and devalues all our "seeking," whether the search be sentimental (for the One True Love), platonic (for the Good), or simply hedonistic (for another, better lover). In a more experimental poet, one willing to let the modern temper inflect the forms of her verse, this nature might be troublesome indeed.

Like her Greenwich Village compatriot Millay, Mina Loy was hailed by the American press as one of those New Women who were, as one reporter said "the cause of modernism, whatever that is."[16] "Sympathetic to efforts for greater sexual honesty, which she saw as a prerequisite for psychic and social liberation," Carolyn Burke explains, Loy followed the struggles of Margaret Sanger and other reformers. In poems such as "Virgins Plus Curtains Minus Dots" she, like them, mocks middle-class marriage. Taught that "Love is god / White   with soft wings," Loy's virgins learn that although "Nobody shouts / Virgins for sale," they're still on the market.[17] But Loy goes further than activists like Sanger and Goldman. They took care to distinguish lo-

from "that poor little State- and Church-begotten weed, marriage," thus following the lead of romantic reformers like Percy Shelley.[18] In "Virgins," Loy takes no such pains. And in her "Feminist Manifesto" (1914), she mocks the cultural and psychological importance of "sex (or so-called love)." Women must "destroy in [themselves] the desire to be loved" in order to be truly free, she writes.[19] "Are you prepared," she taunts her readers, "for the WRENCH?"

Now, Loy was hardly the only modernist poet to speak in naturalist terms of "sex or so called love."[20] F. T. Marinetti, Loy's futurist comrade-in-arms, disdained *amore* that way. But any inability to plot a course between love's reductively sexual origins and its expansive cultural flourishing—the "monotony" of the merely physical and the polytonal human inclination to "twang nobler notes / Of nobler sentiment"—poses a serious threat to poetry.[21] And there may be a deeper "WRENCH" in store. "There is no writing other than the amorous," Kristeva advises, since "the speaking being is a wounded being," whose speech "wells up out of an aching for love."[22] Mock that ache and you may cap the well of words with irony. In her *Songs to Joannes*, written a few years later, Loy put her sense of these threats into practice. As the "I" of this embittered sequence discovers, once love's "superstructure of poetry" has been undermined, the urges that remain prove more far bleak than liberating.

Here is the first, and most famous, of Loy's thirty-four *Songs*:

Spawn   of   Fantasies
Silting the appraisable
Pig Cupid   his rosy snout
Rooting erotic garbage
"Once upon a time"
Pulls a weed   white and star-topped
Among wild oats   sewn in mucous-membrane

I would   an   eye in a Bengal light
Eternity in a sky-rocket
Constellations in an ocean
Whose rivers run no fresher
Than a trickle of saliva
These   are suspect places

I must live in my lantern
Trimming subliminal flicker
Virginal   to the bellows
Of Experience
            Coloured   glass[23]

"Once upon a time" we told love stories, fairy-tale romances, in which sex was kept discreetly out of sight. Now Pig Cupid's rosy snout, a displaced and comical phallus, noses into every subtext, bringing lust to light. But far from being liberated, in love or in verse, this speaker finds herself trapped and choked off. She has lived out her "fantasies," only to see them become a grotesque "spawn." She sees herself not as a New Woman but as one more "weed" in Pig Cupid's garden of "mucous-membrane." And when she tries to articulate her own desires, the syntactic freedom of this verse is her undoing. She gets only as far as "I would"—and then no verb will come. For a moment she pictures herself as an exotic signal beacon ("Bengal light"). But a watchful, "virginal" seclusion proves more attractive. She flees the "suspect places" of her own "Experience" back into her "lantern," and dismisses all she sees as "coloured glass."[24]

"Swill poetry," readers called this. "Hoggerel."[25] They weren't entirely wrong. Loy has no nostalgia for "this tepid wash, this diluted deferential love" in which the body stayed unspoken.[26] But in a world where Whitmanian bestowals of love have turned to coarse accounts of "the appraisable," the older poet's erotic faith is just so much "erotic garbage." As long as Loy's "I" remains at a satirical distance from this "garbage," she seems quite poised. When she figures sex as a combative badminton match in poem 10, for example—"Shuttle-cock and battle-door / A little pink love / And feathers are strewn"—or when dawn's Homeric rosy fingers are transformed into a "little rosy / Tongue" that makes the lovers, like heliotropes, "twiddle to it / Round and round / Faster / And turn into machines," the rhetoric is pointed and accomplished.[27] Unlike the author of the "Feminist Manifesto," however, this "I" wanted sex to be what Victorian "erotic faith" said it *could* be: a bond of soul accomplished in the flesh. Disappointed, she lashes out at herself and her lost ideals. She grows flip and dismissive, and her imagery gutters into talk of "sordid biological process."[28]

What balks the singer of these bleak love songs? Clearly she has tried to take the advice of Loy's "Feminist Manifesto," to quash her own desire to be loved and instead to sing only of "sex or so-called love." She seems equally hampered by the whittling away of the lover's selfhood—of anyone's selfhood—by modern psychologies. It may be, as one critic claims, that the *Songs to Joannes* can be read as a "collage of love's failure that rewrites 'Experience' in flamboyant sexual imagery," mining the Emersonian tradition's "core of doubt."[29] But Emerson's great and crescive transcendental self has been reduced, in Loy, to a mere "ego's necessity," hapless before unconscious urges and instinctual drives.[30] How, then, can Loy's speaker take refuge in the dramas of desire that let the self conquer its doubts in Dickinson's work? To a woman of "the mod ern temper," even the grandest Dickinsonian demand would seem an admission of weakness, a confession that the speaker has not, as the "Feminist Manifesto" ordered, "destroy[ed] in [herself], the desire to be loved."[31] And, though it pains her to admit it, she doesn't really want a Dickinsonian "Master." "Apparently / I had to be caught in the weak eddy / Of your driveling humanity / To love you most," she sighs—the only time in the sequence when "love" is a verb.[32]

There is one final reason for her disappointment, which the sequence explicitly names. Evidently Joannes, the lover of Loy's "I," has refused to have a child with her. Their "consummations" were merely "pubescent," the "I" resentfully declares, since they bear only "irredeemable pledges" that "Rot / To the recurrent moon."[33] References to "birdlike abortions" and "sweep[ing] the brood clean out" in poem 4 suggest that Joannes has not only withheld his "completions" but forced the speaker to have an abortion. At the center of the sequence lies a poem of toneless denials and stunned repetition that may look back to that act:

> I don't care
> Where the legs of the legs of the furniture are walking to
> Or what is hidden in the shadows they stride
> Or what would look at me
> If the shutters were not shut
>
> Red   a warm colour on the battlefield
> Heavy on my knees as a counterpane
> Count counter
> I counted   the fringe of the towel
> Till two tassels clinging together
> Let the square room fall away[34]

Loy keeps the scene out of focus. The source of the pain and the referent of "as a counterpane" are obscured, and we can't tell if the speaker is looking at something red and heavy on her knees, say a skirt or a lap blanket, or if she is on her knees watching the chair legs, then something blood-red, cradled by a towel whose tassels cling to one another as the couple do no more. The loss, though, is unmistakable.

Like the more famous abortion in *The Waste Land*, this abortion both signals and enforces the barriers between failed lovers. "Come to me," the "I" begs Joannes in the next poem, as though language could accomplish the union sex did not. Perhaps she dreams of the intimate exchanges enacted in the love poems of Gertrude Stein, whose work Loy admired. In Stein's utopian *Lifting Belly*, written the same years as Loy's dystopian *Songs* (1915–17), voices interweave and overlap in an easy, intimate, mutually gratifying exchange—one that builds on baby talk, not "procreative truth." But Joannes is no Alice B. Toklas, eager to offer "protection" and "blandishment" to an interlocutor.[35] He wants to stay separate, not to "Disorb inviolate egos" in sexual or linguistic interchange. And Loy's speaker is too caustic and cautious not to answer in kind. "Oh that's right," she snaps, stung by loss and by the "modern temper" they share.

> Keep away from me   Please give me a push
> Don't let me understand you   Don't realise me
> Or we might tumble together
> Depersonalized
> Identical
> Into the terrific Nirvana[36]

As her brittle ventriloquism shows, Loy's "I" finds it hard to believe in her own dream of delight. At least, she can't picture it with *him*.

The "modern temper" infects the speaker of Loy's *Songs for Joannes*. Its demystifying, liberatory impulse draws her into enacting her "fantasies," to her later regret. Its corrosive skepticism leaves her still more vulnerable to disappointment. Too embarrassed to speak of her lingering, old-fashioned "erotic faith," she can find no words for any new form of relationship. "There is something / I have got to tell you," she promises Joannes, but she masks her hope with irony. (What's the "Something taking shape"? "A new use," she shrugs: "A new illusion."[37]) She can only picture a life "together" with Joannes as the childlike innocence of "apple stealing under the sea" or playing "Hide and seek in love and cobwebs / And a lullaby on a tin pan." To live that way, though, they would have "never [to] have known any better."[38] And to "know better" in this case doesn't mean to know a better love than play and solace and endless, easy talk. It means to be, as Maud Bailey puts it, *knowing*: to live in an adult, experienced world where "apple stealing" has all too evident a biblical overtone. A world, that is to say, where a Fall into loss and separateness is the start, not the end, of the story, and where the use of such allusions shapes one's sorrow into art.[39]

Loy's speaker is unable, or Loy herself unwilling, to shape the *Songs* in this way. To use Kristeva's psychoanalytic terms, the sequence refuses to achieve the "primary identification" with "father, form, schema" that would let its speaker "triumph over sadness" by finding in signs some surrogate for her loss child, lost love, and lost ideal of herself.[40] In practice, this refusal means that the poems' allusions ring hollow. Although critics have tried, you can't get Joannes to play Cupid, or even Pig Cupid, to the speaker's wounded Psyche.[41] And you will read them in vain for references to the English sonnet sequence, whose traditions might well give shape to Loy's poetry of loss. Like the Elizabethan sequences analyzed by Carol Neely, the *Songs to Joannes* announce and interpret the poet's affections, engage and recreate the beloved, and muse on "poetry itself—its function, its power, its limitations," as a "substitute for the breeding which is the real goal—the begetting of a response from the beloved—attention, approval, love, consummation, children." Their final cadence offers images of "the immobilized lover, the perpetually tyrannical beloved, [and] the ultimate barrenness of the poetry." And they seem caught in a Shakespearean double bind where "idealization and consummation are equally unsatisfying and no transcendence is permitted."[42] But Loy cedes this literary tradition, like the worlds of the Bible and of myth, to the "professorial" Joannes (67). Unwilling to be duped by "Love — — — the preeminent litterateur," she chooses instead to "go / Gracelessly" (68, 62). She denies her speaker and her readers the reassurance such allusions would provide.

"The secret ways of love"

Loy's *Songs to Joannes* mark an extreme case of the "modern temper." They are the knowing, melancholy songs of a woman who understands that art means, in part, forgiveness: a lifting up and shaping of experience that, in Kristeva's words, fits the "humiliated, offended being into an order of perfection" and reassures her that she is, finally, at home.[43] Alas, she and reformers like her have debunked or unmasked all the available orders of perfection. The affair has been for naught, "biologically speaking," and Loy will not avail herself of compensatory cultural satisfactions. The *Songs* thus spark and sputter, wrench and recollect, and bear witness to the disillusionment that other poets, then and since, have struggled to cure.

In their deliberate failure, the *Songs to Joannes* suggest two answers to the crisis named by Krutch. One answer would be not simply to acknowledge but to *insist* on the mythic and traditional resonance of one's affairs, in the hope that this "assertion and inscription of meaning" (in Kristeva's words) would reverse the "erosion of meaning, melancholy, and abjection" from which the modern lover suffers.[44] The second response would be to write a poetry of modern companionate engagement: a poetry where the dream of a life "together" would not be projected into a childhood before the lovers have "known any better" or into an idealized, allusive world elsewhere. I reach this second answer somewhat later. To begin, I want to look at three poets who explore the first, resuscitating those resources that Loy abandons to Joannes—three poets, that is, of the "secret ways of love."

I have already compared Loy's *Songs*, albeit briefly, to the most famous poem of the modern temper, *The Waste Land*. Of the major modern poets, only Eliot shares both Loy's unease with Victorian "*erotic faith*" *and* her despair at the Pig Cupidity of modern love. But his reasons could not be more different. Where Loy refuses to universalize her speaker's sad case, Eliot embraces an older Christian and Platonic lesson that "*no* human relations are adequate to human desires."[45] In 1919, just two years after the *Songs to Joannes*, Eliot noted "the awful separation between potential passion and any actualization possible in life": a separation founded not on the failures of this or that relationship but on "the indestructible barriers between one human being and another."[46] Pig Cupid may huff, and the erotic faithful may puff, but neither can blow those walls down.

In many ways, Eliot's revolt against Victorian erotic faith recalls Emerson's reaction against it two generations before. Like Emerson, Eliot addresses an audience quite satisfied with the pleasures and meaning and union supplied by ordinary human affections. Like Emerson, he insists that our essential solitude of self gives those pleasures the lie. Drawing on F. H. Bradley, on theology, on biographical disappointments, and on his own experience of union with "The Silence," Eliot insists that another, finer union is possible—an Absolute against which all relative human loves must be judged.[47] We ask too much of one another, he (like Emerson) advises. We must learn "not to expect more from *life* than it can give or more from *human* beings than they can give."[48]

Through most of his career, Eliot weighs the absolute against the relative and finds the latter wanting. Like a Puritan who has weaned his affections too far, he finds little place for the pleasures of the world and the flesh. This is especially true in *The Waste Land*, that poem "about spiritual success which renders sexual failure nugatory, indeed expects it," in Calvin Bedient's counterintuitive but finally compelling description.[49] Indeed, not until late in his "new life" with Valerie Eliot does the poet find that the love of God can underwrite, not undercut, such relative and ordinary bonds as "the breathing in unison / / Of lovers whose bodies smell of each other."[50] Given the poet's earlier sniffy distaste for the flesh, this last seems to me a particularly forgiving image of what de Rougemont calls "the entirely carnal eros, which is not in the least to be deified," of interhuman love.[51]

Eliot's poetry thus shades the sordid naturalist details characteristic of the modern temper into an older poetic of *contemptus mundi*. Rather than reinforcing one another, however, these secular and religious efforts at disillusionment compete for control. Eliot had no patience for the reformers described by Krutch. He scorned "the enervate gospel of happiness," and insisted that the "natural, 'life-giving,' cheery automatism" such freedom underwrites cannot provide the transcendent meaning once supplied by love. "A great deal of sentiment has been spilt ... upon idealizing the reciprocal feelings of man and woman towards each other, which various realists have been irritated to denounce," he observes. But both sentimentalists and realists forget that "the love of man and woman (or for that matter of man and man) is only explained and made reasonable by the higher love, or else it is simply the coupling of animals."[52] Although he had no fondness for Freud, Eliot would no doubt have agreed with his conclusion that with "no difficulties standing in the way of sexual satisfaction," we find ourselves in a melancholy mess. Only strong "reaction-formations," like those Freud said had revived love in the Middle Ages, will bring us to health once more.[53]

In practice, as in *The Waste Land*, the "reaction-formation" of invoking a higher love may leave lower loves in the dust. But in theory this reaction gives modern love the "final cause" it needs: a meaning to events that their origins cannot supply. Through it, even the most sordid, disappointing details may be redeemed, as they are in one of Eliot's other poems, "Lune de Miel." Written shortly after Loy's *Songs*, it concerns two American honeymooners on their European tour. As the poem begins, husband and wife have been united in marriage. At some point, if not on the sweaty summer night of the poem, they have been united sexually as well. But Eliot focuses on images of messy multiplicity—two sheets, two hundred bedbugs, the spread knees of *"quatre jambes molles"*—and the smell of estrus, or continuing demand, wafting over the couple in a *"forte odeur de chienne."*[54] Do these bedbugs and stink of bitch in heat show Eliot's fussiness over the world, the flesh, and the female—a fussiness that flowers in *The Waste Land*, with its now-infamous canceled lines about "the good old hearty female stench" and the way "The same eternal and consuming itch / Can make a martyr, or plain simple bitch"?[55] Well, probably. As Emerson reminds us, "As I am, so I see." But in a complex, compact system of allusions, William Arrowsmith has shown, each detail also takes its place in an economy of salvation. The bedbug bites, Arrowsmith explains, echo "Dante's *morsi*, those 'bitings of love' that draw the soul upwards toward God." Dante had St. Augustine's "itch" of the soul in mind; and Augustine takes that image of the soul's insatiable desire for entire satisfaction from Plato's *Phaedrus*. "When the lover who ... retains an intense vision of his former divine existence, sees a godlike face or bodily form which truly resembles Beauty," says Socrates, he suffers the "sweating, itching, swelling" that symptomize Eros, "the maddening bite of the gadfly." Gadfly in Greek is *oistros*, notes Arrowsmith. Hence the English "estrus," hence the "*forte odeur de chienne.*"[56]

What seems at first and second glance a rather cruel satire—two hapless Indianans on their glum Grand Tour, embodying a fineness that has been lost—turns out, therefore, to grace its targets with an allusive respect. "In its madness," Socrates says of the love-bitten soul, "it cannot sleep at night, it cannot stay in one place by day, but filled with yearning, goes wherever it thinks it might behold the possessor of Beauty."[57] As they toss and turn from the "Low Countries" home to "Terre Haute," Eliot's honeymooners act in radically *meaningful* ways. Their acts seem trivial and abject in themselves, but they (the acts and the couple) retrace the steps of a Platonic ascent. Their disappointment in the union that sex provides spurs a search for the idealist union that sex teases us to remember, but cannot supply. The palimpsest that Arrowsmith unveils thus saves the lovers—or, perhaps more, their author—from the melancholy of Loy and her speaker. They may suffer; but not, like Loy's speaker, from the "Romantic sadness" that cannot believe "in any further object for human desires than that which, being human, fails to satisfy them."[58]

When Eliot offers something like the naturalism of the "modern temper," then, we need to be wary. He uses its debunking and defensive strain as a mask, a Trojan horse. Tucked within it are glimpses and orders of perfection. Other poets took a more direct approach. In the overlapping cases of Pound and H.D., the effort to restore romance began with the old code closest at hand: the studied Pre-Raphaelite medievalism and the vogue for the occult that during their adolescence were the native language of "artistic" love.[59]

From his teen-age years, as many biographers have discussed, Pound was both swayed by the Pre-Raphaelite cult of the beautiful and, as Kevin Oderman explains, "preoccupied with the 'mediumistic' potentiality of sexuality, its ability to stimulate visions."[60] Like the Rossettis, like Swinburne, like Morris, like the early Yeats—like all his models for what it meant to be a poet, in fact—he was determined to set a premodern notion of poetic inspiration against a world gone crass, industrial, and dull. He wanted not just to see visions but to have them granted by a "Lady," a muse, as they had apparently been to the poets of Italy and Provence. During his collegiate romance with Hilda Doolittle, starting in 1905, the couple read an appropriately inspiring set of texts: poems by William Morris, Balzac's Swedenborgian novel *Séraphita*, a set of "Yogi books," and the story of Tristan and Isolde. In 1906 Pound reviewed *Le Secret des Troubadours*, by the French Rosicrucian Josephin Péladan. He seized upon its notion of the troubadours as "the last guardians and practitioners" of a "secret religion, in which sex, or rather the mental enlightenment supposedly achieved through sex, was worshipped rather than repressed."[61] What "Provence knew," he would write in "Und Drang" (1911), was "not a game that plays at mates and mating" but a way, inspired by the "powers" of love for "my Lady," to discern "the subtler music, the clear light" of "the gods."[62]

By 1911, of course, Pound was weary of Pre-Raphaelite rhetoric. How, though, to shake off this archaic discourse of love without yielding to the debunking, materialist modern temper? "When poetry comes down to facts," as Pound puts it near the end of "Und Drang," will the old, inspiring affair between the muse and her poet survive?[63] The key, Pound found, was to insist that his visionary *ars amorica*, based on restraint and the use of the beloved as a "mantram," was itself scientific, a technology as much as an occult technique. The muse is a "charged pole" who sparks the poet's "human mechanism," he thus writes in *The Spirit of Romance*. Just as "the electric current gives light when it meets resistance," he would write in "Psychology and the Troubadours," a "delay" in sexual consummation—whether of intercourse or of ejaculation, as in Tantric yoga, is unclear—can produce poetic illumination.[64] Indeed, the latest in "glandular" science *proved* the truth of ancient erotic mysteries. In Remy de Gourmont, who had rejected the naturalism of Zola on similar grounds, Pound found a corroborating vision.[65] Properly disciplined, eros could lead to something just this side of "union with the absolute."[66] And, which is more, to lasting art.

Everything old was new again, founded in fact—including the relationship between poet and muse. Hence the methodical progress of his early poem "Of Jacopo del Sellaio" (from *Ripostes*, 1912), its couplets crisp as a lab report:

> This man knew out the secret ways of love,
> No man could paint such things who did not know.
>
> And now she's gone, who was his Cyprian,
> And you are here, who are "The Isles" to me.
>
> And here's the thing that lasts the whole thing out:
> The eyes of this dead lady speak to me.[67]

That lovely phrase "the secret ways of love" comes from Pound's early master Swinburne, from "A Ballad of Death." Here, though, it has a literal, quasi-Tantric meaning. From the spark of connection that flies between ancient and modern artists to the central invocation of Venus, the Cyprian, the poem is meant to sketch a visionary experience, not a graceful compliment. The poem is less concerned with praise of its Lady, in fact, than with the use she can be put to. The poem, like Jacopo's painting, tags its maker as a member of an erotic—and therefore aesthetic—elite.[68]

Throughout his career, Pound asserts the power of this equation between erotics and aesthetics: the compositional force supplied by the Lady as "Mantram." In his youthful poems, it proves a way to make love poetry heroic, not sentimental or deliquescent. If the Lady will participate in the quest for erotic visions, well and good: she will be "the song-drawer," summoned up by the poet's own soul.[69] If she refuses even his "word kiss," he will avenge himself, building (as Pound's "Na Audiart" advises) " 'Una dompna soiseubuda' a borrowed lady or as the Italians translated it 'Una donna ideale.' "[70] By the time of "Hugh Selwyn Mauberly" you can trace the decadence of the age by the progression of failed relationships between artist and muse. The *Cantos*, for their part, repeatedly return to moments of initiatory intercourse between the human and the divine. There is the flaming embrace of Canto 20, with its language borrowed from St. Francis's canticle of marriage to the divine "sposo" who descends to embrace him.[71] And there are the more common moments when the "sposo" is a goddess—Aphrodite, Circe, Mother Earth—and the poet descends or is himself raised up, as in Cantos 47 and 90. The way down and the way up are, in any case, the same: a "Sacrum, sacrum, inluminatio coitu," as Canto 36 has it, in which earth and heaven, fact and ideal, poet and muse are restored to fertile union.[72]

Like Eliot's Christian Neoplatonism, Pound's theophanic vision of sex counteracts the reductive naturalism of the modern temper. Presumably it also holds to the literal in a way that Eliot's allusions do not, finding in the actual beloved at hand an "adequate symbol" for the illumination sought. But does it? Critics stiffen or scoff, for a number of reasons. As Rachel Blau DuPlessis observes, Pound's "secret ways" leave little room for women to be anything other than icons. "Poets. Publishers. Patrons," she writes. "To idealize these culturally active women is to transgress upon their particularity" in a way that vitiates Pound's "announced, professed poetics."[73] And is there really room for love? "Pound's early writings suggest that he has some difficulty with the idea of erotic spirituality through the medium of two equal subjects," claims Thomas Simmons. "The nature of the erotic experience for Pound was to lift the single soul into spiritual communion with all that was beyond its singleness. Erotic communion was not, for him, a mutually reinforcing encounter between two human subjects. . . . Nor was it an encounter with a fundamentally different yet equal human being."[74] As de Rougemont puts it, rather more gracefully, "Once she is man's equal, woman cannot be 'man's goal.' "[75]

Because of its focus on the lover, and its insistence that the beloved stay fixed as a "goal," Pound's notion of "love" has seemed to some recent critics "an impersonal force" or "ideological position," even in the most personal moments of the Pisan Cantos.[76] On this reading, the poet's need to be illuminated breaks into moments of brusque pathos, and turns them to mythic pronouncements.

> O white-chested martin, God damn it,
>   as no one else will carry a message,
> say to La Cara: amo.
>
> Her bed-posts are of sapphire
>   for this stone giveth sleep.
>
>   and in spite of hoi barbaroi
>   pervenche and a sort of dwarf morning-glory
>   that knots in the grass, and a sort of buttercup
> et sequelae
>
> Le Paradis n'est pas artificiel[77]

The speed of transformation here is a tribute to the redemptive force of La Cara. Invoked as a "mantram" of natural paradise, she refocuses and restores the broken poet's mind. Does that very swiftness, though, make her essentially instrumental, a means to the end of "amo"? "Nothing matters but the quality / of the affection," Pound writes in Canto 76. The *quality* of the affection, not the object, is what lasts and gives being. By the end of the epic the objects of that love have grown unclear. "M'amour, m'amour," Pound murmurs in a late "Note," "what do I love and / where are you?"[78] Only the fact of loving is secure.

I am not entirely convinced by this reading. Is Pound's "use" of his Lady worse, somehow, than Anne Bradstreet's "use" of her husband Simon? Transforming him into an "idealized spouse, an earthly counterpart of the Christic Bridegroom," Hammond writes, Bradstreet placed him "within a salvific framework that superseded worldly particulars."[79] Shall we rally to Simon's defense, or protest her transgression of his particularity? The answer may be yes—but mostly because Pound's method offends our commitment to a competing modern ideology of love: the companionate ideal, whose poets I will reach in a few pages. I raise the question here, however, because the choice between a "literal" woman at hand and a Poundian muse in mind will come back to haunt the poets of my next chapter, the Roberts Creeley and Lowell. It also proves crucial to reading Pound's former love, and fellow poet, H.D.

In her later accounts of their courtship, the memoir *End to Torment* and the roman à clef *HERmione*, H.D. is both nostalgic and somewhat ambivalent about the "secret ways of love." She and Pound shared much of its creed. Both remained attached to an intensity of erotic faith that other moderns found archaic or "Victorian."[80] Both held that a secret tradition ran from Greek mysteries to Provence; both saw the erotic as a physical means to union with superhuman forces, and stayed faithful above all to what she called "Love that is mateless, / Love the rite."[81] But if both Eliot and Pound spin "erotic garbage" into gold, recovering the truth behind those tales of love from "Once upon a time" (Loy), H.D.'s work does something rather different. First, it goes back to those tales and revises them, to make them match the lived experience and compositional needs of a woman poet. Second, it takes up a Dickinsonian challenge that Loy's *Songs to Joannes* put aside. Writing out the crests and troughs of particular love affairs, H.D. learns to find in their pattern of idealization, betrayal, and imaginative reconstruction a source of poetic power.

In *HERmione, End to Torment,* and her most moving poems of love, H.D. explores the pleasure and danger of defiant devotion, of self-conscious idolatry and poetic escape. To do so she must brave the presumably "feminine" desire to find in love a loss of self, a fervent absorption in the beloved. "When H.D.'s erotic attachments are subjected to a historical, social, or gender-role analysis," as Adelaide Morris observes, they play out a "dismal script of obsession, sexual polarization, dominance, submission, and betrayal" of the sort that Rachel Blau DuPlessis calls "romantic thralldom."[82] The poet clearly knew it. Many of her finest works, especially *HERmione,* are written out of such insights. In a poem such as "Toward the Piraeus," you can hear them counterpoint her impulse to write in an acceptably "female" cultural tradition of idolatrous love. The results string hesitant, qualifying adjectives on a glinting wire of Dickinsonian bravado. "My weapon," she calls her art as the poem ends: "my own lesser, yet still somewhat fine-wrought, / fiery-tempered, delicate, over-passionate steel."[83]

H.D. knew what her loves would look like in a skeptical, debunking light—illuminated, that is to say, by the feminist elements in the modern temper. And yet, Morris continues, it is "precisely from this point of view that 'love-affairs' began to seem to her 'rather tiresome and not very important.'" The dismal scripts and emotional flights of "thralldom" were *not,* for H.D., to be exposed and avoided. Rather, like the failures of the flesh in Eliot, they could be *redeemed,* given transcendent meaning when incorporated into a larger, palimpsestic reading of the present. They were, after all, reenactments of large mythic tales: the idealization and betrayal of Helen, the struggle of Calypso and Odysseus, the arrival and departure of Eros, and so on. The beloved, whether male or female, can be seen as "a metaphor realized or ritualized," writes Morris, "not primarily a historical nor even a personal presence, but a momentary incarnation" of an actual force.[84] Love's transcendent dimension, dispelled as illusory by the modern temper, is thus restored.

With her faith that myth, because fundamentally true, may be revised to accord with experience, H.D. develops, by her later work, a powerful poetic strategy unavailable to Loy: one more appealing to recent readers than those of Eliot or Pound. Like Eliot, she is able to set the enthusiasms and failures of love in a broader framework of meaning. Unlike him, she recasts and reclaims received mythology and literature, turning the masculine "secret ways of love" to feminist ends. Like Pound, she pledges her allegiance to love and to the inspiration love brings, rather than to a particular beloved. Unlike him, she does so in response to still-appreciable threats to her psychological health and her art. In a world where women's strength is still, as for Dickinson, challenged from inside and out, there's a savvy strategy at work in her declaration that "Love is my master" while "you," the "tyrannous" beloved, are merely "his lesser self."[85] The "lop-winged," earthly tyranny of an Aldington or Pound may still pose a lasting psychological threat. But it now casts no shadow on Eros per se.

Because it seems more defensive than offensive, it is as easy to endorse H.D.'s version of "the secret ways" as it is to cast a cold eye on those of Eliot or Pound. But does she really escape the charge leveled by feminist critics against her male counterparts? Does she *not* disrespect particularity, abandoning the "driveling humanity" and dream of mutual presence that Loy, however desperately, invokes in the *Songs to Joannes*? In answer, we may look to the book that H.D. called her "textbook" and "Bible": de Rougemont's *Love in the Western World*. H.D. read the book avidly, first in French, then in translation, seeing herself as a poet in the great Western tradition of "amorous passion" that de Rougemont describes.[86] Passion is, for de Rougemont, an "infinite desire which takes as its object or pretext a finite individual." It turns the emotional intensity of "adolescent love when this is yet chaste and hence all the more consuming" into "a vehicle of the detailed though ambiguous realities of an erotico-mystical discipline."[87] It needs distance or obstruction to maintain its lyric flame.

Now, for a woman whose introduction to love came through the tale of Tristan and Isolde and the Pre-Raphaelites—and, perhaps more important, who grew up in an America where respectable young lovers were expected to caress but not *quite* copulate—this notion of passion would have had an obvious appeal.[88] "No 'act' afterwards, though biologically fulfilled, had had significance of the first *demi-vièrge* embraces," she recalls in *End to Torm* "The significance of 'first love' can not be overestimated."[89] In a poem "The Dancer," you hear not only a Dickinsonian demand to "retain integri and an authentic American urge to remain "wild and free" but also a longi for love perpetually "taut," never sullied by mere speech or by the off-chance actual sex.[90] And in an achingly beautiful passage from "Winter Love," dressed by H.D., then in her seventies, to Pound, you can see this poetic passion at its finest. "There is something left over," "Helen" tells "Odysseu something left from the days when she and Pound experienced

> the first unsatisfied desire—
> the first time, that first kiss,
>
> the rough stones of a wall,
> the fragrance of honey-flowers, the bees,
> and how I would have fallen but for a voice,
>
> calling through the brambles
> and tangle of bay-berry
> and rough broom,
>
> *Helen, Helen, come home*;
> there was a Helen before there was a War,
> but who remembers her?[91]

In the eyes of the modern temper this near fall would be into romantic thra dom. In a mythic reading, it's the gnostic Fall of the soul into matter and forg fulness. Romance asks a simpler question. To be caught at the moment of fa ing, taut, unsatisfied, yet dizzy from a kiss: is there a finer, more invigorati vision of passion?

There are, however, other traditions of love.

"Being here together is enough"

In the hands of an H.D., the "secret ways of love" have all the grace and p gnancy of any Victorian romance. If they had proved the dominant response the "modern temper," A. S. Byatt's Maud and Roland would have had no ing to fear. But though they brought the dream of the lady as muse into modern period, particularly thanks to Pound's essays and Robert Graves's *White Goddess,* the "secret ways" stayed largely secret. The debunking mod temper has taken its toll. Readers find them increasingly hard to take at f value.[92] With a few scattered exceptions—Robert Duncan and Robert Creeley among them—they have had little lasting influence on American poets. The response that continues to shape us, as readers and as poets, must be looked for elsewhere.

To find it, let me draw once more on *The Modern Temper.* Krutch makes, as we have seen, two arguable assumptions. First, he assumes that by 1928 reformers have successfully debunked the old codes of Victorian "erotic faith." Second, and more important, he assumes that if you strip love of mystery, you strip it of meaning. Neither is necessarily so, and for such theorists of love as De Rougemont and de Beauvoir, the existential ideal of authenticity sufficed as a "final cause" to give love meaning. Unlike the idealist goal of fusion, which was "increasingly interpreted as an illusion, a failure, or a projection of oneself," realist goals such as authenticity and contact could survive disillusionment without appealing to some other, finer romance.[93] Like Dickinson's poems of "the Daily Own," modern authentic love will sacrifice the imaginative free-play of passion to enact a chastened, reciprocal *relationship.*

The most famous poets of such "authentic" encounter are Rilke and Lawrence. Both spurn the dream of fusion; and whether or not they practice it, both extol the encounter of separate equals, in which sparks may fly. (The immediate shared influence is probably Nietzsche, but behind Nietzsche may stand Emerson, with Dickinson a long-lost secret sharer.) In American poetry, this modern realism is widespread. I find it tucked among the ironies of Marianne Moore's "Marriage"; Stein features it, more comically, in *Lifting Belly* and "A Sonatina Followed by Another"; and it underwrites Louis Zukofsky's maddening *Bottom: On Shakespeare,* a prose collage of voices from Shakespeare and Spinoza and elsewhere, arguing love and epistemology. (All of these texts, it is worth noting, feature at least *two voices,* challenging the traditions of lyric. I will return to this.) By the end of the twentieth century, it is safe to say, this revision of the old Puritan companionate ideal has become an unquestioned norm for both poets and critics. Books that flout it, such as Lucy Brock-Broido's Dickinsonian *The Master Letters,* are rare and even suspect. To bring its ethical and aesthetic issues into focus, let me turn to Wallace Stevens and William Carlos Williams.

It may seem strange to start with Stevens. Often, after all, he seems a poet of "the modern temper" in all its ironic and reductive force: think of "Le Monocle de Mon Oncle" or the "Apostrophe to Vincentine" or "Romance for a Demoiselle Lying in the Grass." Elsewhere he seems a poet of the "secret ways of love," drawing on Neoplatonism to write the spousal verse for his new "weddings of the soul."[94] Neither Pound nor H.D., finally, is a more passionate cele-

brant of desire. Neither muses quite as memorably on how one composes a s[
from one's longings—or as reassuringly on the way those longings may be sa
isfied through poetry.

As a poet of love, however, Stevens's power and influence lies less in h
poems of disillusionment or the "secret ways" than in his willingness to cha
lenge those poetics from within. In a way that helped shape poets as different
Creeley and Merrill, Stevens is deeply *eigentlich*, or authentic, about the loss
and choices on which his poems depend. As he records his flight from love
desire, from encounter to imagination, Stevens outlines the difficulties and t[
attractions of a poetry that would *not* make that flight. He also insists, with
chastened, believable faith, on the worth of what he's done instead.

We start, as so often, with the problem of disappointment. The sadness
Stevens's marriage is by now well known. Milton Bates sums up the case juc
ciously: Stevens "betrayed less by Elsie than by his own imagination; she . . . b
trayed more by insecurity than by her own spouse"; the poet transforming h
estranged wife into "the genius of reality, calling him back to Reading, and t[
genius of imagination [or Interior Paramour], inviting him to share h
candle-lit chamber."[95] In his troubadour poem "Na Audiart," the twenty-tw
year old unmarried Ezra Pound sketched a similar response to rejectio
Dodging his lady's scorn, the poet retreated to build "'Una dompna soise
buda' a borrowed lady or . . . 'Una donna ideale.'" Stevens, older, wiser, stops
reflect on this transformation of pain into art. He is more "authentic," and t[
poem, "Gallant Château," is a small, heartbreaking masterpiece.

Like Keats in the "Ode to Psyche," Stevens's poet has turned inward, d
scribing his poem as an inner room. Perhaps he had hoped to leave a windc
open, to "let the warm Love in." As the poem begins, however, no love has a
peared—which may be for the best. "Is it bad to have come here / And to ha
found the bed empty?" he wonders as he looks about the room.

> One might have found tragic hair,
> Bitter eyes, hands hostile and cold.

> There might have been a light on a book
> Lighting a pitiless verse or two.

> There might have been the immense solitude
> Of the wind upon the curtains.

Had the other been re-created feature for feature, as the troubadour's "bc
rowed lady" re-created the woman he left behind, she would have been here
reject her suitor. The "immense solitude" of the couple's bedroom might ha

accompanied her. But from that chilly bedroom scene Stevens brings only some "pitiless" verse, and he takes pains to keep us from identifying its owner. Perhaps it belongs to the bitter, hostile wife, fractured into a blazon of hair and eyes and hands by the poet's anguished gaze. Perhaps to the poet himself, its verses describing a scene of ideal union or naming, in bleak detail, the failure at hand.

As he projects his (and her) solitude onto the wind and the curtains, the speaker turns away from this "painful kingdom" of domestic disillusion. He also asks a question. Is his *verse* "pitiless," after all?

> Pitiless verse? A few words tuned
> And tuned and tuned and tuned and tuned.
>
> It is good. The bed is empty,
> The curtains are stiff and prim and still.

Slowly and repeatedly tuned, these verses create an alternate world, the world of the château. They display, at least and at last, the harmony this couple lacks. "It is good," their creator may say, examining his well-tempered creation. Yet there, the poet's conscience tells him, the victory ends. The *poem* may be good, but the bed in it is still empty. The curtains of its inner room are as "stiff and prim and still" as the woman left behind.[96]

In "Gallant Château" Stevens confronts his flight from the once-beloved and finds it productive of a single, limited good: the good of reflective, conscientious verse. Elsewhere he isn't sure even of that. "Part of Stevens knew that solitude is not the whole story," Mark Halliday explains; hence his many poems of pain and self-incrimination.[97] Does the poet truly come home to a "wild country in the soul" when he leaves the other's "Guatemala"? Does he return to a country, that is to say, just as rich and vital as the one he leaves behind? Or does he simply fly to an illegitimate solitude "Where the wild poem is a substitute / For the woman one loves or ought to love, / One wild rhapsody a fake for another"?[98]

As such lines ought to remind us, Stevens will be as hard on his poetic as any critic. Does he tell a beloved, reprehensibly, to "speak, even, as if I did not hear you speaking / But spoke for you perfectly in my thoughts, / Conceiving words"? Yes—but only to turn on the doll he has created, condemning his own impulse as "puerile."[99] "Good Man, Bad Woman," he calls another poem, throwing its self-justifications into ironic relief. Even the late, peaceful meditation "Final Soliloquy of the Interior Paramour" gets much of its pathos from Stevens's determination to "own," and own up to, his actions. Only a "small reason," he acknowledges, provokes him to assert that "The world imagined is the ultimate good." The lacerating self-depreciation of that first adjective calls up the soothing, salvific assurance of the poem's proof of the second. "It is in that thought [that the world imagined is the ultimate good] that we collect ourselves," the Paramour tells her poet. We might well read the line in the vulgate as "we pull ourselves together," regain some emotional assurance, after the fear that the world imagined is only a *partial* good, after all. Consider a likely alternative, the world of acknowledged, reciprocal relationship, where "being there together" involves two people, and not the poet and his internalized muse. If *that* were the ultimate good, Stevens's appeal to the imagination might seem "small" indeed![100]

And yet, the power of the Paramour's assertion stands. Because the poet "owns" his gestures, accepting the shame of his flight, the smallness of the reason slips from sight. Because the poem has such absolute, tender authority, we credit its claim about, if not the plenitude, then the *sufficiency* of the imagination's power. In this poem Stevens builds a "dwelling," a house of stanzas, where the poet-paramour couple may meet, and we may feel we join them. For past the tumult caused by sexual and emotional demands, unfulfilled and possibly unfulfillable, this imaginative "being there together" seems not only possible, but "enough."

The "Final Soliloquy" is thus a deeply reassuring poem. Without appealing to the myths, theological structures, or occult experiences of "the secret ways of love," it gives a glimpse of redeeming orders of perfection. "Providing us with encouragement is central to Stevens' project," Mark Halliday observes, since in doing so the poet "reminds us of our own moments of solipsistic bliss, or at least of our aspirations for such moments," and he allows us to say of such moments, "It is good."[101] If our moments of "being together" seemed, finally, solitudes shared, Stevens gives us verse in which our remaining "deeply by ourselves," "Supremely true each to [our] separate self" is an acceptable ideal, without the struggle separateness entails in, say, Lawrence.[102]

"Stevens has thus bestowed a calming kind of hope and pride and self-esteem," Halliday concludes, "upon me and thousands of other English professors and future English professors."[103] This is a little harsh. But is there not something limited in Stevens's vision of an "Inescapable romance, inescapable choice / Of dreams"?[104] In his thoughtful and heartfelt "moral critique," *Stevens and the Interpersonal*, Halliday gives voice to the basic objections: "Stevens earnestly seeks to imply and to believe that the solitary self has an ample, good life within reach, and that the absence of distinct other persons is not only undetrimental to this good life but essentially unimportant, if not beneficial." His poetry "suggests that he was a man who resented being agitated by any other person, especially by a woman, and more especially by a woman who offered or expected romantic feeling or sexual desire." The sparks and strains of love as an intersubjective encounter left him "intolerably disturbed," and led him to pronouncements on the impossibility, rather than mere ethical difficulty, of human contact. "One way to deal with the discomfort caused by other selves rubbing against one's own is to assert that such rubbing is an illusion," Halliday observes: an assertion that Stevens could have justified by appeals to Nietzsche, Walter Pater, F. H. Bradley, and of course Emerson.[105]

As with critiques of Pound's use of the Lady as Mantram, I find this reading true, but partial, and finally unconvincing. Stevens's vision of love is deeply platonic—quite similar, in fact, to the thought of George Santayana and other turn-of-the-century theorists of love.[106] Poet and philosopher sense that "the lover uses the beloved as a reminder of some ideal object that she approximates"—the mother's face, the paramour, the "fat girl terrestrial"—and thus "expresses a dual devotion: first to the ideal object, itself an effect of man's imagination; and second to the beloved, whom he appreciates as the partial embodiment of beauty or goodness." To Santayana such idealization is no insult. "By seeing the woman as the epiphany of some ideal, the lover dignifies the beloved beyond those accidental properties that constitute her natural condition."[107] Given what we know of the Stevenses' marriage, it is hard to keep from adding, in a Jake Barnes monotone, "Isn't it pretty to think so?" But Stevens's vision is deeply dignifying to the imagination, without the tones of triumph that inflect the young Pound's. When Stevens's platonizing fails, when "love as possession" falls flat and he retires to the Gallant Château, he does not pride himself on having brought the other with him.

The act of mourning cushions Stevens from moral criticism. (It seems at times designed to.) But it also means that when he confesses his love for something *other* than the woman loved and lost, we can no longer accuse him of indulging in something like de Rougemont's passion, closer to desire than love. Say that desire "seeks to save the object from life's poverty and finitude by loading it with a rich, multiplicitous, potentially infinite value that is ultimately in excess of its limited reality," while love "accepts the cycle of want and fulfillment . . . accepts, in other words, its finitude, and its fundamental nature as a becoming in time."[108] Which better describes the relationship between the poet and his interior paramour? By refusing the temptation to force the other into his verses, and by taking the muse or the poem as a lover instead, Stevens grants autonomy to the only beloved he can. He lets the other *person*, meanwhile, drift from view, where she was headed already, driven, perhaps, by the force of his imagination itself.[109]

I do not pretend that this is a happy scene. "The thought of her takes h
away," Stevens writes in "Bouquet of Belle Scavoir," and though the belove
returns in her bouquet and in figures of speech, "The reflection of her her
and then there," this seems to the poet always merely "another shadow, a
other evasion."[110] (One that he cannot evade, evidently: *her* peeps out, after a
from "*here*," "*there*," "ano*ther*," "every*where*" and "now*here*.") We might e
trapolate from this poem to a general rule: when Stevens looks for anoth
person in signs, she vanishes. When he looks for the muse, she remains. Pr
cisely *because* Stevens holds to an ideal of mutual presence, of "being there t
gether," he chooses the muse. We must not let our own "modern temper" kee
us from seeing the success he wins from failure—and if this is the victory L
refused, it was so much the worse for her work. Whether this choice of "solil
quy or kiss" is finally necessary remains an open question. Of contemporai
poets, James Merrill asked it most productively, and with the most Stevensi
grace.

Yet what would "being there together" look between two people, rather tha
between people and pages? And can such mutual presence be enacted in th
signs that Stevens found betrayed it? These questions preoccupy the poets
my next chapter, Robert Creeley and Robert Lowell. For models and advi
they turned to the poems of William Carlos Williams.

In poem IX of *Spring and All*, Williams raises a number of painful, sel
conscious questions about the relationships between desire, moral error, ar
art. "What to want?" he wonders. "What about all this writing?"[111] Willian
often found, as Stevens had, that writing and marriage proved rivals, and no
just because desire was as unruly as it was inspiring. For the words to "becon
real," he declares in *The Great American Novel*, "they must take the place of wi
and sweetheart," claiming the poet's time and his attention.[112] But a wife ma
out of words could not supply the challenge, clash, and response that he nee
to ratify his ego, and his art. How to resolve this dilemma? Only the poem wri
ten in the American grain, he decided—the poem stripped of borrowed syn
bolism, focused on the resilient fact of things—would let the other exist.
Only the literal wife can grant him the recognition he craves. If she doesn
that too may serve a helpful, deflationary role. At least it proves that she is no
what the poet Doc Thurber, in Williams's *A Dream of Love*, calls "a woman o
of his imagination . . . All right, a poem."[114]

He went in to his wife with exalted mind, his breath coming in pleasant
surges. I come to tell you that the book is finished.

> I have added a new chapter to the art of writing. I feel sincerely that all
> they say of me is true, that I am truly a great man and a great poet.
> What did you say, dear, I have been asleep?[115]

You can't imagine Pound's La Cara saying that, or Loy's Joannes, or even Alice B. Toklas, always ready to second Stein's declarations of genius. The comic, novelistic touch Williams brings from his prose to his verse marks a new and lasting turn in American poetry of marriage—and, more broadly, of love.

Williams's first love poems, of course, are nothing like this. Like Pound, he wrote his early work in an etiolated imitation of Keats and the Pre-Raphaelites. When he fired off an early sonnet for H.D. to his brother, for example, he described her in prose as "the first girl into whose eyes I have looked and forgotten everything about me." In the poem this turns into "Those eyes, those eyes, my love entombed lies / In their deep depths beyond recalling cries." But Williams closes the letter with a laughing caveat: "Don't think that I'm in love or anything foolish; the truth is I am working like a blooming truckhorse."[116] Well before writing *Kora in Hell*, he was already refusing to treat love as a "sordid sort of religion."[117] And by the time of that collection, almost ten years into his marriage, he had been touched by the modern temper. What he took from it, however, was not a bitter debunking strain but an insight into love's rhythms of passion, stagnation, destruction, and, most important, of rebuilding.

"I have discovered that the thrill of first love passes!" Williams exclaims, rejoicing in the disappointment that Stevens and H.D. learned to mourn. He may, indeed, have helped that "thrill" along. "I have been," he proudly announces

> reasonably frank about my erotics with my wife. I have never or seldom said, my dear I love you, when I would rather say: My dear, I wish you were in Tierra del Fuego. I have discovered by scrupulous attention to this detail and by certain allied experiments that we can continue from time to time to elaborate relationships quite equal in quality, if not greatly superior, to that surrounding our wedding. In fact, the best we have enjoyed of love together has come after the most thorough destruction or harvesting of that which has gone before. Periods of barrenness have intervened, periods comparable to the prison music in *Fidelio* or to any of Beethoven's pianissimo transition passages. It is at these times our formal relations have teetered on the edge of a debacle to be followed, as our imaginations have permitted, by a new growth of passionate attachment dissimilar in every member to that which has gone before.[118]

The bluff tone here masks a Keatsian lesson. Marital "periods of barrenness," Williams has discovered, have their beauty too. But Williams isn't merely bluffing when he writes that the "teetering" of the couple's "formal relations . . . on the edge of a debacle" is a veritable *good*. As a modernist, he's inspired by the way such formal instability both clears the ground and provokes the couple's paired "imaginations" to make things new. This "continual and violent refreshing of the idea," writes the poet later in this passage, gives "love and good writing . . . their security." And in that security, Williams finds a "final cause" to inform and give meaning to the struggle that has come before.

As it plays out in Williams's poems, this "refreshing of the idea" entails four overlapping stages of disengagement and return. It begins in separation, a flight by *someone* to Tierra del Fuego. Or, perhaps, to the north room of "Danse Russe," where the poet slips away on an autoerotic, self-ironic holiday. The charm of "Danse Russe" lies less in the speaker's dance before the upstairs mirror, however, than in the joy he gets from the domestic world he's left, but kept in mind. He names it lovingly, carefully, in detail, and takes pains to sing "softly" so as not to disturb anyone. This isn't an escape from the other or from the turmoil of resentment or arousal she may cause. It's a step back that makes the poet a "happy genius *of my household*"—apart but still at home (my emphasis).

The second stage of love's refreshment lies in the fine, appreciative focus it allows, on the rest of the household and the rest of the world. When he steps away from his domestic life to practice medicine, for example, Williams discovers objects of desire sprouting everywhere he looks, from a "murderer's little daughter / who is barely ten years old" ("Sympathetic Portrait of a Child") to the old jaundiced woman of poem XVI in *Spring and All*.[119] He describes the latter with deliberate slowness, so that we find her as sensually present as "Kiki," the younger woman he attends to sexually elsewhere in the sequence. The work of art, Williams notes just before poem XVI, "places a value upon experience." To reuse a term from my discussion of Whitman, it *bestows value*, as the lover bestows value on his beloved.

At best this second stage, the awakening of appetite and attention, ought to send the poet back to the home he left behind. But Williams knows there is something self-serving about these freely ranging attentions, something that drives the couple still further apart. The "violent refreshing" of love and poetry leads him past bestowals into a third stage: one composed of the aggressive, often deliberate testing of borders. At times the trespass is fairly minor, a matter of snacking on plums. Elsewhere it involves a series of more-than-metaphysical adulteries, including strange fits of passion directed toward patients. (I think here of the Beautiful Thing passages of *Paterson III*, with their alternations of desire, domination, and abashed tenderness.) In a pattern common to male poets of the generation to follow, Williams's transgressions amount to "a refusal, a negation, the mental experience of 'You do not exist for me,'" directed at times against a woman he desires, at times against the wife he betrays.[120] What he's after, in both cases, is proof that the injured other will remain, at last, inviolate—that she will resist what Myra Thurber, in *A Dream of Love*, yawns to call "the rape of the imagination."[121] "The favorable outcome," Jessica Benjamin explains of such hamfisted gestures at contact, "is pleasure in the other's survival." Only by surviving can she supply the *"constant tension"* between sovereign subjects that proves their "authentic" encounter.[122] Or, in the ending Williams prefers, only thus can she forgive.

According to the map Williams lays out in *Kora in Hell*, this survival and reunion marks the fourth and final stage of love's "violent refreshing." In the return to one another it entails, the couple will arrive at a "new growth of passionate attachment"—in effect, a remarriage, with a second honeymoon. Like a modern poem, they will grow into a new pattern of "formal relations" as well.[123] In practice, however, at least in his early work, Williams prefers to hover at the threshold. Consider "Waiting," which I read as a less charming, more "authentic" revision of "Danse Russe." "When I am alone I am happy," this poem begins. But this speaker is not now, nor has he recently been, upstairs singing "I am lonely, lonely":

> The air is cool. The sky is
> flecked and splashed and wound
> with color. The crimson phalloi
> of the sassafras leaves
> hang crowded before me
> in shoals on the heavy branches.
> When I reach the doorstep
> I am greeted by
> the happy shrieks of my children
> and my heart sinks.
> I am crushed.

Here as in "Danse Russe," solitude has spurred desire, and thus attention to detail. But the suggestion of wounding in "wound / with color," like the sexual blush of those "crimson phalloi," suggest a guilt not found in "Danse Russe"—

perhaps guilt over an adulterous encounter, from which the speaker returns. Thrown back on himself, repeating "I" and "my," he finds his bestowals of value askew. "Are not my children as dear to me / as falling leaves," he wonders—

> or
> must one become stupid
> to grow older?
> It seems much as if Sorrow
> had tripped up my heels.
> Let us see, let us see!
> What did I plan to say to her
> when it should happen to me
> as it has happened now?[124]

At a loss for words—how clumsy those lines about sorrow are, for example!— this man isn't about to say, blithely, "I wish you all were in Tierra del Fuego." Nor, though, do we picture him slipping off in his imagination to a Gallant Château. When "Waiting" ends he will have to speak up and address his wife, someone before him to see and to know. And he will be answered by her, as some new cycle, however painfully, begins. If "Waiting" begins in solitary happiness, it ends in something other than solitude, other than happiness, yet somehow better than both. That "something" is what Stevens found impossible, and Stein makes seem too easy: a moment of what Cavell calls "acknowledgment," and Benjamin, "mutual recognition."

In his late love poems, Williams frequently crosses the threshold he stops at in "Waiting." He addresses his wife, calling on her to join him in rebuilding their marriage—or, at least, to listen to his pleas.[125] He offers her aphorisms usually meant to turn the pain of their marriage into evidence of its "authentic," existential heroism. "The business of love is / cruelty," he assures her in "The Ivy Crown," though a cruelty "which / by our wills, we transform / to live together." Invoking, but revising the carpe diem tradition—the season of spring, the plucking of the rose before it fades—he sketches instead a love that can exist only in summer and after, only in and through time—a love shaped by the imagination, which lifts husband and wife "across," and not above, "the sorry facts."[126] If the thrill of first love passes, if the poet has helped it to pass through his "cruel / and selfish / and totally obtuse" acts of withdrawal and illicit desire, another love follows to bring restitution. The "jeweled prize" of reciprocal love and mutual presence need not be projected, as Loy's Songs to Joannes sug gested, back to a time before one knew any better. Nor need the passion of an Antony and Cleopatra stand opposed to the briars and burdens of companionate marriage. "We have," the poet promises his wife,

> no matter how,
>> by our wills survived
>>> to keep
> the jeweled prize
>> always
>>> at our finger tips.
> We will it so
>> and so it is
>>> past all accident.

The poem hangs like a mobile, threaded, like their marriage, on the couple's conjoined "wills." And the setting up of that form constitutes, in itself, an act of forgiveness: the forgiveness that, as Kristeva assures us, "giv[es] shape to relations between insulted and humiliated individuals" even as it gives shape to their "signs."[127] Loy's modern temper kept her from finding such forgiveness, and the poets of the "secret ways of love" found it only under the auspices of some old code of romance. With his faith in the ability of the imagination to inform, and thus transform, the "sorry facts," Williams offers a promising alternative to both.

Williams's late, confessional poems of love answer disillusionment by announcing an "authentic" interpersonal ideal, where love is the art, at least in part, of cruelty transformed. But the "we" of "The Ivy Crown" is an awfully fragile construct, always threatened by the temptation of a more comfortable, more salvific, and less "authentic" love. In "The Ivy Crown" the couple's plural "wills" produce the mobile of their marriage. "*We* will it so," the poet crosses his fingers and proclaims. Elsewhere, and more often, Williams relies on his own will, and on a poem's implicitly forgiving "design."[128] In poems like "The Orchestra" and even "Asphodel, that Greeny Flower," the companionate vision of "The Ivy Crown" rubs elbows with a vision of amatory salvation that *assumes* forgiveness, often simply on the basis of confession. The poet comes "proudly / as to an equal / to be forgiven." But when he fears forgiveness will not come, he turns his wife from an equal to "my queen, / my queen of love / forever more."[129]

I don't want to be smug. "It is the artist's *failing* / to seek and to yield / such forgiveness," Williams writes, after all; and perhaps he is right to tell his wife

that such extravagant bestowals "will cure us both."[130] But as they demon-
strate Williams's ability to overcome the crisis of idealization that makes up
the modern temper, such moments also turn Floss Williams into a La Cara, an
archetype, an ideal. Her merely human pain at hearing his confession fades,
and with it, the chance of authentic connection. With none of its delicate hesi-
tancy, such idealizations remind me of Williams's early poem "Rain." Here the
speaker can't stop thinking about the woman he's betrayed. But he can't bring
himself to leave "the priceless dry / rooms / of illicit love," either. Instead, he
lingers over its furnishings, "all the whorishness / of our / delight," pacing
and breaking his lines so that the delight, not the whorishness, stays in mind.
But why, at that, *should* he leave? The *licit* love he's stepped away from drops, as
the title suggests, as mercifully as the gentle rain from heaven, washing him
clean. As he muses on "the spring wash / of your love / the falling / rain," he
drifts from this first-person address to the "you" to a safer, less self-indicting
third-person description. As he "spreads / the words / far apart" to let in this
now "unworldly" love, it can't help but grant his words "its / liquid / / clear-
ness," bringing them "into form." It's exquisite writing, some of Williams's
best. But as Stevens would ask, is it bad to have come here?[131]

The moral and aesthetic questions raised by these late love poems are cen-
tral to recent poetry of love. Can a lyric poem represent love as a relationship
between two sovereign speaking subjects? How can the poet address the moral
complexities involved in writing of such love—and can he or she avoid turning
the poem's "few words tuned and tuned and tuned" into an alternative, more
dearly beloved?[132] Must the poet choose between extravagant bestowals and
authenticity, the aesthetics and ethics of love?

The most famous, or infamous, answer Williams gives comes from *Pater-
son*—a poem that repeatedly returns to themes of destruction and rebuilding,
and to questions of contact.[133] In Book 2, Williams's "Dr. Paterson" is up-
braided by letters from a woman the poem names "Cress"—excerpts from let-
ters the poet himself had received from the poet Marcia Nardi.[134] The Doctor,
it seems, has trespassed against her. He has refused to respond to her letters,
treating her to what Benjamin rather blithely calls "the mental experience of
'You do not exist for me.' "[135] She has survived, but barely. "That whole side of
my life connected with those letters," she tells the Doctor, has "take[n] on for
my own self that same kind of unreality and inaccessibility which the inner
lives of other people often have for us."[136] The Doctor, too, is undercut by this
failure of mutual recognition. The book ends with a faltering dialogue between
a "He" and "She," a poet's bathetic efforts to write a love poem (despite his sense
that "the language is worn out"), and at last the promise, in what seems a

quoted lyric, that love may now at last "enjoy its play." Then, as a five-page coda, one last, biting letter from Cress, which undercuts and overwhelms the hopes mustered moments before.

With its use of these letters, *Paterson 2* suggests that to represent an inter-subjective encounter, the poet may need to turn his back on the monologic traditions of lyric. Stein's love poems had come to that conclusion nearly twenty years before. "A Sonatina Followed By Another," for example, is "a poem a conversation an address and a dialogue and a rebuttal"; while *Lifting Belly* interweaves two voices who play out the games and lullabies and baby talk that Mina Loy's speaker, back in the *Songs to Joannes*, failed to enjoy.[137] Moore's "Marriage" is a collage of sometimes bantering, more often bickering voices; and even the lyrical Hart Crane turns to prosopopoeia at the climax of "Voyages," giving voice to his beloved in a desperate effort to keep him from slipping away. Such gestures are risky, as Crane's speaker discovers. (*"Never to quite understand,"* his beloved sighs, leaving the "I" quite abashed.) But they have an obvious appeal. Since they so clearly represent love as a matter of two subjects, two voices, in relationship, dialogic love poems may well seem more "authentic." And they offer escape from Stevens's fear about the isolation incumbent in writing. How can "the thought of her take her away" if the other gets to *speak*?

I will take up the risks of this aesthetic in detail in my next chapter. They are central to Lowell's *The Dolphin*, which was influenced by *Paterson 2*. For now, let me speak to Williams's rather troubling success. As we read, we shuttle from the failure of recognition between the characters in the poem to the apparent *success* of recognition—certainly there's a "constant tension"—that gives shape to the poem itself. Dr. Paterson may have missed his chance with Cress. Dr. *Williams*, though, seems at least at first to have risen to the task. By ending his poem with a voice from "outside"—one that responds to "incursions" with anger, and with cause—Williams asks us to conclude that he knows the truth of Dr. Paterson's opening lines, "Outside / outside myself / there is a world," in a way that his complacent alter ego does not. Through the poem's "design," that is to say, Williams digests, transforms, and forgives the transgressions that lie at its heart. For us to admit that, however, we need to do just what Cress (and Marcia Nardi) accuse Dr. Paterson (and Williams) of doing: that is, turning her letters into "literature, as something disconnected from life."[138] Williams hopes that the formal relations of an "authentic" marriage will be matched by the formal relations of the poem, but *Paterson 2* suggests that the two may be at odds. Must "design" be sacrificed, in the end, for "authenticity" to bloom?

In the next chapter I look at how such questions inflect the work of Robert

Creeley and Robert Lowell, both deeply indebted to Williams's vision of love. In both, the question of a beloved's separate subjectivity will be central. In both, a woman who refuses to be treated as a mythic, forgiving ideal will chasten the poet's overweening male selfhood—chasten him in the context of a *lyric* poem, one lacking the artful dodge of Williams's "Dr. Paterson" and "Cress." I find the seed of their work in a short, neglected poem by Williams called "The Act." Reversing the usual gender roles in the carpe diem scene, Williams transposes the urge to gather rosebuds from the male poet-as-seducer, bewitched by youth and beauty, to his mature interlocutor: a woman cut and gathered some time before:

> There were the roses, in the rain.
> Don't cut them, I pleaded.
>   They won't last, she said.
> But they're beautiful
>   where they are.
> Agh, we were all beautiful once, she
>   said,
> and cut them and gave them to me
>   in my hand.[139]

"She / *said*," Williams breaks the line, shocked at her words and her implicit reminder that "the rose is obsolete," that "love is at an end—of roses," and that the traditions of love in which women are flowers are "borrowed" traditions in which she "ha[s] no existence."[140] This is the sort of response that one imagines elsewhere in Williams, say, after "Waiting," and which announcements of forgiveness and the talk of "queens of love" tends to elide.

The way a "hand" like this will write, handed its own flowery words, will be my next concern. A poetry of contact and of authenticity, it is also, alas, a poetry of divorce.

Four

Real Crises in Real Homes

"Do you really know what you have done?"
—"LIZZIE," IN ROBERT LOWELL'S "EXORCISM 2"

Early in 1993 the *New York Times* announced "The Death of Eros." It was not from natural causes. Like Psyche's jealous sisters, Allan Bloom explained, sexologists and feminists have tricked us into peering where we shouldn't. Eros flees the disenchanted scene, leaving us clutching starkly empirical or contractual terms to speak of our desires. What other language could we use? "There have been hardly any great novelists of love for almost a century," Bloom laments, and the texts that linger from a more romantic time have now been debunked as "pernicious and sexist." Hardly inspiration, aid, or comfort for modern lovers nursing an outdated "ideal longing."[1]

This polemic ought to sound familiar. By and large Bloom echoes the warnings of J. W. Krutch's *The Modern Temper*, sixty years before. And indeed, since the 1930s, American poets have concerned themselves far less with "ideal longings" than with the sparks and stumbles and domestic cares that Dickinson called "the Daily Own of Love." As we saw in the last chapter, a number of modernist writers turned the old Puritan dream of companionate marriage into a drama of existential contact. Here the poet-lover may no longer use the beloved primarily as a mantram, a redeeming icon of the ideal. Rather, he or she must address both the pleasures of Miltonic fit conversation and the bickering discomfort that arrives when conversation fails. Not love as a "mode of salvation," but as "a human interrelation" draws poets' interest, to borrow de Beauvoir's phrases: a federal relationship "founded on the mutual recognition of two liberties."[2]

Bloom is unimpressed. Talk of recognition implies, he complains, that "human connectedness can arise only out of a motiveless act of freedom." Worse, it marks a "disastrous decline in the rhetoric of love." "One has to have a tin ear to describe one's great love as a relationship," he sniffs. "Did Romeo and Juliet have a relationship?"[3] One's impulse is to answer, "No. They died." But if the rhetoric of relationship now sounds dated, as uninspiring as Pre-Raphaelite sighs in 1912, it once seemed radical, even redemptive. The "New World" of 1961, Robert Creeley announced, was a place where "relationships, rather than the hierarchies to which these might refer, are dominant." Poetry might still prove "An Intensely Singular Art," as another title had it. But its accounts and embodiments of the "attempt to move into form, again, with others, with one's wife, husband, children—the sudden instances of relationship, the worn ones, all of it" might ease or end "the isolation which the American so often carries like a sore, marking him as lonely, lost, and a little pathetic."[4]

At its happiest, in the work of poets like Mona Van Duyn, May Swenson, and Marilyn Hacker, the "attempt to move into form, again, with others" yields a poetry of intimate wit and sensual rapprochement. The unequal subject and object of Emerson's "Experience" meet on a level playing field, the "Other than self / O inconceivable" an "O believable" at last.[5] What, though, if that meeting proves hard to arrange? Let the self's defenses prove too powerful, or its instinct to turn the other into a forgiving "queen of love," and the attempt may fail—or at least demand an abashed reappraisal of oneself and one's art.

The first major poets of this latter, unhappy tradition are men, Robert Creeley and Robert Lowell. Although admirers of Williams, they find it hard to muster the older poet's faith in his own innocence and in the forgiving power of poetic "design." They turn instead to a breaking of staffs and a putting off of robes: a resignation of suspect masculine mastery in favor of a looser, more improvisational poetry or the literal incorporation of the other's words. Whether this resignation is successful, either as ethics or as aesthetics— whether it can succeed as both at the same time—is the question I turn to in this chapter. I take my texts from Creeley's work of the fifties and sixties (*For Love, Words, Pieces,* and *A Day Book*) and then from Lowell's later poems of love and marriage, especially *The Dolphin* (1973), whose desperate measures bring to a bitter fruition the poetry of what Creeley calls, in "The New World," "real crises in real homes."[6]

The Edge of Contact

Although he is the younger poet, it is helpful to begin with Creeley. Late in 1945, home from the war and needing "something to locate me . . . just to be real, to take up a real role as I assumed it to be," the nineteen-year-old poet married Ann MacKinnon.[7] They moved to an artists' colony, then a small New Hampshire farm, then southern France, then Mallorca, supported mostly by Ann's slim trust-fund income.

There in Mallorca, in the summer of 1954, Creeley wrote "A Character for Love": an essay-review of Williams's *The Desert Music* that spells out a crabbed, conflictual philosophy of marriage. Married love must resist arriving at an "understanding," he explains. Such "mature" and "responsible" bonds gloss over love's true struggle, a "hammering at the final edge of contact." "There is no woman either to be kind or to live with a kind man," the essay declares. "The man who would come to her comes with his own weapons, and if he is not a fool, he uses them."[8]

Where does this hardscrabble spite come from? You won't find it in Williams. "In spite of the 'wrong note' / I love you. My heart is / innocent": that is the tonal center of *The Desert Music*. The marital meeting promised in "Asphodel, that Greeny Flower" seems an embrace, not a championship bout. Even when writing of the "hard / give and take / of a man's life with / a woman," Williams keeps his eyes on the "thing . . . beyond / and above" such exchanges that will survive and give meaning to them.[9] A likelier source is D. H. Lawrence, whom Creeley cites both in "A Character for Love" and in several sour letters to Charles Olson. Lawrence taught an "aloneness" hard to balance with the "valid / actual: responsibilities" of marriage, Creeley observed. More broadly, though, he taught "LOVE. Jesus, he knew it cold. And how they hate him, the ladies for that. . . . I used to sit on the couch reading this stuff, and my wife cd tell what BK by the expression of my face ... [. . .] She used to get worried—that I got insufferable after same."[10] For a poet who grew up among women, and "didn't have a clue as to what men did, except literally I was a man," Lawrence proved an attractive, but dangerous, tutor.[11]

The poems of *For Love*, which span the failure of Creeley's first marriage and the wary start of his second, show the poet putting his vision of contact to the test. Their hesitant address to a silent "you" expertly captures the brittle emotional state that taking on the "real roles" of postwar husbandry and Lawrentian manhood entailed.[12] Consider the relationship between the third and fourth poems of the book, "A Song" and "The Crisis." Both turn the poet's "projective" verse, all breathy darts and withdrawals, into a reflective radar map of a resistant other, a muse of reproach. In the first, he keeps hushing her, turning her into a metaphorical "thrush" and treading the eggshells of lines like "and so, at peace, so very much now this same quiet."[13] When he trips, as in the second poem, a different scene slips through:

Let me say (in anger) that since the day we were married
we have never had a towel
where anyone could find it,
the fact.

Notwithstanding that I am not
simple to live with, not
my own judgment, but no
matter.

There are other things:

to kiss you is not
to love you.

Or not so simply.

Laughter releases rancor, the quality of mercy is not
strained.[14]

Can we reconstruct the scene? "Let me say (in anger)," the speaker begins, but
by the time we reach the short fourth line, "the fact," that permission has been
withdrawn. He raises his voice and talks over the other, rattling off that "not-
withstanding," then retreats to a sullen mutter, "but no / matter." As its tone
shifts, growing more musing, more appealing, the poem turns ambiguous. Is
"To kiss you is not / to love you" one of the "other things" he wishes to com-
plain of, or a response to an interrupting kiss? Has the other laughed, and if so,
was that to ease his "rancor" or just *at* it? Such puzzles suit the speaker's ambiv-
alence, and they prepare us for the way that "strained" undermines "laughter"
on the page. (Certainly there is neither "laughter" nor much mercy in the *Mer-
chant of Venice* speech he sententiously quotes.) But the poem simply cuts off, un-
resolved as emotion or as art, neither achieving nor even really aspiring to the
forgiving formal accomplishment that Williams called "design." If this is the
best that the speaker can do, as a husband or as a poet, he's in trouble—and the
progress of *For Love* shows that Creeley knew it.

From the later poems of *For Love*, it's clear that missing towels are not the
cause of "The Crisis." As the speaker says, "There are other things," notably a
deeper clash of marital expectations. At a time when love seemed "a kind of
down payment ... on a house, or perhaps a refrigerator," the "Unsuccessful
Husband" of Creeley's early verse and prose finds himself unable to join in the
business of affection.[15] This failure, at once economic and emotional, sours his
efforts at lyrical art. Many of the poems of *For Love*, especially in its first two
sections, are more or less bitter and satirical self-portraits. They sketch a satur-

nine man stranded in a pained self-consciousness. False notions of concord whisper him off cliffs—in the poem "Wait for Me," Creeley off-rhymes "marriage is" with "hypocrisies"—and in "The Bed," fantasies of middle-class recognition co-opt his native, limpid eloquence.[16] In "The Gift" another frangible "He" takes on a role that's beyond him: the masterful and understanding husband at his wedding, or (in a grimmer, more humorous reading) on his wedding night. How the poem teeters on its narrow foundation:

> He hands
> down the gift
> as from a great
> height, his
>
> precious
> understanding clothed
> in miraculous
> fortitude. This
>
> is the present
> of the ages, all
> rewards
> in itself.
>
> But the lady—
> she, disdain-
> ful, all
> in white for
>
> this occasion—cries
> out petulantly, is
> that all, is
> that all.[17]

The "she, disdain- / ful" here is one of Simone de Beauvoir's *grande amoreuses*, arriving at her moment of "searing disappointment" in the man she has adored. The man's prestige "may collapse at the first kiss, or in daily association, or during the wedding night," the French writer observes.[18] With its puffing of "his" to "this"—it will deflate in a minute to a mere "is, is"—the poem turns the woman's question back on the "he," and perhaps on the poet behind the curtain. Is this pretension all there is to him? And, by implication, might another marriage blossom once he's been cut down to size?

In "A Dilemma," written a few months after the essay on Williams, "A Character for Love," Creeley tries to tell himself that failure at business—or sex, or simply love—is required for the hammering of contact to occur. "Between a man and his wife," he writes, "there must be constantly some means whereby she can spit on him—and he, likewise, on her."[19] It's a sour, unconvincing piece. But it shows the poet's hope that somehow a good fight, hammering or spitting at contact, will bring him down from his inauthentic "great height."[20] Like the Williams who quotes Marcia Nardi's letters in *Paterson 2*, Creeley needs a voice from outside to snap him out of solipsism and pretention. Only by going *through* petulance, disappointment, and resentment can the couple meet as equals and restore the equitable, enlivening relationship of mutual recognition.

On the evidence of Creeley's letters and his loosely autobiographical novel *The Island*, it's clear that this shock treatment didn't work. Whatever Lawrence and Williams advised, the poet's bursts of anger prompted only a disheartened or seething withdrawal on the part of the other at hand. In Creeley's poems, these refusals strand male speakers in inauthenticity, for they deny the vital tension between sovereign subjects which alone will ratify both.[21] "The Warning" seems to answer one such refusal to have it out, its speaker determined to keep love alive:

> For love—I would
> split open your head and put
> a candle in
> behind the eyes.
>
> Love is dead in us
> if we forget
> the virtues of an amulet
> and quick surprise.[22]

The candle is no doubt phallic, and the violence implicitly sexual. As Charles Bernstein notes, "For Creeley, the sexual conditioning creating maleness appears to be correlative to the social conditioning creating identity."[23] When the latter is threatened, the former rises to defend it. But if by "putting it in" the poet hopes to restore a light or interest in the other's eyes, he can do so only at the cost of turning her into an "amulet," killing off the woman truly sought. Her stillness is a death's-head monument to the speaker's desperation, his longing for her to survive and respond. And yet—in a paradox that haunts his later work—this anger also snaps "The Warning" into focus. Compared to "The

Crisis" or "The Gift," it is taut, charged, crisply turned and immediately mem-
orable. One of Creeley's finest early pieces, it exemplifies the clenched but un-
happy aesthetic that the poet of *Pieces* would leave behind."

The Woman at Hand, the Woman in Mind

"Truly our hero," Creeley calls Williams in "A Character for Love." Here, as in
"The Dilemma" and poems like "The Warning," he shares the older poet's
faith that "The business of love is / cruelty," or at least a cruelty transformed.[24]
Jessica Benjamin sees the cruelties of love—from the sublime violence of eros
to an everyday couple's quotidian spite—as at heart a "struggle . . . for recogni-
tion." They show a couple struggling to balance "dependence and indepen-
dence" within the self and between self and other.[25] Aside from the appealing,
uncharacteristic opening of "Ballad of the Despairing Husband," however,
Creeley finds it hard to represent this balance in his work. Only nostalgia lets
the Despairing Husband picture a relationship where husband and wife turn a
slanging match to Miltonic "fit conversation": "I fought with her, she fought
with me, / and things went on right merrily." The speaker nods and smiles, in-
viting us to take his side and see old conflicts as a Punch and Judy show. And,
indeed, the broad Chaucerian humor of their exchanges makes this husband
and wife seem quite suited for each other. Why *shouldn't* they lace up and go at
it again?

As the "Ballad" goes on, however, the poet's staged dialogue shifts into ex-
tremes of bathetic entreaty and exultant self-defense. The complex tension be-
tween two sovereign subjects unravels into an easier, less profitable splitting of
terms. "Oh wife, oh wife—I tell you true," sings the Husband, "I never loved
no one but you." "I'm free of you, you little prick," the Ex-Wife responds, "and
I'm the one can make it stick." His childish diction is no match for her muscular
vulgarity, and his later allusion to Portia's speech about mercy dropping like
rain—a look back to "A Song," if not to Williams's "Rain"—falls flat. By the
final stanzas, the quickening banter of the start is long gone. Creeley has called
these closing lines an attempt to rouse the other's "sense of humor," at which
point the poem grows "whiningly sincere."[26] Humor there is, in forced, un-
likely rhymes: "Oh lovely lady, morning or evening or afternoon. / Oh lovely
lady, eating with or without a spoon." And delicacy, too: "Oh most lovely lady,
whether dressed or undressed or partly. / Oh most lovely lady, getting up or
going to bed or sitting only." But as the litany of ladies grows more and more
elaborate—"Oh lovely lady," "Oh most lovely lady," "Oh loveliest of ladies,"
and "Oh most loveliest of ladies"—it pushes the couple farther and farther

apart. The speaker drifts into dreamy entreaty, and despite his gallantry, you may want to shake him awake on the barstool. (Mister, that's no lady. That's your *wife*.)

As it turns the other from a sparring partner to a lady, "The Ballad of the Despairing Husband" signals a deeper turn in Creeley's vision of relationship—one that corresponds with his first divorce, and with the addition of a new name to his roster of tutors of love. "My heart has been limping, for months now," the poet confides in "On Love," a piece written soon after his divorce. "In that way, I tend to forget the lady, a little. . . . For an instant, no matter more—there are these several juxtapositions possible, e.g. H.D.'s saying, *I go where I love and am loved* . . . ; Williams' *what, shut grief in from us? We who have perhaps nothing to lose?* And the, *myself forgetting violence, and long betrayal*—of Robert Graves, the poem which introduces the first edition of *The White Goddess*."[27]

Creeley's quick cento insinuates that he is a suffering poet-lover in the highest tradition. Like the H.D. of *The Flowering of the Rod*, he may survive pain to "mount higher / to love—resurrection," his life as an artist renewed. And, more important, like the muse-poet of Robert Graves he may yet prove "headstrong and heroic," ready for "the next bright bolt" of inspiration.[28]

Creeley's limping heart will "forget the lady, a little," then, by taking refuge in what I have called the "secret ways of love": a tradition where the other may be muse or mistress, but never just a wife. Six years later, in his review of *For Love*, Robert Duncan honed in on this Gravesian strain. The Lady of Creeley's poems, writes Duncan, ought to be read as that "power in women that Dante once knew in his Beatrice, and that, before Dante, troubadours of Provence addressed in their love songs and petitions." Since the turn of the century, he explains, there have been poets who addressed "the woman as both Lady and wife in one": poets like Hardy and Lawrence and Williams for whom "the Lady is both archetypal and specific." According to Duncan, Creeley exploits a similar play between archetypes and human specificities, noble and vulgar dictions, to capture this romantic "perplexity of life."[29]

As the fullest postmodern inheritor of Pound's and H.D.'s mythic method, Duncan is drawn to the spirit of romance in Creeley's work. Creeley, though, seems more troubled by it, and by the strain of treating the woman at hand as the woman in mind. The Lawrence he admires, after all, is not a worshiper of the White Goddess. He's a diagnostician of the domestic, of companionate turmoil. "If your wife should accomplish for herself the sweetness of her own soul's possession," he advises in a passage Creeley quotes, "then gently, delicately let the new mode assert itself." With "the apple of knowledge at last di-

gested," the couple may establish a new, more authentic "mode of relation." Not
that this will prove easy or pleasant. "What belly-aches meanwhile. The apple
is harder to digest than a lead gun-cartridge."[30] The Lady may be the "most
persistent other of our existence," a figure who "eschew[s] male order,
allowing us to live at last," as Creeley writes in "Her Service Is Perfect Free-
dom," a review of Graves's *The White Goddess.*[31] But if this mystical other frees
Creeley from the "real role" of husband and provider, she makes none of the
merely human demands entailed by the other person met in an authentic com-
panionate relationship.[32] Her "service" includes no "bellyaches"—which may
mean, no human love.

The Lady poems of *For Love* dodge the purely human demands of de Beau-
voir's authentic love—that love built on the bellyaches of intersubjective rec-
ognition. This does not mean they are not beautiful. Think of "Air: 'Cat Bird
Singing,'" with its Elizabethan self-deprecation and faltering appeals. By
humbling the male speaker, dedicating him to the Lady's "Service," they hope
to get him a hearing, and thus spring him from his emotional lockup. But the
great divide that always lay between Petrarchan poets and their Ladies sur-
vives. In the age-old courtly double-bind, the other's nearness may become as
much a threat as her withdrawal. Both make recognition impossible; both leave
the poet alone.

With his uneasy embrace of the "secret ways of love," Creeley resembles nei-
ther Williams nor Lawrence nor Graves so much as a fourth male modernist,
Wallace Stevens.[33] Like the poet of "Gallant Château" and "Arrival at the Wal-
dorf" and "Bouquet of Belle Scavoir," Creeley suspects that the turn to an ide-
alized other may be an evasion, its rhapsody a fake. When "the imagination
projects for itself a world more real than that which it literally experiences,"
then "contact is broken, becomes the touch of the mind," and that love which is
a form of "being-with" becomes "impossible," the poet will warn as he writes
the poems collected in *Words.*[34] But you can see his qualms as early as "The
Whip," in part 1 of *For Love.* The speaker of "The Whip" is cut off from his
"specific" love, the woman sleeping beside him, by his inability to capture her
in metaphor. "My love was a feather," he begins, only to deflate the already mal-
adroit figure by calling her "a flat / sleeping thing." In other poems—"The
Warning," for example—the other's "flat" stasis prompts a flash of violence.
Here it makes the poet think of a woman "above," whom he "had / addressed . . .
in / a fit she / returned."[35]

In his review of *For Love* Duncan equates this other, unspecified woman with
Dante's archetypal "gloriosa donna della mia mente," the "glorious lady of my

mind." An exchange of "fits" with this Lady might solve the poet's problems with metaphor, or ease the nervous flicker of his lines. It might even lead him to some paradisal vision, like the one that follows Pound's appeal to La Cara. It *can't* supply Miltonic "fit conversation," and that seems a sticking point. As the poet draws back from the woman in mind, his delicate diction breaks off: "I yelled, / / but what is that? Ugh, / she said, beside me, she put / / her hand on / my back." This yell brings him back to his literal place in the bed, to the literal woman beside him, and to a flat, ungainly scrap of what Margaret Homans calls "literal language," that language "in which the presence or absence of referents in the ordinary sense is quite unimportant," since it aims primarily to signal presence and reassurance.[36] A language, as the critic explains, at odds with figuration ("my love was a feather"), at least insofar as figures depend on discarding the literal for symbolic substitutes. In Freudian theory, after all, that's how a boy masters his loss of Mama, entering the realm of metaphor, symbol, and sign. No wonder the speaker "think[s] to say this / wrongly" as the poem ends. Whipped by guilt, he longs to set aside the "rightness" of more polished verses, in which the Lady would take untroubled dominion.

The moral spasm of "The Whip" does not accompany all of Creeley's dabblings in the secret ways of love. Often the poet keeps his eye on the developmental connection between his mother and the unnamed other, and this gives him a gentle and appealing sense of humor. The speaker of "The Way" knows that his courtly bent reveals, at heart, "a small boy's notion of doing good." The sad-sack ex-husband of "The Wind" recalls the mother who gave him such comforting, inaccurate expectations of what "love in homes" would mean. That memory stirs up others, including screaming fights with another woman, presumably an ex-wife. These in turn "betoken" the arrival of a goddess—whose resemblance to his mother he now laughs to recognize. The archetypal lady is thus rooted in the literal, while the literal other is invoked precisely inasmuch as she will "betoken . . . all mothers or potentials thereof." Such poems forecast the poet's later effort, especially in *Words*, to excavate the foundations of male identity, not through a Freudian tour of the family romance but through attention to the verbal, rhetorical construction of masculinity: what voices, heard in boyhood, now whisper in his "I." Elsewhere, however, the tension between "La gloriosa donna della mia mente" and the inglorious literal other remains, and with it a split between the secret ways of lyrical love and the "ugh" of speaking "wrongly." The tact, restraint, and abstraction of "The Wife" suggest Creeley's plight, as he weighs the claims of "two women": the first "tangible substance, / flesh and bone," and the other who "in my mind /

occurs" and "keeps her strict / proportion there."[37] The poet will choose flesh, and trust it to find a new proportion, less strict, more inviting, and more "literal."

Into the Literal

The poems of *For Love* are set in a loosely chronological and biographical sequence. From poems of crisis and divorce the book moves to such hesitant verses of remarriage as "The Hill," "For Fear," "Love Comes Quietly," and the closing poem, "For Love," dedicated to his second wife, Bobbie. Unlike the edgy poems of contact and the graceful courtly poems for the Lady, Creeley's verses of remarriage step back from anxious or self-abasing masculinity. Straying from what he would later call "man's estate," the poet turns his back on the "tedium, / despair, a painful / sense of isolation and / whimsical if pompous / / self-regard" that received notions of manliness bring.[38] Alongside the poet's emotional progress lies an aesthetic one: a search for a poetic that can "say this / wrongly" and approximate the contact available to flesh without resorting to a language of yelling and "ughs" alone. Creeley will now dwell on the flesh that the thinking self inhabits, on the life it lives in bodily company, and on the words that both enact and testify to the chance of unforced connection. These are conjoined in a return to something called "the literal."

In the last chapter I looked at one such "literal" poetic: Loy's decision to "go / gracelessly." Gertrude Stein's language of blandishment and intimate copresence bears comparison as well. I find the most helpful approach to Creeley's poetics of the literal, however, in a less likely place, a study of nineteenth-century women writers, *Bearing the Word*. Here Margaret Homans sets out four strategies or situations characteristic of these women's interest in the literal. With some stretching, two fit Creeley's efforts. The first she calls "the literalization of a figure," which "occurs when some piece of overtly figurative language, a simile or an extended or conspicuous metaphor, is translated into an actual event or practice": a translation I want to look at in the context of Creeley's poem "Rain," and which is vital to the treatment of sexuality and the notion of "emptiness" in *Words*. The second strategy, which leads me to the poetry of *Pieces* and the prose of *A Day Book*, involves the "translation, transmission, copying, and so on" of words from other authors in an attempt to "convert the unwomanly selfishness of writing into the selflessness of transmission."[39] In Creeley the turn away from selfishness—an effort to disown his all too manly will to mastery—appears in a dedication to the selflessness of serial composition and a notebook poetry. (By the end of this chapter we will meet another text that tries, again with mixed success, to "translate" another's voice and thus renounce male mastery: Lowell's *The Dolphin.*)

Some pages ago I noted an allusion to Portia's courtroom speech in the "Ballad of the Despairing Husband," and at the end of "The Crisis." Implicit in both allusions was the figure of mercy, which "droppeth as the gentle rain from heaven / Upon the place beneath" and so on (3.4.183–84). The local distributor for these allusions may be Williams's "Rain," which I discussed near the end of Chapter 3. In any case, in the third part of *For Love* Creeley literalizes this figure to write one of his finest poems, "The Rain." Here the "ease" and "hardness" of a "quiet persistent rain" reminds the speaker of his lack of either, and with it of the merciless self-consciousness that has left him locked in himself for so long. To anatomize his condition the poet draws on a highly abstract diction. But to *escape* it he turns to the other, not just as a figure for the rain of mercy but as mercifully "wet" in her own right, an incarnation of the earlier figure. "Love, if you love me," he pleads,

> lie next to me.
> Be for me, like rain,
> the getting out
>
> of the tiredness, the fatuousness, the semi-
> lust of intentional indifference.
> Be wet
> with a decent happiness.[40]

To find the beloved "wet / with a decent happiness" would prove her response and approval: a happier, gentler version of the recognition sought in the fights of "The Crisis" and the "Ballad." It would at last open the way to a contact "twice bless'd" since, like Portia's mercy, it "blesseth him that gives and him that takes." And, in a step beyond Williams and his demand for forgiveness, it would acknowledge receipt of something that the woman cannot be assumed to bestow. Stanley Cavell's remarks on "the woman's satisfaction" as "the essential object of the skeptical question" in *Othello* and *Antony and Cleopatra* seem relevant here. "It is a conclusion that must be conferred, given," he writes, "not one that I can cause or determine. . . . To elicit this gift, the extreme claim of male activeness, thus requires the man's acceptance of his absolute passiveness."[41] Such wetness is both metaphor and metonym for an eased, appeased relationship with the world.

In *Words*, it seems at first that Creeley's quest to drop the metaphorical "rocks of thought" and return to the passive, the literal, the body, has succeeded. In the second poem, "The Rocks," a wife is beside the speaker, her "warm / moistness" suggesting that the prayer of "The Rain" has been answered.[42] The speaker of "Something" recalls a "woman I loved / then, literally," who a moment after she had been "completely / open to me, naked," grew embarrassed at her need to pee. Unnamed, framed by memory and by the poet's third-person, this woman is still the most human and memorable other in Creeley's early poetry. The speaker does his best to hold his focus on her upper body as she goes to the basin across from the bed:

> Squatting, her

> head reflected in the mirror,
> the hair dark there, the
> full of her face, the shoulders . . .

His gaze drifts downward, but the phrases that come to his mind put a tenderly ironic spin on the distance between the earlier literal lovemaking and the scene as she

> sat spread-legged, turned on
> one faucet and shyly pissed. What
> love might learn from such a sight.[43]

One thing that love might learn is that while all wetness may be physical, literal, not all wetness is sexual. One moment "spread-legged, turned on," is not a promise of perpetual ardor and access—and yet, this separateness does not signal a threatening withdrawal or perpetual exile, but the dawn of a delicate courtesy.

Words is, in many ways, a transitional book. Its "I's" and "He's" are still, often, "disturbed / and fumbling" men, given to acts of anger and even violence.[44] The volume shows Creeley coming to terms with the origins of that kind of masculine self *in terms*, quite literally, as he attends to the words and phrases that sponsor his fantasy life.[45] The woman in mind has "tits, not breasts," he muses in "The Woman"; he is, to himself, a "He / I" whose first stab at making love leaves him alienated from his own body: "Cock, / they say, prick, dick, / I put it in her, / I lay there."[46] The "they" that speaks in Creeley's "I"—like the third-person "I" that speaks whenever the first-person does, as "The Pattern" has it—seems given to fits of passionate violence, less because his instincts drive him than because the "they" that underwrite masculine identity keep urging him on. "Fatty / Arbuckle, the one / hero of the school, / took a coke bottle, / pushed it up his girl," the poet recalls in "The Hole," drifting into a schoolyard rhythm; and a few stanzas later, an imagined or recalled sexual partner reinforces the lesson: "she didn't want / it, but said, after, / / the only time / it felt right. Was / I to force / her."[47] After the figurative attack of "The Warning," such force seems only natural—or, at least, both assaults would have a place if love is cruelty transformed.

Now, though, Creeley retreats from cruelty, even figurative cruelty, even when the assault takes part in a struggle for recognition. When the poet slides from memories of Fatty Arbuckle to his own fantasy, in "The Hole," his first thought is of the literal, brutal scene—"Broken glass, / broken silence, // filled with screaming"—and his second, retreating from the rape fantasy, is a memory of other, familial bodies, untouched.[48] Attending to spelling and phonemes, the literal letters he writes on the page, he echoes the "her" of "Force / her" in the next word, "Mother." Was she, then, the real object of assault, the woman in mind, for whom the woman at hand has become a mere victimized figure? "The Dream," a few pages before, makes that insight quite explicit, and it connects attacks like these with a childish fear of being left, abandoned, or simply turned away from. Met head-on, admitted and addressed, those fears might fade—and with them the gripped, arid rigidity of his old tumescent selfhood. It's when Creeley's "I" feels least himself, least heroic on the Fatty Arbuckle model, that he feels most "alive and honored," according to "The Flower," a poem that dances away from the "I" to dwell on the self as transitive object, a "me."[49] That the poem gets a little sentimental is, perhaps, its point. To picture the beloved as a flower, or even just her sex as one, is no less conventional than to picture her as a lady. But it's not an especially masculine or heroic convention, particularly since the modern period, and it is one that the poet of *For Love* would have shied away from, wary and torn.[50]

In *Words*, then, Creeley sets himself the task of writing a poetry not of "real crises in real homes," but of achieved relationship. He wants his work to capture his new emotional state, the meditative, mindful process through which he is arriving there, and the new "literal" language that will embody and enact it. Often, however, the poet relies on assertions of change or desire to bring his poems to their close, in a way that makes them carry more weight than their language will bear: the vows that close his "Enough," for example, or the declarations of love and presence that round out "A Birthday" and "A Tally." As *Words* ends it remains an open question, I think, exactly how the poet will "sing / days of happiness" and "make / a pardonable wonder / of one's blunders."[51] The solution he begins to explore in poems such as "Enough" is an agglomerative serial poetic, a version of Homans's second strategy of literalized

language, that of selfless transmission. With this nonintentional composi-
tional style—and, by extension, a non-intentional stance toward the world—
the tender mercies of the literal are extended to the literal process of composi-
tion. "With each intentional act the subject isolates itself from the world, from
possible absolute involvement, from love," Harold Mesch explains of Creeley's
logic. As "Things / come and go" and the poet says, "Then / let them," Creeley
captures involvement and encounter in his work.[52]

Two books from the late sixties—*Pieces*, published in 1969, and *A Day Book*,
written from November 1968 through the following February—demonstrate
Creeley's first major work in this new mode. Both turn their backs on the
clipped, intense work that he had specialized in until then. Both draw your at-
tention to the literal act of writing; both describe that act as a return to the
poet's literal body and through it to an unforced contact with others.[53] Like
Stein and Loy and Whitman before him, that is to say, Creeley denies that we
fall into language, banished forever to a melancholy symbolic realm. If words
are "full / / of holes / aching," they are therefore *like* the body. The right *sort* of
language could accomplish the sort of mutual presence that poets of authentic
love dream of, or claim to: "No one / there. Everyone / here." If wetness is the
keynote of *Words*, then *with*ness is the keynote of Pieces: a companionate rela-
tionship with others and the reader, permitted by a genial, general defenestra-
tion of mastery. "I had / an ego once upon / a time," the poet confides—and
then adds, not hung up on egolessness, "I do still, / for you to listen to me."[54]

Those who love *Pieces* often praise this open ease of gesture. Nothing in the
book is fraught. When Creeley invokes the "goddess or woman / become her,"
he does so with an equanimity utterly foreign to Graves, or to his own earlier
poems, such as "The Door." When the poet writes or dreams of "fucking,"
he's not relying on sex to end his solitude, or even concerned with the patri-
archal discourse of his drives. Indeed, the only flash of his old anger comes
when he thinks of *language*, snapping (in exhausted exasperation), "I hate the
metaphors. / I want you. I am still alone, / but want you with me." Those who
prefer Creeley's earlier work—I am one of them, I'll confess—find that *Pieces*
asks you to set aside criteria I am too "locked in" to release. The closing lines, a
quadrille where the phrase "what do you" bows in four crisply different direc-
tions, depending on the verb that follows, is charming, even brilliant: a triumph
of unforced attention. The book's declarations of "happy love," however, like
those in the later serial poem *In London*, seem to my ear a little insistent, more
sentimental than their context supports.[55]

I hesitate to pass such judgments. The poems, after all, ask to be read in the spirit that wrote them, with a mild, compassionate attention that watches the poet dip into bathos, confident he'll towel himself off in a few lines, though never briskly. On the whole, however, I prefer *A Day Book* to *Pieces*, and to much of Creeley's work in verse from the early seventies. A prose poem in thirty entries, *A Day Book* is preoccupied with marriage. Its subjects are rangy, some familiar from *Words*, some quite new: fantasies of other men making love with the poet's wife; the construction of masculinity; the pleasure of writing, and of having written; sex as a *return* to self, at least after orgasm, and not as a means to union. In the four months' entries you watch the poet move from an unhelpful blunt language trapped "in the head"—a glance back to Lawrence, perhaps—to musings on the limits of that language ("shit, fuck, cunt, etc.") when divorced from the literal context of affection: "She delights, you are held in the succulent wonder, fondled, teased, and just those words come whispering into your ear."[56] Where the organization of *Pieces* seems linear, but not developmental—the speaker has not changed by the end, either in concerns or in tone—in *A Day Book* you watch him letting go of fear and jealousy and a desire to get past the opacity of the female other. The fantasized gang bang of the first entry, where the husband "flips her [his wife] to the other, in the mind" and "the man, men, maul her body," stands in sharp contrast with the tender ménage à trois twelve entries later:

> and as they both in an awkwardness moved toward her, she eased them by smiling, and reached to take the other against her, so that he now took position beside them, back of her, reaching over the arch of her back to stroke her tits, as the other was now down on her, sucking, the cunt, as she moved against him, making soft sweet moans, as one says. . . .
>
> .   .   .
>
> Slowly, almost gravely, it went on, while on the bed, he watched, felt his own cock tense with it, could not see the eyes facing also toward the sight, hers, erotic, lovely, tight with interest, his own, fucking, fucking in the knowledge of animals, in delight and permission of animals, gravely, sweetly, humans without fear or jealousy, but intensive increasing provocation.[57]

"Gravely, sweetly," this passage captures for me the return to body and relationship that others find in *Pieces*, and with the fine attention to manners more common in Creeley's earlier work. I find its chewy detail a welcome contrast to the poles of abstraction and didacticism of his other late-seventies work, with its repeated invocation of that "sticky sentimental / warm enclosure," the body which builds, for love, "a home / on earth."[58]

The Use of the Other

In my reading of Creeley I have not, I realize, attended to questions of composition nearly as much as the poet would like.[59] It's a curious but not unpredictable fact, for example, that his poems are best served for closure by looks back to the condition of being "locked in" emotionally, even when the poem sighs with relief that he's been freed.[60] Rather than treat him in further detail, however, working on through to his books of the last twenty years, I want to turn my attention outward once more. For Creeley is not the only postwar poet to imagine a redeeming connection between love's and writing's improvisations. I find a similar equation in writers who share none of Creeley's faith in serial composition—poets who leave the link metaphorical. In Mona Van Duyn's "Toward a Definition of Marriage," for example, you'll find an image of marriage remarkably similar to that worked through in Creeley's serial work. Marriage is, she proposes, "essentially artless," a serial composition in which "line after line plods on, / and none of the ho hum passages can be skipped." Van Duyn, too, imagines this art as best when "embodied," since

> digression there
> is meaningful, and takes such joy in the slopes and crannies
> that every bony gesture is generous, full,
> all lacy with veins and nerves. There, the spirit
> smiles in its skin, and impassions and sweetens to style.

As she hunts up a model for such "embodied" art, complete with "ho hum passages" and joyful digression, Van Duyn joins Creeley in a shrugging off of mastery. Marriage is, she proposes, like the work found in notebooks "after the master died," where the "great gift" of this "charred, balky man" was let loose one day to "play / . . . on a small ground" until it "rounded the steeliest shape / to shapeliness, it was so loving an exercise."[61]

During the late 1960s and the early 1970s, a "charred" Robert Lowell turned his great gift loose in the poetry of his *Notebooks*: masses of unrhymed sonnets that explore, with much else, the poetics of marriage and "divorce! divorce!" Like Creeley, Lowell is determined to make his work capture life lived on the line and in the act of writing. But he cannot take the younger poet's comfort in the "warm enclosure" of his or another's body, literary or otherwise. Lowell is resolutely undeceived, especially about art's ability to tease out love's ethical tangles. However he may rely on the touch or the voice of another to call him back from his own mind's wanderings, Lowell comes to find such contact insufficient. It will not guarantee a world outside that is at once "literal" and meaningful, and it cannot restore his faith in the inner life, either.[62] A crisis for any poetry, but particularly for the poetry of love.

Like Creeley, and like Williams before them both, Lowell is primarily a poet of love in marriage, especially when that love must accommodate forces that would shatter the marriage in a metaphorical or actual divorce. Of the three, however, it is Lowell who most constantly discards the ideal of marriage as an "understanding" in favor of a more difficult but more rewarding "hammering at the final edge of contact."[63] Lowell writes of marriage, Allan Williamson explains, "not as bourgeois stability, but its opposite: the one encounter so unremitting that it breaks down all our normal and solipsistic ways of conceiving our relationships" and "forces us to acknowledge the person as beyond all our frames of reference, an other and the Other": an acknowledgment basic to the modern companionate ideal.[64] Once more, then, the question arises: how can lyric poetry capture such an "unremitting encounter" with "an other and the Other"? What can or should intersubjective love look like in verse?

As we have seen, Creeley moves from mapping the other's reproach or response to a more self-critical project. In *Words,* and still more in *Pieces* and *A Day Book,* he tries to reconstruct his male self so that it is capable of relationship. His efforts to capture relationship itself tend to the epistolary—poems directed to a "you" in tones of more or less believable entreaty and abstraction—and less often to the descriptive, as scenes of courtesy or gentleness come to life. Lowell's first efforts to capture intersubjective relationship are mostly thematic. Starting with *Life Studies,* his "I" constantly risks falling out of touch with the world in general and a particular woman, usually his wife. A century earlier Emerson would have consoled him with the thought that this near solipsism was an incurable condition of being. By the mid-twentieth century, however, thanks in part to the debunking "modern temper," such subjectiveness has become a psychological and not a philosophical condition: one that a truly healthy companionate relationship ought to supersede, not just survive.

As a psychological condition, the fatal subjectivity of Lowell's "I" has a discernable origin and, with luck, a cure. This inability to recognize "an outside reality that is not one's own projection," D. W. Winnicott explains, signals an inability to move from "relating" to the world—"the experience of 'the subject as an isolate,' in which the object is merely a 'phenomenon of the subject' "—to a condition of "using" the world as a "shared" but "independent" reality. Where does this inability come from? To use the world or another person, in Winnicott's sense of the word, requires a faith that the other will survive what he calls destruction: "a refusal, a negation, the mental experience of 'You do not exist for me'" familiar to any parent from the tantrums of a cranky, individuating child. At best these efforts of destruction lead to a happy discovery: Mama (and the world, therefore) survives! Let her capitulate, however, or register no response at all, and the developing subject's faith that he or she can "engage in an all-out collision with the other, can hurtle himself against the barriers of otherness in order to feel the shock of the fresh cold outside" will be eviscerated.[65] The adult it grows into will suffer a paralyzing sense of inauthenticity. It may be incapable of a mature, "authentic," intersubjective love.

Winnicott's theories bring the flashes of violence in Creeley and Williams into new focus. His majesty the baby and his majesty the husband are both unsure egotists, hungry for the chastening response that will show that love and the other have survived. When Lowell looks in the mirror of "Murder Incorporated's Czar Lepke," he thus sees a man whose more than metaphorical, all-too-successful destruction of others has left him imprisoned in a "little segregated cell" that signals a deeper psychological isolation. All sorts of demands have been met—he has "a portable radio, a dresser, two toy American / flags tied together with a ribbon of Easter palm"—but where the social contact and personal resurrection these objects should entail have been denied.[66]

Like Lepke, the "I" of *Life Studies* is medically "tamed" and psychologically disoriented. He focuses on death and disconnection; he has an "air of lost connections." Those connections are restored, however, when an "agonizing reappraisal" arrives in the poems that come after "Memories of West Street and Lepke": "Man and Wife," and "To Speak of Woe That Is in Marriage."[67] The first of these begins with a poet whose "homicidal eye" kills everything it sees by sucking it into himself. ("As I am," says Emerson, "so I see"). Yet in his wife's remembered "invective," and still more in her present "old-fashioned tirade— / loving, rapid, merciless—," he finds an aural connection, partial and painful, that has not been lost. At least one person has survived to hold his hand—and, just as important, has survived his demand for comfort. She holds her pillow, rather than holding him, as he desires.[68] Her distance, invective, and tirade save him from a Lepke-like confinement—and a comparable sentence.

The wife's survival and response in "Man and Wife" and "To Speak of Woe" forms a model for the use of the other elsewhere in Lowell's work. Throughout *For the Union Dead*, as Stephen Yenser and Steven Gould Axelrod have argued, such appeals move the poet from lost connections to contact.[69] In "Night Sweat," for example, he finds himself spiraling back into himself as he writes, heading toward a childhood "will to die." His wife's arrival startles him back to social selfhood, but the shock can't save him entirely. For by the time he finishes describing it, he has harnessed the energies of their encounter for his own compositional use, catching it in a closely woven sail of metaphors. The verse surges forward, but the other's independent selfhood starts to slip, once again, out of sight.

Lowell's instinct to trap the other in tropes always tends to betray him, not least because it is, he suspects, an *instinct*, and not a controlled compositional device. Williams was able to see the virgin and the wife as the same forgiving figure, and Creeley was reassured to the point of laughter by the developmental connection between his mother and the other that his adult thoughts usher up. But Lowell is a true son of the debunking modern temper, and he knows with bitter irony how determined his inner life has been by the family romance. The woman of tangible substance he longs for will thus remain a woman in mind, inspiring but unable to satisfy his hunger for contact—unless, perhaps, she objects, and with such force that the poet's art is shaken down to its instinctual foundations. *The Dolphin* springs from this necessity.

The Use of Error

In 1973, having carved *For Lizzie and Harriet* from the bulky block of *Notebook* and having shaped the poems that remained, with some additions, into his lyric-epic *History*, Lowell published these two books of sonnets along with a third, *The Dolphin*. Reviews, as they say, were mixed.[70] Many focused their attacks on Lowell's decision to incorporate letters from and conversations with Elizabeth Hardwick as she responds to the poet's love affair with Caroline Blackwood, and to name both women in his text. Adrienne Rich found all three books hemmed in by the poet's masculine "encapsulated ego"—the "self-enclosed" Cartesian self, "gliding / safe from the turbulence," whose failure she celebrates in her poem "The Wave," written the same year. Outraged, Rich attacked the letter-poems of *The Dolphin*, as one of the "most vindictive and mean-spirited acts in the history of poetry."[71]

I find Rich's attack off the mark, but only in a single crucial detail. Yes, Lowell's use of the letters grows out of his "encapsulated ego." It comes, though, as a desperate strategy to escape this segregated selfhood, to plunge into the "turbulence" of intersubjective encounter. By quoting "Lizzie's" and "Caroline's" words in *The Dolphin*, Lowell tries his hand at the second strategy of literalization I discussed in Creeley's turn to serial composition. Both are attempts to abandon a tradition of male aesthetic and emotional mastery and arrive at a poetry of contact.[72] Lowell's attempt has far more drama, of course, as the poet records the other's agonizing reappraisals of his behavior. "*Do you really* know," she asks, "*what you have done?*"[73]

I return in a few pages to the moral questions raised by Lowell's quotations. To appreciate the *aesthetic* drama of *The Dolphin* it helps to keep in mind the role that Elizabeth Hardwick plays in the earlier *Notebook* collections and in *For Lizzie and Harriet.* As represented in his poems, this marriage offers the poet the sting and reassurance that he looked for in *Life Studies* and *For the Union Dead.* Lowell's "Lizzie" is not an especially comforting presence. But comfort is less important than contact, and that she surely provides. The quarrels and biting comments that these poems recount seem structurally central to the relationship between the poet and his "Dear Heart's-Ease." A rhythm of "exaggerated outcry" and "rest from all discussion, drinking, smoking" brings this pair their only equilibrium.[74] A fellow writer and, what's more, a critic, "Lizzie" is well suited to provide response and reappraisal, to let the poet see his words afresh.[75] It is "the Samuel Johnson in a wife" that "sends us home kicking each bleeding leaf of the weeds," Lowell writes in "Playing Ball with the Critic"—kicking the weeds the way, perhaps, Dr. Johnson kicked at a stone, and for much the same reason. Both prove the existence of the outside world.[76]

"Writers marry / their kind still, true and one and clashing," Lowell muses in *Notebook 1967–68.*[77] Such marriages have a number of rewards—indeed, Gabriel Pearson suggests that the affairs that Lowell recounts in *For Lizzie and Harriet* are meant to "appeal to Lizzie as fellow writer." She will, as a fellow artist, understand his need for erotic "Beauty-sleep," even sleep with someone else, so long as it restores his authorial vitality.[78] In his descriptions of adultery Lowell's lines do repeatedly blossom from self-deprecation or stings of conscience into lyric ease. They do so with an eye over their shoulder, perhaps on the general reading public, of course; but more likely on the wife who is meant to read and understand that the poet's affairs have nothing to do with *her.* It's painful to picture her facing sensual tributes to the poet's other "you": "you caught me and kissed me and stopped my rush, / your sinewy lips wide-eyed as the honeycomb." Yet would she spot herself inscribed elsewhere in the scene, perhaps in the background music Lowell mentions a moment later?[79] And wouldn't she see how Lowell makes sure that the women who inspire him seem no match for her? They offer a return to the body, an exultant if immoral "redemption." But this life in the erotic moment can hardly replace the poet's life through time with his fellow "Old Campaigner."[80]

The rhythm of transgression and guilty composition that underwrites Lowell's sonnets of adultery echoes, with a guiltier conscience, Williams's patterns of destruction, confession, and assumed forgiveness. Once again we find a love that can exist only in time, in history, lifted "across" but not above "the sorry facts" of "cruel / and selfish / and totally obtuse" acts of withdrawal and renewal. But Lowell's husband and wife seem far more equally matched than those in Williams, perhaps because they are both writers. "Lizzie" is far more resistant than Floss to being turned into a forgiving "queen of love."[81] And love through time in Lowell means love in the face of *entropy*, a threat that is nowhere on the scene in Williams's work. Without the loyalty Lowell feels for his "professional sparring partner"—Hepburn to his Tracy, though this is no comedy—the world would turn "all icy pandemonium," a chaos come again. And even with that love to shelter him, the poet can find only a "firelit hollow" to repair to. He can't avoid the thought that time leaves "neither of us the wiser or kinder," and that his adulterous, poetic affairs will come to naught as well. "Beatrice / always met me too early or too late," he sighs, and when she "pierc[ed] the firelit hollow of the marriage," she appeared as a mere "brightest prong, antennae of the ant." She did not, perhaps *could* not, lead her poet into paradise.

"What my hand did"

As *The Dolphin* opens it seems this entropic shadow has lifted. A Beatrice has finally come on time, and with her the hope of a transcendent world. The Dolphin we meet in the first sonnet, "Fishnet," is at once the poet's lover (and soon to be third wife) Caroline Blackwood and the muse. Both "archetypal and specific," then, in Robert Duncan's phrase, she bids fair to be Lowell's version of Graves's White Goddess, the other who "eschew[s] male order, allowing us to live at last."[82] But Lowell's memory of another vision of love—a companionate ideal where "it was the equivalent of everlasting / to stay loyal to my other person loved"—haunts his search for a new life of erotic inspiration.[83] The energies the Dolphin embodies can perhaps rescue the poet from his self-portrait as an "old actor" who merely "reads himself aloud." But as they tear down his old home with Lizzie and help build his new "house" of poetry, made up of fourteen-line stanza-rooms, they keep exposing the shaky foundations of his new domestic life.

The Dolphin may thus seem a Beatrice. But her passion for Lowell, and Lowell's for her, finds a closer match in Dante's *bufera*, the storm that eternally sweeps up Paolo and Francesca, in the *Inferno*, to punish their adulterous love. I do not know whether Lowell was familiar with George Santayana's commentary on this scene from the *Inferno* in "Three Philosophical Poets," but it seems on point. "What makes these lovers so wretched in the Inferno?" the philosopher asks. "Can an eternity of floating on the wind, in each other's arms, be a punishment for lovers?" Such a fate is what their passion would have asked for;

"it is what passion stops at, and would gladly prolong forever." But the *bufera* of passion is, for Santayana, clearly distinguished from love:

> Love dreams of more than mere possession; to conceive happiness, it must conceive a life to be shared in a varied world, full of events and activities, which shall be new and ideal bonds between the lovers. But unlawful love cannot pass out into this public fulfillment. It is condemned to be mere possession—possession in the dark, without an environment, without a future. It is love among the ruins. And it is precisely this that is the torment of Paolo and Francesca—love among the ruins of themselves and of all else they might have had to give to one another. Abandon yourself, Dante would say to us,—abandon yourself altogether to a love that is nothing but love, and you are in hell already.[84]

Love among the ruins, a love that is nothing but love ... The anti-Dantean "new life" of Lowell's and Caroline's quotidian concerns ("Dolphins"), their often pastoral languor, even their bloody, painful bond in the birth of their son—none of these can quite dispel the poet's underlying fear that their love depends upon a damned abandonment.

This fear makes Lowell chide and chastise himself throughout *The Dolphin*, mocking his own dreams of erotic redemption. "How mean the drink-money for the hour of joy, / its breathy charity and brag of body," he writes in "Flashback to Washington Square 1966." If at one point he finds himself astonished by sensual joy, a sonnet later he will sober up and scoff. Such dark humors are not new to Lowell's work. In "Wind," a *Notebook* sonnet that obliquely comments on the story of Paolo and Francesca, Lowell mourned the fragility of all passion. "Winds fed the fire," he writes, "a wind can blow it out."[85] But in *The Dolphin* the poet is more brutal, even crass, like Stevens at his bitterest or the Loy of *Love Songs to Joannes.* Stung by "conscience incurable," Lowell knows he has no "right to will transcendence" through his affair or, by implication, through the art that it inspires. He knows too well the Freudian templates, the mental illness, and the literature that script his affair: "one man, two women, the common novel plot." Creeley may worry over his doubled love of the woman at hand and the woman in mind. But there is nothing in *For Love* or *Words* or *Pieces* to match Lowell's brutal "Double-Vision": "While we are talking, I am asking you, / 'Where is Caroline?' And you *are* Caroline."[86]

Inasmuch as *The Dolphin* aspires to be a sonnet sequence about the reviving force of its muse, the Dolphin, it fails. As Vereen Bell has argued, this is a book that "wants to be a volume that it cannot be; and it cannot be the book it wants to be, that it dreams of being, because of its author's inability to be self-deceived."[87] To be "authentic," Lowell must acknowledge those forces within the self which determine its actions; and in this book they leave any hope of transcendence through love or art irrevocably tainted. These shaping scripts make the poet's love affair, divorce, and new life seem oddly unreal. Not always—there are moments when Lowell dreams the stormy weather brought by his mermaid-muse will afford him an escape from social and natural laws. "Does anyone ever make you do anything?" he asks her, and she responds with just the blessing he desires, just the reassurance that eros is not bound and determined by the patterns of nature or the family romance:

> "Do this, do that, do nothing; you're not chained.
> I am a woman or I am a dolphin,
> the only animal man really loves,
> I spout the smarting waters of joy in your face—
> rough weather fish, who cuts your nets and chains."[88]

Unfortunately, the fish who "cuts your nets" would also escape the "net" of words the poet has cast from "Fishnet" on. The freer she is, the less available she is to poetry.

As *The Dolphin* goes on, Lowell casts an increasingly cold eye on Caroline. He does his best to see her without romantic illusion, complete with "bulge eyes bigger than your man's closed fist."[89] Such lines gesture towards Winnicott's "destruction," hungry for contact with a world outside. But this purely human Caroline never comes entirely into focus, and as a character she mostly remains "a projection of the poet's dream," drifting with him in "a voluptuous leisure."[90] Since in Lowell's previous work only struggle ratified the self, however, the pastoral sonnets that describe his life with Caroline lie under a threatening shadow. Some sort of crisis seems at hand.

Exactly what crisis, though, is it? In another poet it might have been a split between Caroline as archetypal Dolphin and Caroline as specific new wife. As Calvin Bedient convincingly asserts, Lowell is at his most eloquent "when recalling, however indirectly, the tyrannical mermaid who had impersonated his mother, a creature 'stone-deaf at will' and stone-deaf often." The poet "never loves his craft so much," Bedient goes on, "never writes more undulantly, than when, catching his breath and leaving pick-work metonymic 'reality' behind, he enters the deep uncharted erotic swell" and "with a half-horrified, half-willing rush to destruction, he goes to meet the mermaid who waits in the refreshing depths to ply her 'knife and fork in chainsong at the spine.'"[91] The craft of *The Dolphin*, by contrast, is undermined by conscience: a problem that the poet himself notes early on. "I waste hours writing in and writing out a line," he notes in "Summer Between Terms 2," "as if listening to conscience were telling the truth."[92]

For whatever reasons, aesthetic or psychological or both, Lowell does not split off his muse from his new love. Perhaps to do so required more faith in the beauty and the strength of inner and outer worlds than he could muster this late in his life and writing. Instead, Lowell takes a different risk. He turns to another whose outrage shows that she is well outside his dreamy inwardness, namely his old "sparring partner" Lizzie. In her first substantial speech in *The Dolphin*, just after the sonnet "Double-Vision," she cuts through his mental fog with lines of caustic clarity. "What a record year, even for us—" she snorts. "That new creature, / when I hear her name, I have to laugh." To his self-pitying cry "Family, my family, why are we so far?" she offers a curt and practical response: "This was the price of your manic flight to London." This woman *knows* him, from his childhood traumas to his poetry. And in sonnet after sonnet she cuts through his "sidestepping and obliquities" with her "rapier voice."[93]

Although it is by far the most memorable, Lizzie's is not the only other voice in *The Dolphin*. Caroline, too, gets a say. But it is clear she will be of far less help to the poet in his hunger for contact. He needs a reappraisal, and she offers reassurance; her voice slides all too easily into his, picking up his phrases and lending him figures of speech.[94] For all that Lowell (and critics like Axelrod) credit the Dolphin Caroline as the inspiring other of this book, then, Lizzie plays a more important role. Leaving Lizzie for Caroline is an act of Winnicott's *destruction*: a refusal and negation that will, with any luck, show that Lizzie has in fact survived, thus reaffirming the existence of an otherwise shaky and tentative self and reopening the possibility of recognition. Her letters of response confirm his effect on a world outside him. They wake the poet and profoundly shape the sequence as a whole.

I have put off addressing what has seemed to many readers the most pressing question of *The Dolphin*: the moral propriety of Lowell's use of these letters and conversations and actual names. It clearly caused both women extraordinary pain, especially Hardwick. Twenty years later, however, what strikes me in Lowell's strategy is the way its moral flaws derive from an aesthetic capitulation. If Lowell names names, he does so in an effort to remain authentic, to do love and poetry right, this time, precisely by doing them wrong. At the same time, however, Lowell does not stick to a selfless "literal" transmission of their words or of the affair's chronology, but rather silently revises both for his own purposes.[95] Caught between two strategies, *The Dolphin* thus sacrifices the fictive power of poetry in favor of, if not a *spurious* authenticity, then an unprovable, unnecessary one. When he tells himself that "good writers write all possible wrong" without claiming that they *right* all wrong as well, Lowell undermines any lingering, Williams-like faith in "design" as a means to forgiveness. It falls to other, more artificed poets—notably the Merrill of *The Fire Screen*—to raise that flag once more.

In his pursuit of mutual recognition Lowell has broken open the monologic lyric to let the other speak. When the results prove neither ethically nor aesthetically secure, he has no escape route left to aesthetic forgiveness or the realm of the ideal. Compare *The Dolphin* to Hart Crane's "Voyages," another sequence that runs aground on the shoals of prosopopoeia. Lowell's sequence is a *relationship* poem: disturbing, psychologically acute, richly detailed, novelistic, unwilling to turn to art for solace. Crane's more traditional love poem makes that turn, leaves the other behind, admits it—and lands at last on the Imaged Word's "Belle Isle" of the "imaged Word." Evasive? No, and far more beautiful.

In the middle of the 1980s, just between *The Dolphin* and Bloom's epitaph for Eros, *New York Times* book critic Anatole Broyard mulled over the fate of modern love. "It was just a matter of time," he observed, "before we realized that love can't stand up to poetry. The tender passion has been losing ground for some time, its constitution undermined by more than a century of irony." As for the future? "Without some kind of formal dissembling," Broyard predicted, the truth of love will out: a matter of "tiresome incompatibilities and deadened perceptions," as Louise Bogan put it in a letter that he quotes approvingly.[96]

Lowell and Creeley aim to sweep away an over-masterful "formal dissembling." They trust that the drama of contact with the other and the pathos of process will revive perception in its place. But Lowell's late hope to write a poetry of "something imagined, not recalled" shows the persistence of poesis in his work.[97] It is no doubt significant that more recent poets of domestic love have stepped back from Creeley's love of the literal into a more discursive poetry of interpersonal analysis (C. K. Williams, Stephen Dunn, Mark Halliday, Albert Goldbarth) or have pushed Lowell's awareness of the familial structures underwriting our loves into a less ironic and more mythic mode (Sharon Olds, Louise Glück).

In the final chapter of this book I return to these questions of fiction and "formal dissembling," for in James Merrill I find a fine recuperation of both: a poetry where "speaking wrongly" is not prized, as though two wrongs (one ethical, the other literary) made a right. Merrill unsettles any naive ideal of "contact," and puts an explicitly fictive imagination once again to the uses of love. Before I reach Merrill, however, I want to treat a question I have raised at several points in this chapter and the previous one: the question of mutual recognition as it occurs between women, rather than between women and men. At the same time as Creeley and Lowell are breaking their staffs to make the poem answer to a woman's separate subjectivity, a feminist love poetry is evolving in which the questions of contact central to the poetry of "real crises in real homes" play out in a brighter key. Like Lizzie and Caroline in Lowell's sonnet "The Couple," the women who write and figure in these poems have "a certain intimacy"; their conversations often begin in, but go well beyond, the "simple plot" that Lowell has Caroline describe: "a story of a woman and a man / versifying her tragedy— / we were talking like sisters . . . you did not exist."[98] Must women go through the painful rhythm of destruction and separation that Lowell, Creeley, and Williams detail to write their own poems of mutual recognition? Stein's utopian erotic texts hinted the answer was no. But the poet who most thoughtfully addresses this question, and who does so in part through a self-conscious dialogue with earlier American writers, is Adrienne Rich: a poet of "the edge of contact," but also of "solitude / shared."

Five

Solitude Shared

> In the empty street, on the empty beach, in the desert,
> what in this world as it is can solitude mean?
>
> —ADRIENNE RICH, "YOM KIPPUR 1984"

In the middle of January 1892, Elizabeth Cady Stanton resigned her post as president of the American suffrage movement. Her last address took up the lesson of "self-dependence, self-protection, self-support" that women and men must equally learn, given the "birthright to self-sovereignty" that both sexes enjoy. Or is it endure? That birthright derives, according to Stanton, from an isolation no friend or lover can ease: "a solitude which each and every one of us has always carried with him, more inaccessible than the ice-cold mountains, more profound than the midnight sea; the solitude of self." Like Emerson before her, Stanton calls this inner solitude a "Protestant idea." Like Whitman, she finds that it underwrites "our republican idea" as well.[1]

In the preceding chapters I have tracked this "solitude of self" in American poets of love. In some poets it underwrites the soul's integrity, safeguarding it against the glamour of idolatry and the ecstasy of idealist fusion. In others it serves as a spur to connection, underwriting the idealistic "Americas of love" envisioned by Whitman, Rukeyser, and Ginsberg and the rather messier vision of love as an intersubjective *encounter* characteristic of, among others, Dickinson, Williams, Creeley, and Lowell.

As Lowell and Creeley put their poetics of contact to the test in the 1950s and 1960s, Adrienne Rich began her own career-long exploration of both the "myths of separation" and "the fact of separateness." She shares their suspicion of mastery. The "whole new poetry" she describes in "Transcendental Etude" has just as little to do "with eternity, / the striving for greatness, brilliance" as that of *Day by Day*. And like the poetry of *Pieces* and *A Day Book* it aspires to trace "the musing of a mind / one with her body . . . / . . . / with no mere will to mastery, / only care for the many lived, unending / forms in which she finds herself."[2] But Rich differs from her male contemporaries in two crucial ways. First, she rarely figures love as a sparring match or contest for supremacy, each self affronted by and craving recognition from an equally solitary other. She is thus able to abjure the "will to mastery" while maintaining a commitment to poetic strength and a shaping, analytic intelligence.[3] Second, while Creeley and Lowell find love an answer to the isolation of the American self, neither envisions that love as shaping a Whitmanian "aggregate," an America of love.[4] Rich has not only imagined such an America—she has been part of one: a feminist and lesbian-feminist community of which love is not a metaphorical model but a literal element.

Rich's vision of love as a state of "mutual recognition"—a phrase that occurs in her poem "Turnings," from *Time's Power*—sets her apart from the clenched early Creeley and the despairing late Lowell. It aligns her with the amatory ideals of women writers like Stanton, Margaret Fuller, and more recently Jessica Benjamin. Yet I would do Rich a deep disservice to read her only in this context—or, worse, to praise her as a redeeming corrective to her male precursors, a lesbian New Testament to their patriarchal Old Law. As she negotiates the claims of love, community, and the "solitude of self," Rich has drawn on the examples of both Dickinson *and* Whitman; and like Emerson before them both, she finds that love must be "a little of a citizen, before it is quite a cherub."[5] She is best read, that is to say, as a central recent voice in the broad, ongoing American debate over love's federal paradox of liberty and union, especially in her vision of love as a "solitude / shared."[6]

The Defeat of Isolation

In Rich's first collections, *A Change of World* (1951) and *The Diamond Cutters* (1953), the "solitude of self" looks mostly like a retreat from emotional turmoil. The speaker of "Storm Warnings," who can only "close the shutters" and "draw the curtains" against inclement emotional weather, may look like an isolated Emersonian "me," cut off from others, her own body, and the world—but Rich paints that situation as a fearful "mastery of elements," rather than an ontological condition. Aunt Jennifer is isolated by marriage, the traditional trope for an *escape* from solitude, whether through metaphysical fusion or through companionate love's ideal of "daily mutual devotedness."[7] The unnamed woman of "An Unsaid Word" restrains her urge to contact while "her man" is off in "that estranged intensity, / Where his mind forages alone": perhaps the flip-side of one of Creeley's early poems of withdrawal. This restraint may signal devotion, that "holding-back" demanded of women "to be with a man in the old way of marriage."[8] But we see only estrangement, cold comfort, a hard lesson in silence to be learned.

"Storm Warnings," "Aunt Jennifer's Tigers," and "An Unsaid Word" all foreshadow Rich's later interest in marriages "lonelier than solitude."[9] They are also all preoccupied with mastery, in ways that look both forward, to a feminist critique, and back to male literary models like Frost, Thoreau, Stevens, and Auden.[10] Consider her plea, in "Stepping Backward," to "let our blunders and our blind mischances / Argue a certain brusque abrupt compassion" as we "return to imperfection's school." Although she clearly senses that "our" solitude may resist being "mastered" because it springs from that very will to mastery, Rich won't name that will or solitude as distinctively masculine for almost twenty years.

In these early poems, as in the Auden they draw on, imperfection teaches awkward sociability. "When we come into each other's rooms / Once in a while, encumbered and self-conscious," the poet writes in "Stepping Backward," "We hover awkwardly about the threshold / And usually regret the visit later." Only "lovers— / And once in a while two with the grace of lovers" manage to "let each other freely come and go": a solution which suggests that part of the earlier awkwardness derived from having clutched too desperately at one another, refusing to let contact be partial or temporary.[11] The tighter we grasp, the more we lose our grip: thus Emerson found in "Experience," where "the evanescence and lubricity of all objects [including other people], which lets them slip through our fingers then when we clutch hardest," proved "the most unhandsome part of our condition."[12]

Emerson offers several answers to this unhandsome condition, one of which is implicit in his punning on clutching and *hand*someness. Perhaps if we were less "manipular" in our attempts to reach one another, his phrases suggest, we would be more "handsome"—which is to say attractive, drawing objects and persons to us without the need to clutch or hold them fast.[13] Rich, too, advises a turn away from excessive demand. Like the modernists described by Stephen Kern, she proposes a love that would "not only survive a failure to fuse but could thrive on it."[14] As admittedly "tragi-comic stumblers," partial in contact and knowledge, writes the poet, "perhaps we come to know each other."[15]

Our common awkwardness ought to allow some sympathetic connection. It would open a door into or out of these "rooms of selfhood," if we could only put it into words.[16] Yet in a rhetorical shift that illuminates much of her later work, the poet hedges even this small bet. "All we can confess of what we ," she writes,

"Has in it the defeat of isolation— / If not our own, then someone's, anyway."[17]
The syntax of "defeat of isolation" is, in the best New Critical senses of the
words, ambiguous and paradoxical. The effort to "defeat" isolation through
language thus inscribes its own failure, so that it defeats us (or that nervous
"someone") as much as we (or "someone") may ever win out over it.

What does this mean, and why should it be true? Is it simply that language
is too slippery, that it can always undo itself in double-meanings? So says
Emerson, in his essay "Nominalist and Realist." Deconstructive and post-
Freudian theories likewise insist that language can never do all we ask, born as
it is from absence, lack, and loss. Rich herself has written many poems that an-
nounce a metaphysical skepticism about contact or communication, in lan-
guage or in the flesh—or, at least, they seem to. In those "books we borrowed /
trying to read each other's minds," writing proves an unreliable medium.[18]
Face-to-face communication falters in her work throughout the 1960s, espe-
cially when the faces are those of husband and wife. "Two strangers, thrust for
life upon a rock / may have at last the perfect hour of talk / that language aches
for," the poet observes at the start of the decade. Yet the flood of solution that
language feels like, in such a "perfect hour," must inevitably withdraw. In its
wake? "Two minds, two messages."[19] The contact possible in words, like that
available to flesh, crumbles in "Pieces." "Plugged-in to her body," the poet re-
calls, "he came the whole way / but it makes no difference"; and being "in love
on words" can't keep the couple from "ending in silence / with its double-
meanings." The flat affect of Rich's unpunctuated monosyllables signals her
despair, moving forward, looking for some change: "If not this then what /
would fuse a connection."[20]

To read Rich in this unhappy light, however, slights the *second* meaning of
her early phrase about the "defeat of isolation": namely, that language does
bring contact, after all. The lines I have just quoted are skeptical. But in con-
text, their skepticism *explicitly* arises from the Cavellian insight that sweeping
and skeptical claims about the failure of language stem from a sense that love
and marriage and conversation can't supply the satisfactions of knowing and
being known which we must place upon them.[21] "A Marriage in the 'Sixties"
(1961) and "Pieces" (1969) record a time of tremendous upheaval in marriage,
after all: a time when "some mote of history" was liable to fly into one's eye, and
not just the history captured by pictures of Castro in the *Sunday Times.* In 1961,
as I noted in the last chapter, Creeley describes "our time" and "the new po-
etry" as one in which "the center of *self* (rather than 'we' or 'they')" has become
dominant. Not an exultant or imperial romantic self, but an abashed and pain-

fully self-conscious one, which takes its shape from the experience of "real cri-
ses in real homes."[22] Those "real crises" are an essential part of the "history"
that the couple of "A Marriage in the 'Sixties" must confront.

Like Creeley's *For Love*, Rich's *Snapshots of a Daughter-in-Law* is built
around poems of domestic crisis. Some insist on the practical difficulty of com-
munication, since when a social convention like marriage breaks down "it is
very hard to make one's self understood, most of all by another—sadly, truly,
etc."[23] Others show a woman claiming her self-sovereignty in traditionally
masculine terms of separateness. The book gives us, in effect, a daughter-in-
law's view of those painful but necessary moments when Creeley's early
"locked-in" male speaker is confronted by a newly resistant beloved, longing to
be released from his emotional armor. "Who will unhorse this rider?" Rich de-
mands in "The Knight," wondering, "Will they defeat him gently[?]" The an-
swer comes in "Ghost of a Chance," where the "old consolations" of privilege
and tradition retreat like a tide, giving the hapless man a "raw, agonizing" evo-
lutionary opportunity.[24] A man in such straits might well write poems in
which, as Creeley puts it, the "center of *self*" was dominant. The other he has
relied on to serve and protect him now merely watches, with a flash of galling
pity in her gaze.

In the poetry of divorce which I discussed earlier, the "unhorsing" of the
male subject was a necessary first step toward an authentic interpersonal love
and a corresponding poetry of intersubjective encounter. Defeated, the man
enjoys an end to isolation. Even the clash involved in his defeat serves this end,
since it allows the shock of intersubjective contact that the speakers of
Creeley's early and Lowell's late verse require. Rich's work from the same years
is more wary. With no particular need to be defeated, the "I" of *Snapshots of a
Daughter-in-Law* and *Necessities of Life* rarely finds that defeating male others
brings anything inspiring. The only poem where David Kalstone sees that
Rich "anticipates bringing together the energies of the solitary ego and the en-
ergies of dialogue, of a lovers' relationship" is the closing poem of *Necessities*,
"Face to Face." And despite the critic's confident claim that this poem "hopes
for the nourishment of a marriage through the charged revelation of the inner
life," the verse itself never speaks of its "Early American figure[s]" as husband
and wife, or even man and woman.[25] As for hope—the poem is decidedly am-
bivalent. Its first line, "Never to be lonely like that—," sounds wistful enough,
as though the speaker longed to "scan" a "didactic storm" in her own right, to
savor that "privacy" and then speak in "the old plain words." But if the privi-
lege of privacy depends on a "claim / to be Law and Prophets," on defensively
staking out "one's little all" against a "lunar hilarity," is it worth the cost? Rich

may long for the "starved, intense" meetings that love entails in Dickinson. But the "appetite" here is desperate, the figures parched and burnt, and the speaker unsure whether our secrets are "God-given" after all. For all that Rich invokes Dickinson in her last line, "a loaded gun," the scene takes none of Dickinson's *pleasure* in meeting and eating and ownership. These figures have "dry lips," and there's no "Berry of Domingo" in sight.[26]

The closest Rich comes to a poem where the unhorsing of a man permits a sudden instance of relationship comes at the lovely end of "A Marriage in the 'Sixties." Its final lines are a soothing address in which the "real crises" that history entails are transformed into a new "shared form of life," through imagery that incorporates the couple's separateness:

> Dear fellow-particle, electric dust
> I'm blown with—ancestor
> to what euphoric cluster—
> see how particularity dissolves
> in all that hints of chaos. Let one finger
> hover toward you from There
> and see this furious grain
> suspend its dance to hang
> beside you like your twin.[27]

For a poem which finds that the "perfect hour of talk / that language aches for" still leaves lovers with "two minds, two messages," this is a remarkably sanguine close. But what defeat of isolation has been found? There are, I think, two: and the poem neatly elides the difference. The first dissolves particularity in "hints of chaos." It looks forward to "The Wave," written twelve years later, where the poet would embrace "turbulence" in order to say "we."[28] But in the last four lines of "A Marriage," Rich's rhythm shifts into a tender, unthreatening, hardly turbulent trimeter. She shows us, not hints of chaos, but an image of the wife hanging beside her husband, "like your twin" but clearly separate. The marriage imagined here is not a "euphoric cluster," but a delicate system of orbits. "*Let* one finger / hover toward you" from "There" without ever quite touching, this wife asks her husband, and "*see* this furious grain / suspend its dance." These gracious verbal gestures suggest that, confronted by a "dance" away from him, he would be more likely to look askance. Or, perhaps, to demand a more chaotic contact than she wants or can afford.

From the 1950s to the early 1970s, then, Rich explores the "defeat of isolation" which inhabits the contact and confession we clutch at precisely in order to defeat isolation—at least, that is, when the relationships described are between women and men. The best relationship that can be hoped for, these poems suggest, is the tension and distance of two "twin" particles in a common cluster. This isn't an altogether undesirable relation. It preserves the female self against her acculturated "instinct" that "the ego must dwindle in relationships."[29] But it means that any erotic or communal "dissolution of particularity" remains out of reach as well ("A Marriage in the 'Sixties").

Beginning in the early 1960s, however, the poet began to envision relationships in which these limits would disappear. A New World of contact, communication, and communion would be possible: one where the question "if not this then what / would fuse a connection" would not be simply glum and rhetorical. "We're fighting for a slash of recognition / a piercing to the pierced heart," Rich writes in "Leaflets" (1968). The example she gives of this battle seems, now, a little flat, drawn though it is from Simone Weil: *"Tell me what you are going through."* But this very flatness grows out of the poet's desire to be *practical*, to treat the problem of contact as a simple interhuman difficulty, not a case of "Solitude of Self."[30] By the poem's close, the language is grimly, grandly confident. "I am thinking how we can use what we have," the poet explains, "to invent what we need."[31]

Unlike her earlier poems of "the defeat of isolation," Rich's poems of love in the later 1960s imagine an "America of love" quite comparable to Whitman's. This prophet of democracy as an "adhesiveness or love, that fuses, ties and aggregates, making the races comrades, and fraternizing all" is equally a model for her faith that language *works*, even in poems, and that community may be realized through it. And yet, the most important poems that Rich writes in the 1970s often *challenge* Whitman, too—or at least his *echt* American faith that "sooner or later we come down to one single, solitary soul."[32] As early as 1962, the year after "A Marriage in the 'Sixties," Rich imagined a bond between women that would undo this ineluctable solitude. In "To Judith, Taking Leave" the speaker patches a "pale brown envelope / still showing under ink scratches / the letterhead of MIND." Making the inevitable pun, Rich announces that this epistolary and linguistic connection involves more than simply "literacy— / the right to read MIND—." It means a reading of minds, a communion of selves, the settling of a "little spur or *head*land" (my emphasis) that two will share, despite being "shared out in pieces" by their obligations to others. As Rich turns from the hope that heterosexual sex might "fuse a connection" to the dream of a shared "view" between women she grows unabashedly visionary. Once the salt, estranging flood of patriarchy begins to recede, the poem promises, these women can join without the struggle or disappointment of two separate souls hammering at contact. These women already share a common knowledge, a single covenant. They "can meet," Rich writes, "as two eyes in one brow, / receiving at one moment / the rainbow of the world."[33]

The Myths of Separation; or, The Fact of Being Separate

At the start of this chapter I quoted Stanton on the solitude of self, that "inner being" which is more hidden than the "hidden chamber of Eleusinian mystery, for to it only omniscience is permitted to enter."[34] I did so in part to stress that we cannot call this vision of selfhood "masculine" without being either patronizing or ignorant of history. (Recall Mary Moody Emerson, Margaret Fuller, and of course the sublime Dickinson.)

That said, however, there *is* a curious contrast between the opening and closing images of solitude in Stanton's address—a contrast that answers to Rich's work through the 1970s. The "immeasurable solitude" of a woman's life, writes Stanton near the close, is left untouched by "Man's love and sympathy." Given that solitude "which each and every one of us has always carried with him," who would "dare take on himself the rights, the duties, the responsibilities of another human soul"? The male pronouns are no doubt meant to be neutral. But at the start of the address a different analogy slips in, rich with hopeful complications. "In discussing the rights of woman," Stanton writes, "we are to consider, first, what belongs to her as an individual, in a world of her own, the arbiter of her own destiny, an imaginary Robinson Crusoe, with her woman Friday, on a solitary island."[35] As in the poem "To Judith," something other than "omniscience" enters that "hidden chamber of Eleusinian mystery." When the pronouns are all feminine, footprints turn up on the self's long shore.

This discovery of another, or at least another woman, slipping through the boundaries of self links Stanton with a broad range of more recent feminist thought. The divisions of self and other, subject and object, on which the logic of loneliness depends, seem to these writers masculine at heart.[36] As legal scholar Robin West explains, "the cluster of claims that jointly constitute the 'separation thesis'—the claim that human beings are, definitionally, distinct from one another, the claim that the referent of 'I' is singular and unambiguous, the claim that the word 'individual' has an uncontested biological meaning . . . the claim that we are individuals 'first,' and the claim that what separates us is epistemologically and morally prior to what connects us" are all "patently untrue of women." The reasons are, first and foremost, biological:

Women are not essentially, necessarily, inevitably, invariably, always, and forever separate from other human beings: women, distinctively, are quite clearly "connected" to another human life when pregnant. In fact, women are in some sense "connected" to life and to other human beings during at least four recurrent and critical material experiences: the experience of pregnancy itself; the invasive and "connecting" experience of heterosexual penetration, which may lead to pregnancy; the monthly experience of menstruation, which represents the potential for pregnancy; and the post-pregnancy experience of breast-feeding. Indeed, perhaps the central insight of feminist theory over the last decade has been that women are "essentially connected," not "essentially separate."[37]

The hunger for union that we see in the "surrounded, detached" self of Whitman, the authentic sadness of Stevens, the pitched drama of contact we saw in *Paterson 2* and *For Love* and *The Dolphin*: all start from some version of the "separation thesis." The "woman Friday" on the shores of the self, or the reading of "MIND" in "To Judith," signal less fraught, more easily intimate relations. They don't rely on language to cross the "sheer distances of soul" that separate women. Rather, they call on a shared gender, an implied intimate commonality of experience, despite the "memories / so different and so draining" that distinguish them.[38] As West puts it in her response to the communitarian theorist Roberto Unger:

> women do not struggle toward connection with others, against what turn out to be insurmountable obstacles. Intimacy is not something which women fight to be capable of. We just do it. It is ridiculously easy. . . . The intimacy women value is a sharing of intersubjective territory that preexists the effort made to identify it. The connection that I suspect men strive for does not preexist the effort, and it is not a sharing of space; at best it is an adjacency.[39]

That is the adjacency, one might say, of the couples in "Stepping Backward" and "A Marriage in the 'Sixties," of the frontier couple always about to meet in "Face to Face," or of Thoreau edging so far away from his visitors that he finds it best to meet them outdoors.

If Rich begins as a late-modernist poet of limits and separateness, by the 1970s she is an urgent, unabashedly sentimental prophet of women's essential connection. "Women's gift for relationship is fundamental," the poet asserts in 1974. Although "becoming a man means leaving / someone, or something," for women "there isn't that radical split between self and others, because what was in us comes out of us and we still love it and care for it and we still relate to it. It's still part of us in some way."[40] That this love and care and relation might not be every woman's story—that Rich assumes a radical *sameness* to women's experience—will come to trouble the poet somewhat later. At first, though, the distinction is uncomplicated and inspiring, not least when it lets her draw a clear line between the sexes, as she does in poems such as "The Ninth Symphony of Beethoven Understood at Last as a Sexual Message," and, more subtly, the "Phantasia for Elvira Shatayev." Even Whitman comes in for implicit criticism. He is one more "phantom of the man-who-would-understand, / the lost brother, the twin," one of the "they" who thinks a spider works "patiently."[41] The "gossamer thread" of a line of poetry, the "filament, filament, filament," spun "out of itself" by the "surrounded, detached" soul as it goes "seeking the spheres to connect them": these are too fine, to fragile to make up "the fibers of actual life," the "weaving, ragged because incomplete" of women's community.[42] Women won't just close up the gap male poets struggle to bridge. They will do so as midwives, "help[ing] the earth deliver."[43]

Vision and exasperation make a potent mix. Yet the Hebraic power of this verse, its devotion to "strictness of conscience" rather than the Hellenic "spontaneity of consciousness," in Matthew Arnold's distinction, corresponds to its central weakness. To quote Arnold, it "seizes upon certain plain, capital intimations of the universal order, and rivets itself . . . with unequalled grandeur of earnestness and intensity on the study and observance of them," without devoting itself in equal terms to complication and lively variousness.[44] This exclusion is perhaps deliberate. As Altieri remarks, "the juxtapositional, notational style" that Rich used in the 1960s to capture "the flow of consciousness" proved incapable of producing "the counterpressure by which one establishes individual identity."[45] Nevertheless, "plain, capital intimations" tend to the over-general. It's hard to keep one set of intimations from looking like those they replace. "Inverting rather than transforming patriarchal hierarchies," writes Betsy Erkkila, Rich offers a schema in which "female is substituted for male, body for head, as the superior and transforming terms, and men—and presumably women who do not bear children—are demonized and outcast as 'Other' in the new matriarchal order."[46] There is no place in Rich's poetry of essential connection for the maternal alienation of Kristeva's "Stabat Mater," with its musings on "the abyss between the mother and the child . . . the abyss between what was mine and is henceforth but irreparably alien," or for the helpless watching of Louise Glück's "Child Crying Out": "You were born, you were far away."[47] There is, at that, no room for the dream of separate, sovereign selfhood that Rich herself explored in poems like "Face to Face." The poet

turns back to and admonishes her earlier work. "I am an American woman,
Rich writes in "From an Old House in America," and this means that while sh
may be cut off from other women, she dare not choose "Isolation, the dream / o
the frontier woman."[48] "We come into the world alone," Stanton writes in he
address, "unlike all who have gone before us, we leave it alone, under circum
stances peculiar to ourselves."[49] Rich, by contrast, finds that we come into th
world out of a mother's body, that the status of "an American woman" make
all who share that name in some sense "like all who have gone before," and tha
however peculiar the circumstances of another woman's death, it may b
claimed as her own.

Following the lead of the poet herself, recent criticism has taken issue wit
this assimilating, incorporating gesture.[50] In it, writes Erkkila, the difference
between women are elided, subsumed "into a single white female-centered nar
rative of return to the mother and female unity."[51] Of course, since Rich's visio
of women's community was *not*, at the root, theoretical, it was always liable t
practical challenge and change. "To believe that it was right to identify with al
women, to wish deeply and sincerely to do so, was not enough," Rich learnec
"I still hear the voice of a Black feminist saying with passionate factuality: *Bu
you don't know us!*"[52] The "woman Friday" that Stanton mentions cannot b
treated as merely a part of the white and privileged female Crusoe-self. Rathe
she is a woman with her own self-sovereignty. In the same way, the woma
with whom the poet longed to experience love "as identification, as tendernes:
as sympathetic memory and vision," a "sensing our way into another's skin,
may always object, step back, reassert her separate history and vision.[53] As
beloved will chide her chronicler in "Sleepwalking Next to Death": *"It's a
about you None of this / tells my story."*[54] To claim union and identification i
not necessarily to achieve it. Even love as "sympathetic memory and vision," i
turns out, can reenact the old "defeat of isolation."

Rereading *The Dream of a Common Language* as the century ends, it is clea
that the "fact of being separate" survives the poet's unsaying of male "myths o
separateness."[55] There are moments, the poet writes, when we feel "as if / ou
true home were the undimensional / solitudes, the rift / in the Great Nebula.
This poem, "Transcendental Etude," presents that sense as temporary or tran
sitional. But it recurs, despite every effort to "close the gap / / in the Grea
Nebula, / to help the earth deliver."[56] Stanton speaks of a solitude of self "mor
inaccessible than the ice-cold mountains, more profound than the midnigh
sea."[57] Ice and oceanic or cosmic distances keep coming between women in *Th
Dream of a Common Language*, too, even as they work to defeat their isolatior

"Each / / speaker of the so-called common language feels / the ice-floe split, the drift apart," Rich writes in "Cartographies of Silence," "as if powerless, as if up against / a force of nature."[58] For all that Rich's "as if" insists that history, not nature, is responsible here—that the "lie" with which this conversation begins, and not a flaw in "these words, these whispers" of language itself, is to blame—this attribution of responsibility doesn't make connection any easier. History can divide women from one another *almost* as effectively as epistemology stood between the me and the not-me for Emerson. Even between "two lovers of one gender, / . . . two women of one generation," that rift refuses to heal.[59]

The heart of *The Dream of a Common Language* are the "Twenty-One Love Poems." These have been offered as a radically new vision of love, one that critiques "the notion of lover as subject, beloved as object, and merger as unattainable ideal."[60] Yet if Rich rejects the tradition where a male poet "idealizes the object of desire and sublimates the 'drive to connect,'" leaving the poet and his poem (I use the pronoun advisedly) the true and final couple—if her sequence stands as a reproach to Berryman's *Sonnets*, say, or to the Tristan and Isolde myth of lovers whose *"partings"* are *"dictated by their passion itself"*—she does not thereby escape the painful disappointments that the Petrarchan tradition turns back into art.[61] Wrestling tradition, as we have seen, Creeley and Lowell struggle to break out of isolation. Rich searches for a place *within* relation for her lasting solitude of self.

Given the way "a drift, an iciness, a splitting" intervenes between women throughout this collection, even as they try to claim essential separateness, the "we" with which the sequence begins is notable, fragile, and brave. "We *need* to grasp our lives inseparable / from those rancid dreams" of pornography and "science-fiction vampires," the poet insists. Their life together is also "inseparable" from the flecks of beauty around them, from a begonia on a windowsill to girls on a playground, glimpsed in motion. Wanting "to live like trees, / sycamores blazing through the sulfuric air, / . . . / our animal passion rooted in the city," these selves are at once arboreal, animal, and human.[62] They are not sparks of the divine whose first allegiance is to "the immeasurable and the eternal" where "each soul lives alone forever."[63]

If the first poem in the sequence speaks entirely in the first-person plural, the force of its early imperatives suggests that there are differences in this "we" right from the start. By the next poem they are separate. "I wake up in your bed. I know I have been dreaming. / Much earlier, the alarm broke us from each other, / You've been at your desk for hours." Is it from the longing for an "animal passion rooted in the city" that the poet wakes? From the dream of a "we"?

I know what I dreamed:
our friend the poet comes into my room
where I've been writing for days,
drafts, carbons, poems are scattered everywhere,
and I want to show her one poem
which is the poem of my life. But I hesitate,
and wake. You've kissed my hair
to wake me. *I dreamed you were a poem,*
I say, *a poem I wanted to show someone.*[64]

The friend's arrival recalls the awkward visits in "Stepping Backward," or the waking up "in rooms of selfhood" in "Ideal Landscape."[65] Here entry and encounter seem easily accomplished—without regret, without anxiety—even into the solitude of a writer's imagination. But why the hesitancy, and the subsequent denial that "the desire to show you to everyone I love" ever faltered? Admittedly there are social, patriarchal restraints at work in the poet's oneiric self-restraint: the risk of their unsponsored, culturally unimagined lesbian relationship. But read against the worries of a later poem in the sequence we can see another reason. "What kind of beast would turn its life into words?" the poet will demand. "When away from you I try to create you in words, / am I simply using you, like a river or a war?" To turn the beloved into a poem, even in a dream, even into the poem of one's own life, does a certain violence to her sovereignty of self. The celebratory address to "you" in poem 3 seems a deliberate response to this threat of imaginative imperialism. But its brave claims about the beloved's "everlasting" eyes come perilously close to the tradition of lovers at war with mutability that Rich wants to reject.[66]

From her earliest poems, as we have seen, Rich is concerned with boundaries and limitation. The vision of women's essential connection is so enlivening to her work in the 1970s because it lets her establish one clear border—that between women and men—even as it frees her from the need to accept a "masculine" separateness of self. As the need to wrestle lovers' separation returns from the repressed in the "Twenty-One Love Poems," it first pushes the poet to a utopian political response. In poem 6 her lover's hands, "precisely equal to [her] own— / only the thumb is larger, longer," are given license to work, create, and celebrate. In each case a border is crossed: the child is turned in the birth canal, a ship threads through icebergs, the shards of a cup are pieced together, women stride to a den or a cave, presumably to enter. None of these crossings, however, is a *violation* of boundaries. Unlike the crashings of a boat driven directly into the waves by its male pilot, in poem 14, they would not make the women involved vomit. Even the "unavoidable" violence of this apocalypse will be, the poet promises, respectful of "limits": a sign of its utopianism, and a hint that these lines are pushing some other insight away—but what?[67]

The first third of the "Twenty-One Love Poems" introduces us to the lovers, and introduces some of the outside forces that threaten their union. The central seven poems repeatedly reject literary models for the relationship, and it starts to show intrinsic flaws. By poems 9 and 10 the beloved's silence invites just the sort of imaginative projection that the poet wants so desperately to avoid. In poem 10 Rich borrows an image of marital coldness and stellar separation from her earlier poem "Novella": "separate as minds / the stars too come alight." Here "planetary nights are growing cold" for two women who are "on the same journey," or who once wanted to be.[68] The dream of travel in a feminized sacral landscape of poem 11 and the sleepy near-address of poem 12 seem offered up to counteract such chilly distances. "A touch is enough to let us know / we're not alone in the universe, even in sleep," the speaker reassures herself. But when the poet hears the other's words "as if my own voice had spoken," it suggests not essential connection but a loss of contact. The poem ends in an attempt to see the two as at once separate and one—"we were two lovers of one gender, / we were two women of one generation"—but the past tense of that verb signals that such union is already in the past. Their different voices, bodies, and pasts set them apart, and the insistent physicality of "(The Floating Poem)" serves as an inadequate gesture of renewal.[69]

The last third of the "Twenty-One Love Poems" recount the dissolution of the relationship, albeit in a circumspect, reluctant fashion. "No one's fated or doomed to love anyone," Rich writes in poem 17, although the issue at hand would seem to be, instead, whether anyone is fated to *stop* loving, or any relationship doomed to fail. The poet points to forces ranged "within us and against us" that might account for their "failure"; but the fault seems to lie less with "us" in general than with the beloved in particular, whose silences have repeatedly drawn the poet into problematic attributions and imaginative projections.[70] By the end of the poem Rich defines herself against her beloved, or at least against how she responds to their failure as a couple. "*The more I live the more I think / two people together is a miracle*," the beloved says in poem 18. "Now you're in fugue across what some I'm sure / Victorian poet called the *salt estranging sea*," the poet notes in answer. "Those are the words that come to mind."[71] The words "in fugue" put a brave face on things, as though the lover's flight (Latin, *fugere*) were merely a contrapuntal strain, a second voice added to the poet's own. But the beloved's claim that *"two people together is a miracle,"* requiring divine intervention to succeed, means she thinks that Arnold was right: "A God, a God their severance ruled!" To believe this is to long for a love without struggle, to dodge what Cavell calls "the practical difficulty . . . of coming to know another person."[72] It means a retreat from the ethical problem of acknowledgment into a world where ethics are secondary, a world of miracles. Rich prefers Stein to Arnold as a model, at least implicitly: not the mournful, skeptical poet but the gay lecturer who hymned the British "daily island life" as a source of literature. She proves willing to accept the threat of coldness as she pulls away:

> Am I speaking coldly when I tell you in a dream
> or in this poem, *There are no miracles?*
> (I told you from the first I wanted daily life,
> this island of Manhattan was island enough for me.)
> If I could let you know—
> two women together is a work
> nothing in civilization has made simple,
> two people together is a work
> heroic in its ordinariness.

In the place of miracle, she offers choice, responsibility, work: the work of women loving against the love stories "civilization" offers. And, in a universalism remarkable for this point in Rich's career, the work of any "two people together." Not pathos or passion but ethos is the proper ground for love.[73]

The "Twenty-One Love Poems" sequence begins with a brave and fragile "we," shifts into the musings of an "I" as she addresses a "you," only to discover that this "I" "was talking to [her] own soul," perhaps all along (poem 20). The final poem contains no pronoun but the poet's "I"; and if Helena Michie goes too far in saying that its "privatized vision of self and womanhood conflicts brutally with the opening . . . which emphasizes the ugly necessity of connection with the world," it is clear that the "inseparable" selfhood Rich proclaimed in the first poem has been left behind, however temporarily.[74] Rich does not invoke a transcendent other who will take the beloved's place. She is not a poet-lover like the Crane of "Voyages"—one who turns to the "imaged Word" as the one beloved whose "unbetrayable reply / whose accent no farewell can know." But she also refuses to represent herself as the chastened, conscience-stricken singer of a sequence like Loy's *Songs to Joannes* or Lowell's *The Dolphin,* her eyes fixed on what her hands have done. She is not far, in fact, from the traditions of the Renaissance sonnet sequence, where an idolatrous lover must turn, in the end, to God for satisfaction. But in a deeply traditional American gesture, grounded in the tradition of Stanton, Fuller, and Emerson, Rich must return to her own "Solitude of Self."

"To be fit for relations in time," Margaret Fuller proclaimed, "souls, whether of man or woman, must be able to do without them in spirit."[75] In the "Twenty-One Love Poems" Rich moves from her early "we" into the chill of "speaking coldly" to her beloved and herself. Such coldness might well seem a threat, not only to the relationship (already near its end) but to the vision of connection where she began. "Women's separation from the other . . . and the tension between that separation and our fundamental state of connection," West explains, "is felt most acutely when a woman must make choices, and when she must speak the truth."[76] By the end of the "Twenty-One Love Poems," Rich takes up this burden of separation. She finds that she can read it as the dawn of a new integrity of self—and of a new, imperfect union. The warm reciprocity of "(The Floating Poem)" and the "whole new poetry" promised by "Transcendental Etude" must be built on a "stone foundation": that of "the mind / casting back to where her solitude / shared, could be chosen without loneliness."[77] Only this choice allows her "to stake out / the circle, the heavy shadows, the great light." Only such a choice allows her "to draw this circle," alive with what Emerson described, in the essay "Circles," as an "insatiable desire" for a new birth into the "flames and generosities of the heart."[78]

In the course of *The Dream of a Common Language*, then, Rich learns to see solitude as a transitory stage on the way to women's community and the "whole new poetry beginning here."[79] Women's "essential connection" gives a theoretical foundation for her lesbian-feminist America of love: one that would not begin with the "separation thesis" that even Whitman asserted, and one that would not find itself inevitably "lost" in more or less democratic, more or less masculine individualism. The community of women that feminism forged in the sixties and seventies gave Rich a model for this utopian *civitas* in which she was embraced and read in a way that Whitman could only dream of. As several women critics have testified, *The Dream of a Common Language* did indeed "arouse and set flowing . . . [in] women's hearts, young and old, endless streams of living, pulsating love and friendship," provoking a "new interchange of adhesiveness, so fitly emblematic of America."[80] Yet connection is always threatened in this book, and not just by patriarchal forces that would split daughters from mothers and women from one another.[81] In the "Twenty-One Love Poems" the poet's own vision of love as "a work / heroic in its ordinariness" divides her from her despairing beloved. It throws her back to an inner landscape of stony solitude from which, she finds, any new love or community must spring.

In her poems since *The Dream of a Common Language*, Rich has moved away from the ideal of essential connection. She does not reject it—but she finds that sustained and successful identification with a figure of "the Mother" gives her what Jessica Benjamin calls a "flexible ego": one "which neither fears its desire [for union] nor is inebriated by the ideal [of it], but which finds that "the experience of union is simply an excursion" into a landscape that does not segregate "regressive maternal warmth and the icy paternal outside."[82] This flexibility of ego has allowed the poet increasingly to incorporate the fact of differences between women into her work, particularly those differences of race and class which Stanton's image of the "woman Friday" glossed over. The insistence of these "others" on their own integrity, meanwhile, has forced her to rethink her sense of her own separateness. Although she takes her cues elsewhere, from Whitman and Rukeyser and Lorde, Rich has implicitly taken up the Emersonian challenge to "substantiate [her] romance" through a hefty dose of "the municipal virtues of justice . . . fidelity, and pity."[83] In the last part of this chapter I look at the development of, the tensions in, and the aesthetic issues raised by Rich's recent poems of a love that lives not in hope but in history: her verses of love and solitude in a "substantiated" romance.

Mutual Recognition

In framing this chapter with appeals to Stanton's address "The Solitude of Self," I take my lead from Rich herself, who quotes from the address and from other texts by Stanton in "Culture and Anarchy," one of the key poems in *A Wild Patience Has Taken Me This Far*, the collection that followed *The Dream of a Common Language*. The volume as a whole can be read as a poetic coming to grips with a "sense of limitation, difference, and the *otherness* of other women," especially, but not only, women of color.[84] This new sense of limitation shapes "The Spirit of Place," where Rich steps back from her quest to recover and identify with Dickinson. *"All we are strangers—dear—"* she quotes the older poet.[85] And we see it in "Turning the Wheel," where the poet refuses her impulse to travel to the Grand Canyon, a figure for woman as archetype, in the names of particularity and contact, however strained or partial that contact may be.[86]

Erkkila stresses difference as a problem for Rich: a failure of the earlier dream of commonality. As I have argued, however, by the end of the "Twenty-One Love Poems" it was clear to Rich that a just and lasting love would have to incorporate not only union but separateness. Indeed, her ideal of an ethical selfhood requires such incorporation. Such a self is affiliated with others—you come into human life through culture, and do not live alone with the Alone—but it is also profoundly distinct from them, since we aren't all bits of a unifying, extratemporal One. What Rich needs is a *model* for this ethical self as it engages in a love relationship where solitude and sharing coexist. In *The Dream of a Common Language* she used the image of identification with a mother, or with other women who are, in one way or another, maternal. In "Culture and Anarchy" her resources are the "culture" of nineteenth-century white women and the "Anarchy of August" in which the poet and her lover read nineteenth-century texts, write their own works, and read each other's rough drafts—not in an effort to achieve perfect unconditioned union, as in the earlier poem "To Judith," but rather in search of a new perspective that only the other's difference can provide.

The nineteenth-century texts that Rich quotes in "Culture and Anarchy" are not concerned with love—at least, that is, if love means dreams of union. They revolve around *work*, whether on behalf of abolition and suffrage or in domestic creative efforts. We have the Brontë sisters, for example, who *"walked up and down / with their arms around each other / and planned their novels,"* thus anticipating the political, domestic, and creative life shared by Rich and her lover. Indeed, the lives of the two sets of women begin to answer one another, as though the loneliness of the precursors could be answered by the collaborative efforts and affection of their descendants. The poet who suffered from an "all-alone feeling" in the "Twenty-One Love Poems" is here rescued from it by the "torrent" of words she reads from Susan B. Anthony, and by the "torrent" of the "you" typing upstairs. Anthony, too, seems relieved—or, at least, she would be, by the knowledge that these women, her descendants, would not also suffer from *"short and ill-environed lives."*[87]

In its quotations from nineteenth-century white women, and its images of the twentieth-century women reading them, "Culture and Anarchy" models what Margaret Fuller called "marriage as intellectual companionship," that union in which "two minds are wed by the only contract that can permanently avail, of a common faith, and a common purpose."[88] Although the separation between Rich and her beloved is constant—they are in the same house, but never actually seen together in the course of the poem—it is never a source of anxiety. Their "contract" of common purpose underwrites a lasting "contact" as well. In effect Rich has given a more passionate picture of Emerson's "real marriage," that love which will "exchange the passion which once could not lose sight of its object, for a cheerful, disengaged furtherance, whether present or absent, of each other's designs."[89] The lovers of this poem may be self-sovereign. But their union in *"aim and sympathy"* counteracts any anxiety over their consequent separateness. Borrowing language from Stanton and from her own earlier work, Rich finds that her "dream of a common language" and her "solitude of self" are complementary, not contradictory, like the threads of crimson in the green chard leaves gathered by her lover. She proposes this ideal union, not as a matter of miracles or of postrevolutionary communion, but as one more version of an old necessity. Like Stanton and Anthony, whatever their differences, this couple *"should be together."* A moral imperative frames this amatory ideal, whatever its bestowals of sensual appreciation on the colors of a beet root or another's body.

The poems of love Rich wrote in the 1980s share this moral frame for sexuality. Poems of love in the face of trial, they do not ask for happiness. "Happiness comes and goes as it comes and goes / the safe-house is temporary the garden / lies open to vandals," Rich declares.[90] The sensual pleasures of cattails and sunflowers, and the pleasures of mental contact with a lover, are good in and of themselves. But "more will be asked of us   we will ask more." As for sex—well, it does not figure the end of particularity in a "euphoric cluster" or something that "hints of chaos" ("A Marriage in the 'Sixties"). It means unison, not union, "your fingers / exact   my tongue exact at the same moment / stopping to laugh at a joke." It answers political coldness and disunion, that is to say, with an image of motile mutuality, the shared solitude of a couple "hot with joy."[91]

Lesbian sexuality, and lesbian love more generally, offers Rich a useful image for what Cavell calls "acknowledgment": a relationship with the other in which separation is accepted, the temptations of a relation closer than caring and beyond the realm of human responsibilities is set aside, and the possibility of an existence shared with others thereby opened.[92] When she takes up the question of solitude in *Your Native Land, Your Life*, especially in the poem "Yom Kippur 1984," she does so with this vision of acknowledgment in mind. Our existential "solitude of self" is thus less her concern than the practical, bodily solitude we choose to get work done, to write poems, to muse and meditate: a solitude far riskier for some than it is for others. As the poem alludes to male precursors—Whitman, Wordsworth, Jeffers—Rich opens a dialogue with them. How can I envision a Whitmanian America of love, she asks, while bearing witness to my own America, the one where "the Jew on the icy, rutted road on Christmas Eve prays for another Jew" and "the woman in the ungainly twisting shadows of the street" prays *"Make those be a woman's footsteps*; as if she could believe in a woman's god."[93] How can I, forced to fear, sing of "the bliss of solitude"? And yet, as the poet reflects in "On the Genesis of 'Yom Kippur 1984,'" "if you reject Jeffers's solitude, if you reject that sort of lofty attitude that says I'm going to keep all of humankind at arm's length except my few chosen ones and I'm going to build myself a tower and dwell in it . . . how still do you get the solitude you need for your life and work?" There are times, the poet confesses, when "I crave separateness." But this craving is part of, not a contrast to, her underlying dream of a love put into action, so that the "world as it is" will become "that world as it may be, newborn and haunted," where lesbian and other loves will be secure. To draw *that* solitude over herself is hardly, as "my worst friends / and my best enemies" call it, one of the poet's "mistakes in love."[94]

Rich's poems of love as acknowledgment thus enact, or at least describe, a state where union and distinction overlap. To quote Benjamin, this "I" and her exemplary lovers exchange the "impossible absolutes of 'oneness' and perfection" for a taste for that "degree of imperfection" which "'ratifies' the existence of the world."[95] Such love is hardly a new goal for Rich. In "Stepping Backward," where this chapter began, we heard a plea for lovers to give up "wandering after Plato's ghost, / Seeking the garden where all fruit is flawless" and to learn instead "That imperfection has a certain tang."[96] A similar effort to embrace love's imperfection marks "A Marriage in the 'Sixties" and even, albeit unsuccessfully, the "Twenty-One Love Poems." By the 1980s, though, Rich could present this embrace without high drama, dry wit, or low spirits. In "Sleepwalking   Next to Death," for example, she runs through a brief description of the "daily own" of love—"I am stupid with you and practical with you / I remind you to take a poultice   forget a quarrel," and so on—only to find that the other looks over her shoulder and "calmly" observes that *"It's all about you   None of this / tells my story."* This objection is a distant echo of the "voice of a Black feminist saying with passionate factuality: *But you don't know us!*" that Rich records in the introduction to *Blood, Bread, and Poetry.* Unlike corresponding moments of interruption or prosopopoeia in *The Dolphin* or in *Paterson 2,* however, this causes no great shift in diction, imagery, or direction in the rest of the poem. It's a grace note, no more.

As I argued in the last chapter, male poets like Creeley and Lowell also idealize a companionate model of love. All three poets partake of a general period emphasis on love as an intersubjective relation, rather than an enthusiasm or exaltation of the lover's soul. But if Creeley, like Rich, may announce the *attainment* of this goal, he does not exploit its political, practical resonance. Rich now does both. Her two most recent collections, *An Atlas of the Difficult World* and *Dark Fields of the Republic*, have a Whitmanian vista. They give us models of what love would look like "in action," as it attends to both sensual and social detail. In "Edgelit," for example, the last poem of *Dark Fields*, love is the faculty that holds the "I" back from her desire for six women, each quite attractive, each ethically flawed. (In a deft, delicious gesture, Rich makes them *more* attractive for their flaws. She leaves you wanting them, too.) Because it looks back to so many themes of this book, however, I want to close with a look at the final poem of *Time's Power*, "Turnings": a poem that insists on the foundations in justice of both interpersonal and international relations.

> A public meeting.   I glance at a woman's face:
> strong lines and soft, listening, a little on guard:
> we have come separately, are sitting apart,
> know each other in the room, have slept twelve years
> in the same bed, attend now to the speaker.
> Her subject is occupation, a promised land,
> displacement, deracination, two peoples called Semites,
> humiliation, force, women trying to speak with women,
> the subject is how to break a mold of discourse,
> how little by little minds change
> but that they do change.[97]

Not in bed, but at a public meeting, is love's true character revealed—or, to be more accurate to the scope of Rich's claim, the public realm is a metonymic figure for what these lovers have "depended upon" even in bed. The "woman's face" is "a little on guard," her borders of selfhood staked out and patrolled. Indeed, the lovers have "come separately, are sitting apart." But that signals no break between them. Just as two lovers of one gender and one generation could find themselves divided by silence and historical contingency, so now "two peoples called Semites," Israeli and Palestinian women, share genders, names, even the facts of suffering in their twice-promised land, yet still remain distinct.

"Turnings" does not hope for these peoples or the lovers who watch them to unite in a utopian community. Unlike Winthrop's "Model of Christian Charity," Whitman's "knit of identity," or even Rich's earlier "Sibling Mysteries," this poem refuses the temptation to envision perfect union. It won't even trust, on an intimate level, the union allowed by sex. "We have depended on something," the poet writes, but what? "Sex isn't enough, merely to trust / each other's inarticulate sounds." Rather, invoking the political and theoretical term I

have used in several chapters, Rich will make the relationship between sepa-
rately sovereign selves a model for the one between separately sovereign
peoples, and vice versa: "Call it," she suggests, "mutual recognition."[98]

In many ways, Rich would serve as a natural close to this book. Her early poems
of domestic crisis offer a woman poet's counterpoint to similar poems I have
looked at by Lowell and Creeley: poems in which the tension of encounter with
the other's separate sovereignty was primarily known through, or resulted in,
what Williams called "divorce! divorce!" Her first poems of lesbian community
restate Whitman's dream of an America of love. Her more recent work looks
back through the modernist suspicion of love as a merger to imagine the deep-
est bond as federal, between still-sovereign states: a trope we find in Moore's
"Marriage," in Dickinson's early "Magnum bonum" prose valentine, in Emer-
son's "American Scholar," and in embryo as far back as Bradstreet, with her
hedged and moderated claims of union. Her career-long realist inclination to
insist on love's imperfection certainly has its American heritage. "Look not for
Perfection in your Relation" with a spouse, preacher Thomas Thatcher advised
his congregation; and he, too, preferred words to the "inarticulate sounds" of
eros as a basis for love.[99]

Yet I am reluctant to use Rich in this way. To do so is to discover *conscience*
shining at the heart of American love and love poetry—a true, but partial, ac-
count. Alongside Bradstreet's admissions of the limits of love, after all, was a
powerful interest in the power of "seeming," in love as a species of the imagina-
tion. This interest lifted her amatory verse beyond that of Thomas Thatchers
and John Saffins, and has continued to tug in American verse *against* the dic-
tates of conscience, contrapuntally. If one line of descent connects Bradstreet's
scruples to Rich's, another might link the Puritan's flashes of extravagance to
Whitman's embrace of idolatry, to Dickinson's poems of "Bondage as Play,"
and to Pound's and H.D.'s investigations of "the secret ways of love." This sec-
ond tradition comes under close moral scrutiny in this century, as it has in this
book. Its focus on the bestowals of value that a lover makes on his or her be-
loved and leaves questions of the other's real presence all but out of the pic-
ture.[100] It slights the dream of reciprocity; and although it may well end in "ac-
knowledgment" or "mutual recognition," it does not set off in search of them.

The moral seriousness of Rich's love poems gives them great dignity. But the
poet who said that "you have to be free to play around with the notion that day
might be night, love might be hate," now sticks to the facts, or at least wills that
impression.[101] To object would be to imagine or indulge "a privilege we can't
afford in the world that is, / who are hated as being of our kind."[102] Against this

truth one can't say much, except to add that there is also an American love po-
etry that builds a world elsewhere, far from gay bashing, misogyny, racism,
promised, and occupied lands. This is, no doubt, a poetry of privilege. But in the
hands of James Merrill, it may also be a privileged poetry, with a place within
its "elegance" for what Auden called "the problematic, the painful, the disor-
derly, the ugly."[103] Merrill's movement from self-doubt to aesthetic consolation
connects him to a poet we left behind some pages ago, Wallace Stevens. Even
more than the "vast facility" he worked and worried over throughout his ca-
reer, this erotic pilgrim's progress makes him a fitting final subject to this
book.[104]

Six

Soliloquy or Kiss

Leave a lover with his thoughts for twenty-four hours, and this is what
will happen:

At the salt mines of Salzburg, they throw a leafless wintry bough into
one of the abandoned workings. Two or three months later they haul it out
covered with a shining deposit of crystals. The smallest twig, no bigger
than a tom-tit's claw, is studded with a galaxy of scintillating diamonds.
The original branch is no longer recognizable.

—STENDHAL, *ON LOVE*

        Up from his quieted

quarry the lover   colder and wiser
hauling himself   finds the world turning

toys triumphs   toxins into
this vast facility   the living come
dearest to die in   How did it happen

—JAMES MERRILL, ''AN UPWARD LOOK''

To illustrate how common the ideal of authentic companionate love
was in the 1950s and 1960s, I quoted a brief passage from Mona Van Duyn's
"Toward a Definition of Marriage" (1959). In part 2 of that poem, Van Duyn
pictures marriage a notebook art, improvised, embodied. By the end, in lines
that look forward to Rich, she calls it "the politics of love." To introduce my fi-
nal chapter, however, a central passage is more helpful: a scene where the me
and not-me start by clashing in an intersubjective "duel of amateurs."

These two have almost forgot how it started—in an alley,
impromptu, and with a real affront. One thought,
"He is not me," and one, "She is not me,"

and they were coming toward each other with sharp knives
when someone saw it was illegal, dragged them away,
bundled them into some curious canvas clothing,
and brought them to this gym that is almost dark, and empty.
Now, too close together for the length of the foils,
wet with fear, they dodge, stumble, strike,
and if either finally thinks he would rather be touched
than touch, he still must listen to the clang and tick
of his own compulsive parrying. Endless. Nothing
but a scream for help can make the authorities come.[1]

As we have seen so often in this book, the "affront" of the other's separate subjectivity prompts a violent reaction. The "I" wants the other to *be me* in an impossible union, or be *known to me* in an impossible intimacy. It craves a connection that is "closer than caring," as Stanley Cavell would say.[2] And it finds that the effort to hammer out such union entails a "compulsive parrying" of the other's response.

Since the 1970s, at least, both Creeley and Rich have offered love poems in which "the authorities come" to rescue "I" and the other. As conscience lays hands on compulsion, the couple may embrace at last, and their duel comes to a close. Van Duyn's poem, however, takes another turn. "If it ever turns into more of a dance than a duel," she writes:

it is only because, feeling more skillful, one
or the other steps back with some notion of grace
and looks at his partner. Then he is able to find
not a wire mask for his target, but a red heart
sewn on the breast like a simple valentine.[3]

Saved by manners, not by law, the lover steps back and shifts focus. Not the other's unmasked face—a hidden inner life, a sign of our essential separateness—but an accessible *sign* becomes the target. In a graceful paradox, the couple thus escapes both solitude *and* the "dodge, stumble, strike" of searching for authentic contact. The fencer reconciles him- or herself to the conventions of fencing, the lover to the artifice of love.

Throughout this book we have looked at poets for whom love's artifice has been a saving grace. Bradstreet, Whitman, Dickinson, H.D.: all turned to love's *as if*, its power of "seeming," against the strictness of theology, Emersonian isolation, and the debunking modern temper. With Stevens, however, we found ourselves confronted by a painful, guilty question. Doesn't love's *as if* mark a retreat from true love to desire, from encounter to imagination, from what Stevens described as "that alien, point-blank, green, and actual Guatemala" of the beloved to the "Waldorf" of the poem? If "the thought of her takes her away," as Stevens confesses in "Bouquet of Belle Scavoir," isn't the love poem finally just "another shadow, another evasion"?[4] Stevens himself will say no, and the beauty of a poem like the "Final Soliloquy of the Interior Paramour" bears him out. But few American poets of the next generation followed his abashed, forgiving, sweet-and-sour lead.

One who did, with triumphant results, was James Merrill. Acclaimed even before his death as perhaps our finest postwar love poet, Merrill shows no obvious commitment to the period's ideals of "mutual recognition" and companionate love. Along with the influence of Stevens—the "Final Soliloquy" was to him, he once remarked, what the Twenty-third Psalm is to others—he draws on Proust, Cavafy, and Stendhal. These writers do not dwell on the ethical demands of "being-with" or of "relationships." And yet, as they anatomize the imaginative arts of love per se, these writers are as modern and authentic as Simone de Beauvoir or Denis de Rougemont. And among American poets of love, there is no one more knowing than Merrill: no one more reflective or more undeceived about the sources, limits, and pleasures of his art.

Few of Merrill's poems are the sort we read ourselves into or slyly recite. He has written no "Drink to me only with thine eyes," no "Having a Coke with You." We take his measure in longer narrative, symbolist, and mythographic efforts, where the way life turns into art, and art to life, may be explored in exemplary detail. Although I discuss his later work as this chapter ends, I dwell in detail on three collections, *Nights and Days* (1966), *The Fire Screen* (1969), and *Braving the Elements* (1972), in which the poet works through the unease over artifice and imagination I have traced through the previous two chapters. Each collection may be read as a sequence; together they plot a zigzag course from unease through reconciliation to a new, deeper despair. Only out of these depths would the poet quarry the consoling, chastened vision of his last two decades.[5] To paraphrase Van Duyn, Merrill learns over the course of his career to "step back . . . and look at his partners" with "some notion of grace": not only David Jackson, Strato Mouflouzélis, and Peter Hooten, but also his muse and himself.

The "elate arena"

When Merrill chose five poems from his first, privately published collection, *The Black Swan* (1946), for his first selected poems, *From the First Nine* (1982), he preserved "the earliest inklings of certain lifelong motifs" and revised them into questions that his later work would answer.[6] I begin with a brief look at one such early poem, a reflection on lost love and artistic gain called "The Broken Bowl."

The title of "The Broken Bowl" alludes, it's safe to say, to the shattering of the golden bowl in the Henry James novel. In the novel, this moment reveals the flaw in the gilded crystal *objet*, and in the marriage of Maggie Verver and her Prince, but it also allows their marriage to be mended at the last. This tale of shattering and reconstruction is paradigmatic for poets and novelists of authentic love, but the younger Merrill does not make much use of it. "Our last joy" in the affair, he tells his lost beloved, lies in "knowing it shall not heal."[7] Thirty-six years later, schooled in his heart's insistent drive to aesthetic restitution, the poet turns his youthful answers on themselves. "Did also the heart shatter when it slipped?" he now demands. Yes: "Shards flash, becoming script"; the heart, the bowl, falls from "lucid, self-containing artifice" to a vision of "fire, ice, / A world in jeopardy," only to be restored as the "we" of the later poem "build another, whole, / Inside us." In the best New Critical fashion, this "new space" looks a lot like the well-wrought and highly allusive poem itself.[8]

With their vision of the poem as an "elate arena" in which "Love's facets" reassemble, "The Broken Bowl" recalls the abashed reconstructions of *The Golden Bowl* less than the confident structure of Keats's "Ode to Psyche." This ode, Helen Vendler observes, promises "a victory, complete and permanent, over loss" through "the constructive activity of the mind."[9] An appealing faith: one that Merrill has trusted, however warily, throughout his career. For if the phrase "Love's facets" looks back to the shattered bowl, to the lovers transformed into diamond, another phrase in the final stanza turns those facets into "monuments, or tombstones." It is as though the act of preserving faces in facets, love in art, either *is* or *requires* the death of love as well.[10] Building art's inner room may have more to do with the repair and expansion of one's own psyche, that is to say, than with building a temple to Psyche with "a casement ope at night, / To let the warm Love in!"[11] In a way that was not true for Williams, but rings true with the sadder Stevensian tradition, the act of aesthetic "design" intervenes between the lovers.

In his memoir, *A Different Person*, Merrill mused on the motives behind these mournful early motifs. *"Like the colt that, genetically programmed to be broken, nevertheless throws its first riders,"* he writes in the book's reflective italics, *"I shied away from being saddled with a lover capable of seeing into my heart, for would he not then despise the confusion he saw there? Far better the unrequited pangs I knew so well, which guaranteed me 'no little innocent bliss,' as Tonio Kröger put it, and could always be used as fuel for a poem."* This sense of internal confusion stemmed in part from the poet's homosexuality, the memoir makes clear. But it also grew out of the young poet's embrace of a "grand renunciatory model" of love, learned from opera and from other poems. Schooled to believe that *"Strong feelings are the stuff of art. They belong not in the home but on stage,"* the poet adopted a compensatory, theatrical vision that was all but guaranteed to undermine the love at hand. *"At fifteen—at twenty-five, for that matter—"* Merrill recalls, *"I trusted suffering to improve the style, the lover's loss to be the artist's gain. Don't I still?"*[12]

To trust in suffering this way is, of course, to place oneself in the finest and most lyrical traditions of both love and poetry. The link between love song and elegy, in which song is a substitute and self-delighting satisfaction, is as old the myths of Pan and Syrinx, Daphne and Apollo. But when the composing imagination itself shatters the peace, the act of writing shades its eyes in shame. "Is it bad to have come here?" Stevens wondered as he looked about his inner room at the start of "Gallant Château." In this poem he was able to conclude that at least the poem that resulted from his retreat from the bitter beloved "is good." Elsewhere, however, he wasn't so sure—and his doubts were shared by many poets of modern love.[13]

Over the years Merrill's tone also shifts uneasily. If to "draw" is also to "withdraw," as "For Proust" rhymes to suggest, is that also why "the loved one always leaves"?[14] Merrill's fourth collection, *Nights and Days*, wrestles with such questions from its ambiguous first poem, "Nightgown," to the tentative resolution of its closing love song, "Days of 1964." Does the "dear heart" invoked at the start of the volume address another person, after all, or is it the poet's heart alone who will "come forth" in the poems to come?

> Whom words appear to warm,
> Dear heart, wear mine. Come forth
> Wound in their flimsy white
> And give it form.[15]

The paired, unsettling intimations here—that words may only *appear* to warm this heart, and that the heart may therefore turn out to be "wound" in words, like a corpse in its shroud, coming forth still cold—counterpoint the verse's warm entreaty. This contrast prepares readers for the more striking split in the speaker of the poem that follows, "The Thousand and Second Night." Robert von Hallberg sees this poem's "true, and buried subject" as "the difficulty one has reconciling ideas about love with erotic experience itself."[16] Ideas about love seem less important, however, than ideas of love *poetry*. His face half paralyzed, his narrative insistently self-interrupting and ironic, the speaker of "The

Thousand and Second Night" pictures the transformation of life into art in brutal metaphors. Now that the poet is not writing out of those *"unrequited pangs I knew so well, which guaranteed me 'no little innocent bliss,'"* he turns on his own sense that love *"could always be used as fuel for a poem."*[17] Here writing involves "stripping the blubber from [his] catch" and burning that oil, so that "Mornings, a black film lay upon the desk."[18] The "elate arena" is far off, any reconstructive structure, out of sight.

Merrill is hardly the first poet to have rebelled against his poem's claim to be an object of desire. Like Loy rejecting "Love ——— the litterateur" and Lowell calling *The Dolphin* "a sheaf of tapeworms," Merrill turns art against art, using brutal or sardonic metaphors.[19] In "The Thousand and Second Night," writing the love poem entails a reductive boiling down of the beloved, as blubber is boiled down into lamp oil—and since "blubber" can mean to weep noisily or speak while weeping, to strip the blubber from one's catch is colder still. In "Between Us" the poet wakes up in bed to find his hand, a metonym for writing, fallen asleep and looking like a shrunken parody of the beloved's head. Poetry does not connect the lovers, but mocks them with its reductive and "inhuman" trophies from love's fray. As "Between Us" ends, Merrill begs the hand to open and "deliver" him, in both redemptive and transportational senses of the word, and the poem that follows in *Nights and Days*, "Violent Pastoral," tries with its single sinuous sentence to convey the rush and blurring boundaries of such deliverance: an erotic connection described in terms of a Jove-like eagle and a Ganymede-lamb. Yet the moment is brief, the syntax strained, and the poem so ambiguous we cannot tell if it describes a moment of union between lovers or *within* the poet's all too conscious self.

"The self's a fine and private place," quips F. W. Dupee, "Yet none, I think, do there embrace."[20] In *Nights and Days* Merrill's stance is mostly one of solitary self-division. He seems far less concerned than Lowell, Creeley, or Rich with forcing the lyric to accommodate a beloved's resistant presence. Yet I find it hard to accuse him of Romantic solipsism, or even to second him when he takes himself to task. He seems free of hauntings by Alastor, the spirit of solitude who stalks poets from Shelley to Stevens. This is first of all a matter of aesthetics. Praising Stevens as a model for how to populate a poem, Merrill turns a common accusation on its head. For Hugh Kenner, among many others, "the Stevens world is empty of people"; for Mark Halliday, Stevens "deliberately ignores or deftly avoids opportunities to consider romantic love as a relationship between two distinct, separately subjective human beings."[21] I have offered one counterclaim: namely, that Stevens renounces at least one "person," the bitter wife of "Gallant Château," in order not to make impossible claims on her or on the art of poetry. Merrill's rebuttal, on the other hand, addresses what human company, *in a poem*, looks like. To the apprentice poet, he explains, Eliot and Pound offered "figures like poor Fräulein von Kulp, frozen forever in a single, telling gesture," and "John Adams wound like a mummy in a thousand ticker tape statistics." Figures in Stevens, by contrast, were "airily emblematic, yet blessed with idiosyncrasy. . . . They served their poet and departed undetained by him."[22] Psyche, in "From the Cupola," is Merrill's Stevensian masterpiece. At once a part of the poet and a realized character, she is both "sheer / projection" and a true "correspondent" with whom the poet must establish a relationship. Merrill's evident tenderness toward Psyche counters Dupee's wry couplet. He enacts an acknowledged embrace within the self—one that neither masks nor undermines the embrace of an external beloved. Near the center of the poem, as she despairs, the poet intervenes. "Psyche, hush," he breaks in:

> This is me, James,
> Writing lest he think
> Of the reasons why he writes—
> Boredom, fear, mixed vanities and shames;
> Also love.
> From my phosphorescent ink
> Trickle faint unworldly lights
>
> Down your face. Come, we'll both rest.
> Weeping? You must not.
> All our pyrotechnic flights
> Miss the sleeper in the pitch-dark breast.
> He is love:
> He is everyone's blind spot.
> We see according to our lights.[23]

Along with the distinct and lively voices of Psyche and her sisters, such musings by the poet populate his inner room to such an extent that his solitude, by the end of the volume, seems hardly to deserve the name.

But artistry alone does not keep Alastor at bay. As Stephen Yenser observes, the "coexistence within the self of Eros and Psyche is not the same . . . as a union of the self with the Eros without; the integration of sensuality and spirit within the self does not assure—though it might facilitate—a close relationship between self and other . . . . The 'touch' of the actual always cracks the mold of the dream."[24] What saves the poet, at least for now, is a new stance toward his art: one that cushions him against that shattering touch. In the process of reassuring Psyche, after all, Merrill also reassures himself that his art is not simply cruel or reductive, a matter of collecting stamps or stripping blubber from a catch. Art's motives may be mixed: "there is no pure deed." But to figure it *only* as reductive and isolating is partial, "black only," inaccurate and partial.

> We've seen what comes next. There is no pure deed.
> A black-and-red enchanter, a deep-dyed
> Coil of—No matter. One falls back, soiled, blurred.
>
> And on the page, of course, black only. Damned
> If I don't tire of the dark view of things
>   .   .   .
>   My hands move. An intense,
> Slow-paced, erratic dance goes on below.
> I have received from whom I do not know
> These letters. Show me, light, if they make sense.[25]

Lines like these ease Merrill's earlier irony and disappointment. They soothe him with the thought that the self-love inherent in art—typing as masturbation, a "slow-paced, erratic dance" of hands "below," producing letters—will not *necessarily* impede the love of someone else. "In love," writes Kristeva, paraphrasing Rimbaud, " 'I' has been an *other*."[26] Merrill's ability to speak as Psyche and the other characters of the poem allows the love for another person we find in the last poem of this volume, "Days of 1964"—a poem that tests the poet's developing assurance against the specifics of an evidently intersubjective romance.

"Was love illusion?"

The end of "From the Cupola" turned the inner room into the external amphitheater of the typewriter. "Days of 1964" continues that push to the exterior. Set almost entirely outdoors, in a Greek world that literalizes the "Greek / Revival" architecture mentioned in the poem before it, "Days of 1964" is lit at the start not by the "lamp" of artifice but by sunlight, which has "cured" the poet's neighborhood. Far from banishing Eros, lamplight here illuminates intimacies: "We lay whole nights, open, in the lamplight / And gazed." Daylight proves just as revealing. At the midday crux of the poem the poet encounters his cleaning woman, Kyria Kleo, on her way to a rendezvous. He has already hinted that, despite looking "like a Palmyra matron / copied in lard and horsehair," she's a type of Aphrodite, just as he figures Aphrodite's son Eros. But the apparition of her face among the pines startles him into another myth of love's lineage, one that bears on the tension between love and art that Merrill has explored throughout the volume:

> Poor old Kleo, her aching legs,
> Trudging into the pines. I called,
> Called three times before she turned.
> Above a tight, skyblue sweater, her face
> Was painted. Yes. Her face was painted
> Clown-white, white of the moon by daylight,
> Lidded with pearl, mouth a poinsettia leaf,
> Eat me, pay me—the erotic mask
> Worn the world over by illusion
> To weddings of itself and simple need.
>
> Startled mute, we had stared—was love illusion?—
> And gone our ways.[27]

Was love illusion? The question has haunted Merrill's book, and this one, too. "Too pathetic, too pitiable, is the region of affection," Emerson lamented in "Illusions," "and its atmosphere always liable to *mirage*." But Emerson wants to contrast the world of illusion with a reality inhabited by the solitary soul and faceless, impersonal "gods" quite different from Merrill's lively pantheon. His insistence that we see one another through the "colored and distorting lenses" of a subjectivity so radical it "ruins the kingdom of mortal friendship and love" carries him well past the poet's more forgiving acknowledgment that, in love, "we see according to our lights."[28] Likewise, when Lynn Keller explains that Merrill here "admits that all human love may be merely illusion, a facade applied to beautify crude physical need," she brings to this poem an ironic, even reductive tone (*"merely* illusion") appropriate to a range of poets of the "modern temper" from Loy to Lowell, and even to earlier poems in *Nights and Days*, but far too caustic for this tender context. In the process she discards the poet's carefully chosen marital metaphor, and misses the question's implicit answer.[29]

The "wedding of [illusion] and simple need," for which this poem is an ambivalent epithalamion, gives *birth* to love, just as "Resource and Need" bear Eros in Plato's *Symposium*. Part illusion, then, love is part necessity also, and the two elements are inextricable strands in its genetic code. The modern temper's effort to sweep love free of illusions ended in naturalist reduction precisely because it ignored this double inheritance, mistaking love's erotic polyphony for a disguise of monotone libido, rather than its humanly inevitable complication. Keller's architectural terms (love as a "facade") are equally misguided, and certainly out of touch with the details of this poem. Need in this poem is not "crude," as she would have it, but "simple," and even then not lacking in imagination. As Irving Singer attests, it is only "through the amorous imagination" that "one person becomes sexually attractive to another," since "our instincts alone would not enable us to love or even to lust in the way that human beings do."[30]

Far from disenchanting love, then, or revealing it to be a mere "superstructure of poetry" covering up a "biological urge," as the poets of the modern temper did, Merrill suggests that the structures of enchantment infiltrate biology, and blossom in bestowal.[31] Although he is hardly a Whitmanian poet, Merrill shares Whitman's sense of the enlargement of both self and other in the radiant amatory imagination. Like Bradstreet, he understands the richness of affection that our elaborate ascriptions of attractive, powerful qualities on one another come to underwrite. "Love makes one generous," he explains.[32] The gift it gives, Merrill's image for bestowal, is a mask.

Why should the mask be an image of bestowal? Here Keller's commentary is more helpful. Masks sustain love, writes Keller, because they "enrich our inner lives by transforming everyday perception"—a transformation intimately linked with the poet's "theatrical aesthetic."[33] "The *as ifs* of love," like those we indulge at the theater, "are imaginative, not delusional," according to Singer, so that "the amorous imagination bestows value upon a person as the dramatic imagination bestows theatrical import upon an actor."[34] Bradstreet's as-ifs were biblical: she loved her husband as if he (or sometimes she) were Christ, and as if two could ever be one. Emerson's were philosophical, concerned first and foremost with the "godhead" or "reality" of noumenal selfhood, which one can only know directly in oneself. Merrill's as-ifs, his masks, might well be those of a classical drama, played out in a Greece that writes large the "shrunken amphitheater" of the poet's typewriter. It's not just that masked, poet and beloved can tell the truth. Rather, masked by fictions, these young lovers may be divinely inspired. The internal embrace of "From the Cupola," in which self became other and was healed, can thus be lived out between lover and beloved. "Where I hid my face, your touch, quick, merciful, / Blindfolded me. A god breathed from my lips," the poet sighs.[35] A winged Cupid painted blind, the poet is also Socrates covering his head to speak of love in the *Phaedrus*, where we learn that love's enthusiasm recalls the "possession or madness" that Socrates' jaded contemporaries call "not manic but *mantic*."[36] Merrill adds, so to speak, an extra syllable, restoring the divinatory value lost in that classical precursor of the modern temper. *Romantic*, then, the poet speaks his piece. In a world of love as possession, the touch of the actual can be a brush of angels' wings. Is love illusion? "You were everywhere beside me, masked," comes the poet's answer, "As who was not, in laughter, pain, and love."[37]

"Her appraising glare"

In its ease with bestowal, "Days of 1964" marks a high point in Merrill's early love poetry. And yet, such love is not without its risks. If at some moment, Roland Barthes explains, I as a lover "see the other in the guise of an inert object, like a kind of stuffed doll" on which I bestow virtues and value, that is enough "to shift my desire from this annulled object to my desire itself," so that "it is my desire I desire, and the loved being is no more than its tool."[38] How awful to wake up and find one's fine romance, inspiring and inspired, reduced to an imaginative play that is *mere* play, an overdressed rehearsal of *idées reçues.* On such a morning the poet might want to uncover his head and recant his earlier testimony. "False, false the tale," Socrates calls out against himself in the *Phaedrus,* proceeding to a second myth of love.

Merrill might have placed that quote as the epigraph to his next volume, *The Fire Screen.* Where love and imagination seemed entwined by the close of *Nights and Days,* in this collection Merrill once again explores the strain between them. He does so by setting up a love triangle in which the muse is not an exalted or idealized version of the beloved (a problem Lowell explored in *The Dolphin*) but rather a powerful rival for the poet's allegiance and affection. At the close of the last volume love made one generous in bestowals, in the as-ifs of amatory idealization. Here, "lacking her blessing"—that is, untransfigured by art—the beloved is no longer attractive, but rather "Stout, serviceable, gray. / A fishwife shawled in fourth-hand idiom."[39] If the opposite of bestowal is, in Singer's terms, *appraisal,* no wonder the poet worries:

> I fear for us. Nights fall
> We toss through blindly, drenched in her appraising
> Glare, the sibyl I turn to
>
> When all else fails me, when you do—
>
> The mother tongue!

The turn from a failed engagement with the other to the surrogate satisfactions of writing will thus, in this book, be represented as the turn from the beloved to "the mother tongue." Four years before Lowell's *The Dolphin,* Merrill's *The Fire Screen* similarly wrestles a figure who incorporates both the impersonal determinisms of language, the literary determinisms of the muse, and the determinant dynamics of the family romance, and with far greater aesthetic success.

Why this threefold concern with the determining factors of love and poetry? By the time of these poems I suspect Merrill had soured on his own facility with bestowal, and with the familiar plots his affections played him through. Barthes describes the poet's lot: "The body, from head to toe, overwhelmed, *submerged by Nature*, and all this nonetheless: *as if I were borrowing a quotation*."[40] Suppose my sacred drama turned out to be a "household opera" written by others and learned in childhood? "Long beyond adolescence," Merrill writes of himself in "Matinees," "Tissue of sound and tissue of the brain / Would coalesce, and what the Masters wrote / Itself compose his features sharp and small."[41] And even this paints the danger in too broad, too comforting a stroke. By the time we reach "Matinees" in the sequence of *The Fire Screen* we are *happy* to hear that some earlier artist has arranged our affairs. That at least leaves room for someone's creativity, if not ex nihilo than through variations on a theme. In "To My Greek," near the start of the volume, Merrill faces the still more alarming fear: that language itself dictates the course of our affections. When he writes of "common sense veering into common scenes, / Tears, incoherent artifice," we hear the all *too* coherent artifice of the words "sense" and "scenes," as though their proximity made the outburst inevitable. "God and the imagination are one," Stevens's interior paramour declared. Merrill puts language in divinity's place, but joylessly. "The mother tongue! / . . . / Her automation and my mind are one."[42]

The violence of early poems in *Nights and Days* was directed against the poet himself, taking the forms of ironic or cruel metaphors. For fear of his words' revelations, the speaker of "To My Greek" turns to violence as well, but his focus is apparently outward. He threatens to slit the muse's windpipe; he twists against syntax and stanzaic structures, warding off clarity and closure. The poet knows the conventions of the amorous sequence all too well, how they end with lovers far apart, their love preserved in verse alone.[43] And as we read *The Fire Screen* we learn other reasons why knowledge is so threatening: flaws in the beloved that the poet cannot bring himself to leave unnamed in verse. In "The Envoys" the beloved torments animals who persist in loving their tormentor. In "Part of the Vigil" the poet enters the "little, doorless, crudely lighted chambers" of the other man's heart and is unable to find his image there. "We must step boldly into man's interior world or not at all," says Stevens, but Merrill's step leads to nervous hope, no more. "Didn't your image / Still unharmed, deep in my own saved skin / Blaze on?" he asks. "You might yet see it, see by it. / Nothing else mattered."[44] The fact that "blazon" means both a dazzling display and a merely showy, ostentatious one, however, suggests the poet's ambivalence, the falsity of his claim. Does this vigil mark the funeral of their love? The last four lines deny it, but their tone gives them the lie.

Love poets have always known how love enacts its bestowals through language. Emerson mocked that ascriptive power: "We unjustly select a particle, and say 'O steel-filing number one! what heart-drawings I feel to thee! what prodigious virtues are these of thine!'" Whitman accepts ascription as he soothes our vanity. "None has done justice to you," he reassures us: "O I could sing such grandeurs and glories about you!"[45] But neither comes to grips as Merrill does with the peculiarly authorial fear that language might be, not just the slippery medium, but the motivating force of his affections. Perhaps because of his inclination to archness, Merrill is also painfully aware that his rhetoric of praise is *a rhetoric*, too. The poet possesses, and fears, a "vast facility," able to process love into language and, perhaps, the other way around.[46] One way or the other, he fears, the mother tongue will have its way with him.

I find this fear nicely addressed in "Flying from Byzantium," where the poet first acknowledges the end of his affair. In the second section of this poem Merrill takes the imperative word play of "common sense veering into common scenes" to a tragicomic extreme. Here "the man in the moon," a male muse, speaks in nothing *but* trouvailles. Rhymes slant with dizzying rapidity; and the poet responds in kind:

> Up spoke the man in the moon:
> "What does that moan mean?
> The plane was part of the plan.
> Why gnaw the bone of a boon?"
>
> I said with spleen, "Explain
> These nights that tie me in knots,
> All drama and no dream,
> While you lampoon my pain."[47]

At this point in his affair Merrill might call on his art to preserve love's memory, or simply to keep himself afloat in seas of erotic travail. Yeats in such distress aspires to "the artifice of eternity." But flying from, not sailing to, a Yeatsian solution, the poet exchanges the coruscating densities of "To My Greek" for bravura wordplay or for minor, amenable forms like the foot-per-line-longer limerick stanza, borrowed from Yeats, that he deploys in section 1. The poet would rather turn the force of art on himself, as he did in "The Thousand and Second Night," than on his lost beloved. Perhaps he fears he's been more in league with the muse, the mother tongue, than her victim. Like the Lowell of *The Dolphin*, Merrill seems haunted by a sense of being "maneuvered on a guiding string" as he "execute[s] his written plot," and he similarly mourns his having listened to "too many / words of the collaborating muse."[48] If Merrill declares himself the "animal" of his lost love, he also knows that he's "the young ringmaster," a man who puts himself and his beloved through the hoops of an predestined, predictable circus. Is that line an echo of Yeats's "The Circus Animals' Desertion"? The affair may have embodied "heart mysteries," but Merrill, too, suspects that "Players and painted stage took all my love / And not those things that they were emblems of."[49]

At the close of *The Dolphin* Lowell despairs of the artistic renewal he once expected from his half-human, half-mythic muse. He hopes only for the satisfactions of memorial accuracy. "Flying from Byzantium," by contrast, ends with Merrill "kneeling" to declare his allegiance to the muse. Or, at least, part of him kneels, while another stands off a little, keeping the muse's powers half at bay. The end of "Flying from Byzantium" is set in the *third* person, that is to say, and not the first: a rhetorical move that lets Merrill qualify his ringing plea for death and rebirth as a "vague, compliant song." The youth of the ringmaster, which signals his distance from maturing experience, is thus *preserved* rather than *restored* in the final figure of "Flying from Byzantium." As in "Last Words," which follows "Flying from Byzantium" as a sort of coda, part of the self will always suffer identifications and ecstasies while another sighs that "There's nothing I don't know / Or shall not know again, / Over and over again."[50]

Not all love poets are repulsed by repetition. "Almost every one loves all repeating in some one," says Stein in *The Making of Americans*; the notion that both life and writing might find our loved ones playing out some pattern, acting according to type, bothers her not at all, as it did not trouble the poets of "the secret ways of love."[51] But in *The Fire Screen* Merrill finds such patterns hard to take. Through them he glimpses a bleak, unhappy vista where we play out love's dramas, but they're hardly sacred, or even operatic. As *The Fire Screen* continues the poet loses his faith in the once-inspiring theatrical metaphor for love. By the time we reach "Remora" he abandons it entirely, and returns to the brutal aquatic metaphors of "The Thousand and Second Night." The poet of "Remora" plays clever parasite to his beloved's blundering shark. The deus ex machina of a skindiver (another lover? a rival?) intercedes, and the poet's cold

and "dapper" self can slip away unscathed. "Thanks for the lift," he all but
sneers. "There are other fish in the sea." Merrill arrives in "Remora" at a cyni-   *173*
cism toward himself and his art at least as deep as the one in which *Nights and
Days* began. If only because of its repetition, the emotional impasse is worse.
"One begins by unlearning how to love others," as Nietzsche observes, "and
ends by no longer finding anything lovable in oneself."[52]

Restatement of Romance

Like other disillusioned sequences and books I have looked at in this study—
Loy's *Songs to Joannes*, Creeley's *For Love*, Lowell's *The Dolphin*—*The Fire
Screen* shows a poet deeply suspicious of aesthetic finish and achievement. Such
artifice can seem to betray the particulars of a love relationship; worse, it wins
a morally suspect literary victory from emotional loss. Only an art that
"go[es] / gracelessly" or speaks "wrongly," in this view, can capture the real-
ity of intersubjective encounter. Only such art can reach the goal of authentic-
ity—a goal far more deeper and more valuable than that of mere aesthetic ac-
complishment.

As I have shown, the goal of authenticity grows out of the modern ideal of
companionate love, with its emphasis on a *faithfulness* to the other, even in the
poem. This modern companionate ideal itself arises, again at least in part, as a
reaction-formation against disillusionment, a way to reassert a meaning for
love in the face of the debunking, disenchanted, melancholy "modern temper"
without appealing to premodern theologies and literatures and other "secret
ways of love." But there may be other answers to that crisis. In *Tales of Love* Ju-
lia Kristeva suggests a postmodern ideal that will self-consciously abandon au-
thenticity—one that gives a postmodern spin to Anne Bradstreet's old strat-
egy of "seeming thine" when time and conscience and theology would render
her not "thine" at all. "Let the seeming take itself seriously," Kristeva advises.
"Let it remain floating, empty at times, inauthentic, obviously lying. Let it pre-
tend. . . . What is at stake is turning the crisis into a *work in progress.*"[53]

As he struggles to restore the value of love as bestowal—which means, in
part, love as illusion—Merrill works to exorcise his self-image as an ever-
untouched "young scribe," a "cold man," or "Jack Frost." He may thereby grow
reconciled with the jealous mistress of *The Fire Screen*, the mother tongue as
muse. His efforts span the close of this volume and the love poems of the next,
Braving the Elements (1972); and precisely this transformation of "the crisis into
a *work in progress*" enables the emotionally poised, consoling vision of "The
Book of Ephraim" and the poems that followed. They offer a powerful alterna-

tive to the ethics and aesthetics of authenticity I have traced from Williams through Creeley and Lowell to Rich: a vision of Eros that proves more hospitable to the artifice and illusion—or, say, the imagination—essential to both poetry and love.

Let's return to the impasse Merrill faces in *The Fire Screen*. If we wished to diagnose the poet's plight, we might say that he suffers from melancholy, that local onset of the modern temper which, as Kristeva explains, "demystifies wisdom, beauty, style, and eros itself." A full-blown case, she continues, includes "a constant *anxiety* on the moral level, a painful *impotence* on the sexual one," the patient poised before an "abyss into which one can read the unsurmountable ascendancy of a stifling mother." In its final stages we find that the lively reversible roles of voyeur and exhibitionist, sadist and masochist, gutter out in an undifferentiated "aggregate . . . of stagnation and despair."[54] Merrill displays none of the flat affect and numbed, repetitive speech that the theorist leads us to expect and that I have shown at work in the melancholy text of Loy's *Songs*. But Kristeva's outline is helpful in reading the close of *The Fire Screen*, and the struggle with the mother she hints at—for Merrill at once the muse, his mother, and the mother tongue—will in fact prove central to the poet's cure.

Recovery begins in "A Fever," where the two muse figures of "Flying from Byzantium," the man in the moon and the mother tongue, merge to form a single intruder into the poet's inner room. The room has been otherwise occupied, evidently: Merrill has apparently begun sharing it with a new friend he names, at the close of the poem, "my girl." When "she leaves," however (the beloved always leaves), the Muse sweeps in to tidy up and chastise:

> Enter the moon like a maid in silence unsheeting the waste
> Within, of giant toys, toy furniture.
> Two button eyes transfix me. A voice blurred and impure,
> Speaks through lips my own lips have effaced:
>
> "Back so soon? Am I to wish you joy, as usual,
> Of a new friend? For myself, not quite the nice
> Young thing first given to your gentleness,
> These visits are my life, which is otherwise uneventful."[55]

Less jealous than hurt and neglected, no longer the imperious force she appeared to be at the end of "Flying from Byzantium," the Muse wants her poet to acknowledge both that she needs him and that he treats her badly.[56] In her defense, and to defend that part of him that she represents, she undertakes an apology for the imagination. The less-deceived and unforgiving gaze of appraisal, which the poet feared in "To My Greek" (it seemed an "appraising glare") and embraced in "Remora" (where it seemed, however bitterly, a "heavenly sunshine")—such appraisal seemed attractive and compelling because it promised the truth about the loved one and the self. It was a mainline injection of what Henry James called "the real ... the things we cannot possibly *not* know, sooner or later." When the brisk delights of accuracy fade, however, the chill of self-hatred sets in. And is there in beauty no truth, no knowledge granted only in disguise? "The point was to be one on whom nothing is lost," the Muse reminds him. "But what good is gained by one more random image // Crossed with mine at one more feast of crumbs?" Appraisal may be a necessary *part* of love, but on its own it ends in cross-reference and accretion, meager fare for poetry. What's lacking in appraisal, and in Merrill's harshest appraisals of his art, is a place for what James calls "romance"—that which "can reach us only through the beautiful circuit and subterfuge of our thought and our desire."[57]

I bring up James because the Muse's "point" is quoted from the novelist: not the preface to *The American*, my own source so far, but "The Art of Fiction," where James explains what the advice to "write from experience" might, in practice, mean. "Experience," he notes, "is never limited, and it is never complete." Rather, "it is the very atmosphere of the mind; and when the mind is imaginative ... it takes to itself the faintest hints of life, it converts the very pulses of the air into revelations. The young lady living in a village has only to be a damsel upon whom nothing is lost to make it quite unfair ... to declare to her that she shall have nothing to say about the military. Greater miracles have been seen that, *imagination assisting, she should speak the truth* about some of these gentlemen.[58] It is as though the poet had until now recalled only the admonition to write from experience, to "be one of the people on whom nothing is lost!" (as James concludes the passage), without recalling how much of experience is mental, imaginative, an extrapolation from crumbs back to the feast. "The tears, the mendings—they all hurt," the Muse admonishes, perhaps to reassure him of her sympathy; she adds that mending, or artistic reconstruction, "entirely consumes."[59] Like her reference to a feast, her admonishments play on the poet's frustrated drive to devour experience—to "live, love," as the man in the moon admonished in "Flying from Byzantium," not "shake [his] fist at the feast"—as well as on his desire to be consumed by passion once again.

Touched by her words, the poet falls to his knees a second time. He awakes from one spell—call it a spell of disenchantment—into another, yet without satisfaction:

> A long
> Spell seems to pass before I am found in a daze,
> Cheek touching floor. From a position so low,
> Colors passionate but insubstantial fill the window.
> Must it begin and end like this always?

The insubstantiality of those colors and the solitude of his position ("so low" as "solo") suggest the incompleteness of this scene. How can the poet, "imagination assisting, speak the truth" from this abashed, unprepossessing stance? "A Fever" ends with an image of dawn, and the next poem begins with one, but we sense no new day at hand.

However much the poet may return to the world of desire and bestowal, after all, he still fears that a part of him will remain aloof and critical, watching the rhythm of subjection to and defiance of the Muse start up again. This "young scribe" self seems to compose "Mornings in a New House," with its detached description of the fires of eros lit once more, "By whom a cold man hardly cares." A great deal depends on our reading of "Mornings," which brings the book to an emotional crisis. Yenser finds the poem essentially optimistic, moving "from stiffness through routine to emotional perception" as the poet discovers once again that "passion and craft are knotted, crossed, *double*-crossed, partly because the exercise of the art discovers or creates the emotion." The poet shields himself from a "tamed uprush / (Which to recall alone can make him flush)" by introducing this poem's version of the mask, the fire screen. The poet's mother's "crewel-work," embroidered by her as a child, this screen is for Yenser a figure of the poem, just as the "tamed uprush" is "the 'fire' of inspiring emotion."[60] But suppose that fire were one more "tamed recall," as Kalstone proposes, "of the shattered (or spent?) affair"? In that case the fact that the poet is recalling *by himself*, "alone" in that sense, makes him flush. The different senses hint at very different scenes.

"It is hard to disentangle the impulses which contribute to this poem," Kalstone says.[61] *Caveat lector*—and yet, at the risk of sounding like a poor man's Paglia, I find the cruel work of poetry giving the poet pleasure because in it he at last admits a certain sadomasochistic enjoyment of his ongoing battle with the mother-muse. The poem sparks into life as the poet imagines himself as a doll to his mother as a child:

> Still vaguely chilled,
>
> Guessing how even then her eight
> Years had foreknown him, nursed him, all,
> Sewn his first dress, sung to him, let him fall,
> Howled when his face chipped like a plate,
>
> He stands there wondering until red
> Infraradiance, wave on wave,
> So enters each plume-petal's crazy weave,
> Each worsted brick of the homestead,
>
> That once more, deep indoors, blood's drawn.[62]

These lines are pivotal, and their tone quite slippery. Kalstone speaks of an "identification with the 'tiny needlewoman' mother": a "discovery of . . . entwined destinies" accomplished "without guilt." Yenser describes the mother "comforting a doll that she has dropped—and therewith foreshadowing her love for her son."[63] Both glosses seem to me false, however, to the scene Merrill describes. She lets him fall and howls because she has been deprived—after all, something belonging to her has been chipped, neglected, damaged. We never see her pick the doll back up. The "Infraradiance" that warms the "worsted brick" of Merrill's new inner room is preeminently his anger at having been bested by a muse who glares at and seduces, cradles, and drops him, brings him to his knees. Roused by this anger, he strikes back, pricking the mother-muse's crewel-working finger. If God and the imagination cannot be joined, the poet seems to say, let my mind and her automation at least be set asunder. Perhaps the pain of that divorce will warm the cold man the poet fears he is, and return him to some vital, charged relationship with both the mother tongue and mother-muse.

After this burst of pain and pleasure, painfully won, "Mornings in a New House" ends with a retreat. "Days later" the poet adds an apologetic footnote, a preview of the note to "Mrs. Livingston" that the boy-poet of "Matinees" must, on his mother's orders, copy out and send.[64] But *The Fire Screen* does not end in dutiful self-abasement. It ends instead with a coda, "The Summer People," which recapitulates the volume's battle between poet and muse, love and art, at the safe aesthetic distance offered by its ballad form and its setting in the "village white and neat" of "Caustic (Me.)." If the previous poems were exhibits from the Caustic town museum, that designation applies equally to the characters of this one: Andrew and Nora, who "had elsewhere played with fire";

Andrew's wife Jane, a painter of sorts; Margaret, Nora's widowed mother. A new inhabitant arrives, linked by rhyme to the failures of love. "I wish I weren't a widow," says Margaret. "I wish you weren't divorced— / Oh, by the way, I heard today / About a man named Frost." Jack Frost's own affections are hammered into us. He "loved four-hand piano," "Loved also bridge," "Loved to gossip, loved croquet, / His money loved to spend / / On food and drink and flowers / Loved entertaining most." Or does he have some other first allegiance?

> "Proud Grimes, proud loyal kitty,"
> Jack said, "I love you best."
> Two golden eyes were trimmed to slits,
> Gorgeously unimpressed.[65]

In his feline indifference, and in his later cruelty, Grimes is the muse cut down to ballad-stanza size.

As long as Jack stays on alone through the off-season, taking the spareness of winter as an opportunity for imaginative embellishment, all goes well. In his eyes bare boughs become "gnarled crystal": an image that recalls Stendhal's version of bestowal, "crystallization," in which the lover alone with his thoughts transforms his beloved the way that Salzburg salt miners toss a leafless winter bough into the mine in order to retrieve it, unrecognizable, "covered with a shining deposit of crystals."[66] If winter is the season of intellectual creativity, as the epigraph of "The Summer People" states, it is perhaps because the season writes large the creative impetus of absence. (Inasmuch as the swan is sacred to Venus, we may find a trace of love's departures in the "Flights of the midnight Swan" that decorate snow-white Caustic all season long.)

Like the Muse, though, Grimes is a jealous master. The moment Jack's summer neighbors decide to stay through Christmas, Grimes reacts by clawing his master's thigh (as close to a castration threat as a cat-sized muse can muster). When Grimes attacks someone *else*, the forces of sociability recoil. "Two good whiffs of ether" and—as the doll's and poet's eyes closed in "Mornings"—the cat's "gold eyes shut on Jack." But the cycle of punishment is not quite closed:

> That same night, Grimes in ermine
> And coronet of ice
> Called him by name, cried vengeance,
> Twitching his long tail twice.
>
> Jack woke in pitch dark, burning,
> Freezing.[67]

We recognize these symptoms of from "A Fever" and "Mornings." Unable to balance hot and cold selves, winter's art and summer's social pleasures, Jack flees.

Yenser calls Jack Frost "Merrill's Mauberley," for like the character from Ezra Pound's "Hugh Selwyn Mauberley," he is for the poet a distancing, exorcising fiction.[68] Merrill must move beyond Jack's alternating quarrel with and subjection to the muse into a mature equanimity. This movement will entail an education in—and grudging acceptance of—what Emerson called *succession,* one of the limiting Lords of Life. When Jack tries to segregate cold and warmth, solitude and society, he forces coherence on time's and inspiration's passage—an effort that finds its equally sterile counterpart in his later wish to unite the two in something like a Spenserian "continual spring, and harvest there continuall, / Both meeting in one time."[69] The fruits of this union, in the "November mildness" that follows Jack's departure, are the doomed spring flowers planted by Jack's Japanese "houseboy," Ken. Ken's suicide follows their unseasonable bloom.

"The Summer People" ends on a worn-down, tragic note. In the course of the ballad, though, a new source for the poet's troubles has been identified, one that shifts our focus from the internal struggle with the muse that has held our attention so far. The "Chemical Plant" whose glow floats over the village harbor at the end of "The Summer People"—"gloats" is Merrill's portmanteau pun—foreshadows the world of impersonal forces that the poet will face in subsequent volumes, and it signals a new vision of the world we cannot in the end *not* know: a world of entropy, of atomic and geologic powers, of threats more external than internal. Learning this new realism, the poet drops his futile rage against the way love's illusions go up in smoke. Near the center of the ballad, in a first-person digression, he thinks of Job. "Logs burned / The sparks flew upward," Merrill observes, then he strikes the new note, startling in its lack of archness or irony: "Time passes softly, scarcely / Felt by me or you. / And then, at the odd moment, / Tenderness passes, too." As we will learn in *Braving the Elements,* love's impermanence and reverberations hardly stand out in a world where "nothing either lasts or ends." Indeed, as cycles go, the muse's circuit can seem beautiful, familiar, comforting.[70]

The Art of Love

The first lines of Merrill's next book, *Braving the Elements,* return us to the burning log we left a moment ago in "The Summer People," and to that book's final muted tone. "Then when the flame forked like a sudden path," the book begins, "I gasped and stumbled, and was less."[71] Throughout the book the poet returns to now-familiar scenes, only to find them diminished, too. In "After the Fire," for example, we revisit Greece. But Kleo, whose appearance startled the poet into his vision of bestowal, has aged into troubles. Her mother, "the yiayia, nearly ninety," screams curses at her children: the son once identified with Eros is "a *Degenerate! a Thieving / Faggot!*" just as daughter Kleo is a *"Whore!"*

Now, in *The Fire Screen* these not-inaccurate appraisals would have called the poet's accusing mother-muse to mind. Here they remind him of his "mother's *mother's* illness," with its "Querulous temper" and "lucid shame."[72] Skipping a generation, Merrill frees his mother from the burden of being purely mytho-logical, an inhumanly terrible and demanding figure for the muse. The merely human yiayia, demanding though she is, calls up a warmth of pity, not a slow burn of resentment. He kneels to embrace her, as in the last book the young page-poet knelt before the Muse, and a mutual transformation occurs. *"It's Tzimi! He's returned!"* the yiayia shouts; "—And with that she returns to hu-man form, / The snuffed out candle-ends grow tall and shine, / Dead flames encircle us, which cannot harm."[73] Out of diminishment (the flames are dead, not reborn) comes the book's first image for a new bond between poet and mother, poet and muse, outside the realm of sadomasochism—and for their joy in the new relation.

Joy is, perhaps, too strong a word. Certainly the poet has not lost sight of the truths he learned in his long sojourn in appraisal. When those "dead flames . . . which cannot harm" reappear in another poem near the end of *Braving the Ele-ments* they take their place in a disquisition on "Proust's Law." "What least thing our self-love longs for most," he observes, "others instinctively with-hold." Thus the corollary: "only when time has slain desire / Is his wish granted to a smiling ghost / Neither harmed nor warmed, now, by the fire."[74] By now any mention of a man who is not warmed should raise a flag; but Jack Frost is nowhere in sight. Warmed by other fires than desire's, Merrill can sub-ject Strato, the heretofore unnamed beloved of *The Fire Screen*, to tenderly ironic scrutiny:

> I look hard
> At both the god and him. (He loves attention
> Like gods and children, and he lifts his glass.)
> Those extra kilos, that moustache,
> Lies found out and letters left unanswered
> Just won't do. It makes him burst out laughing,
> Curiously happy, flecked with foam.[75]

That foam signals a memory of sensual release, recalling as it does the shallows the pair braved in "To My Greek"— and, since the poet has read his love affair through Yeats before, perhaps also the foam where nymphs and satyrs copulate at the end of "News for the Delphic Oracle." But the even tone of "Strato in Plaster" is so different from the earlier passion and divine possession that such feathery touches of allusion, at which Merrill is past master, scarcely bring the lovers' bliss to mind. It seems distant, almost unbelievable.

This even gaze and lack of bitterness, toward the once-beloved *and* the self, depends on the poet's having reconciled at last with the muse. It shows that the poet has come to terms with fiction, or at least with the beautiful circuit and subterfuge that Henry James called "romance." It evinces a victory, in verse if not in life, over melancholy. But when did this victory take place? To answer that, it helps to remember that what the melancholic lacks, at least according to Kristeva, is the basis of love itself: a sense of belonging to an ideal order, to an imaginary, ideal other who loves us and with whom we identify. Following Freud, Kristeva names this figure an ideal father: the sort that Merrill's mother remarries in a poem from this volume, a "gentle General." But "he" is essentially a combination of both parents, in idealized form; and I spot a combination like this in the poem of Merrill's cure, "Days of 1935." In this ballad, which recuperates in its very form the sad plot of "The Summer People," Merrill as a boy dreams of being kidnapped by an affectionate surrogate family: Jean, who watches the boy "as no one ever had"; and Floyd, who loves Jean with a passion the child knows only from movies. That Floyd initiates the boy into sex puts an unexpected spin on the Kristevan imaginary father's "warm but dazzling, domesticated paternity."[76] But their encounter seems part of the boy's growing ability to indulge in fantasy—in this case, to imagine an ever-broader sense of "how much [he's] worth to [his] old man"—and of the adult poet's reconciliation with the beautiful circuit of desire. When imaginary mother Jean asks the boy for "real stories—but not real I mean," she invites him to exchange the appraising glare for a "golden haze," and she validates the paradoxical pleasures of romantic bestowal and Jamesian romance.[77] The child, as Kalstone observes, discovers his own "vitality" in the moment he exercises "his storytelling powers." The adult poet, recalling the dream, learns that "through fiction his parents become available to him in ways never possible in life"—a lesson that applies to lovers, too.[78]

Although "Days of 1935" reasserts the inspired, truth-telling power of illusion last seen in "Days of 1964," Merrill's sojourn in appraisal taught him a few lessons. The boy-poet's speech on the witness stand recalls poems of cold-eyed rejection from *The Fire Screen.* The execution of Floyd and Jean reads like a libretto out of "Matinees." But the poet's attitudes toward both love and poetry have matured. Thinking of his treatment of kidnappers in fantasy, and of his parents in the narrative frame, the poet stakes a new claim for the value of the slip between life and its recreation. "True to life," he writes, the boy has "played them false." The golden haze of fiction may illuminate a world "past belief," but it is "past disbelief" as well. It's just not that the poet nothing affirmeth, and therefore never lieth, as Sidney says. Rather, in a world of boards "painted like board" and of loves that act out sonnet sequences, art's false play is true.[79]

"Life," therefore, "was fiction in disguise."[80] The paradox is easily observed in Merrill's work *too* easily, I think. We need to remind ourselves of the alternative visions he has tested: that art is a world restored in the poet's inner room ("The Broken Bowl"); that art is essentially reductive ("The Thousand and Second Night") or a matter of plots and types and repetition ("Flying from Byzantium"); that the union of art and sociability, while devoutly to be wished, would prove a disastrous forced bloom ("The Summer People"). Merrill's aestheticism stems as much from hard poetic trial and error as it does from innate inclination. The emotional growth behind it shows in his watchful self-portraits in *Braving the Elements.* Instead of looking on as a timelessly "young scribe" or that cold man, Jack Frost, Merrill appears as a love- and dream-struck little boy and, in "Willowware Cup," as a father "minding less and less"—and who must, therefore, have minded more before, as the "young scribe" never could. The poet masks his fear of detachment with insouciance. But even this briefly donned paternal persona is significant. As boy and adult, Merrill is allowed a range of closer relationships with the mother. "She kisses him sweet dreams" in "Days of 1935"; in the second part of "Up and Down" they meet in the vault of a bank called "Mutual Trust."[81]

Given what he's learned about succession, Merrill abandons the attempt to capture moments of amorous union. He may begin "Up and Down" with a vertiginous climb in a chair lift, but as he notes, "Au fond each summit is a cul-de-sac"; and, "The rest was all downhill." The puns have a wistful ring. Merrill forsakes erotic sublimity, or "boundlessness," for the comforts of a "Cozy Cabin": an ironic figure for those consolations art and memory provide.[82] He finds the transformative, distilling power of art in quotidian intimacies, now, like giving a haircut, and his lines conjure the sheet-wrapped beloved into a snow-covered mountain, melting as summer comes. Not that he's grown sentimental: the sheet wound round the lover is a winding-sheet as well. "Sheeted with cold, such rot and tangle must / In time be our affair," Merrill writes; and all affairs in this book take place, as the others did not, "in time."[83]

And Merrill's education in love's repetitions seems equally a lesson in forgiveness. He forgives himself for "minding less and less"; forgives himself and his lover for their inevitable separation; forgives them too, for being unable to settle for the "feast / of flaws" that love amounts to in the end. *"Forgiveness is aesthetic,"* Kristeva announces, for in it we reconcile ourselves with the realm of the ideal. "Recognizing the lack and the wound that caused it," she writes, forgiveness "fulfills them with an ideal gift—promise, project, artifice."[84] Like the late work of Stevens and Williams, then, Merrill's mature love poetry finds that the most pressing task for love is somehow to order the sorry facts of experience into a redemptive design.[85] This means that the poem of love owes its first duty of faithfulness or accuracy to the act of commiseration and to the "forgiving ideal," rather than to those facts. But it also means that the poem, for all its promise and project and artifice, may turn out to be one of the sorry facts that lovers must bring themselves to forgive. "Take these verses," the poet thus invites his lover at the end of "From Nine Sleep Valley," "call them today's flower, / Cluster a rained-in pupil might have scissored. / They too have suffered in the realm of hazard. / Sorry things all. Accepting them's the art."[86]

Forgiveness, acceptance. The love such terms describe is closer to the affectionate world of "From the Cupola" from *Nights and Days* than to anything we saw in *The Fire Screen.* But there's an emotional resiliency to these love poems foreign to Merrill's earlier verse. If all poets, as W. H. Auden suggests, are loyal to either Ariel or Prospero, to the truth of beauty or to the more-than-beautiful value of truth, then Merrill has put on Prospero's robes with an ease and authority that suggests he was never entirely in Ariel's camp to begin with. For all his commitment to poetry as "a verbal earthly paradise," he has in this volume included those elements of "the problematic, the painful, the disorderly, the ugly" that for Auden mark the Prosperian strain. And he does so precisely *by virtue of* the "artifice" of forgiveness, rather than by sacrificing artifice to authenticity.[87] The relationship that includes this disorder, these problems, even this ugliness, yet is not shattered by them, Merrill calls *friendship.* At first a little nervously: "And we are friends now? Funny friends," says the Black Mesa to its landscape; "I, he hazards, have made other friends. / The more reason, then, to part like friends" ("Strato in Plaster"). But the volume as a whole moves from an initial address to the lover as "dear light" to "Syrinx," the final poem, addressed to a "dear friend."[88]

The "story of love changing into affectionate companionship" that David Perkins finds in "The Book of Ephraim" thus retells more than the course of Merrill's decades-long love for David Jackson.[89] It suggests a wise and tender model for art. The very existence of heaven, the Other World with which JM

184

and DJ communicate, depends on the upkeep of human affection. Not of *erotic* love—for though "Ephraim's name / is Eros" in JM's novel, we can't take that name at face value. Rather the heart of the book is "DEVOTION": a devotion at once "TO EACH OTHER TO WORK TO REPRODUCTION TO AN IDEAL," as though these could not, in fact, be opposed to one another.[90] Accepting the shame of composition, the way art wins its "Ill-gotten gains" from life, *The Changing Light at Sandover* turns out to be Merrill's great poem of companionate love, as committed to that ideal as any poem I have looked at in this book. As the poet puts it to DJ in "Clearing the Title," *Sandover* is "Our poem now. It's signed JM, but grew / From life together, grain by coral grain." And if "Building on it, we let the life cloud over," then the saddened return from composition to life was equally "for heaven's sake."[91]

Merrill's love poems do not undertake the grand, political projects that connect visions of an America of love from Winthrop to Whitman to Rich. They also lack the local high drama of mutual recognition, at least as we find it in Williams, Creeley, and Lowell. Instead, after testing a series of melancholy alternatives, they find that both love and poetry are "V work," lifework, antientropic tropings of the "sorry things" of life into forgiving design. Like his contemporaries, that is to say, Merrill forsakes the poetry of ideal love to dwell in the "too pathetic, too pitiable . . . region of affection" that Emerson lamented in "Illusions." Unlike many of them, however, he takes heed of the essayist's later warning never to let "thought [be] daunted in the presence of the world."[92] When Merrill escapes pathos he does not head in the direction of ethos, the republic of conscience where Rich presides as poet laureate, but into a world of bittersweet romantic comedy.

At its luckiest, the art of love we find in *Sandover* and the late lyrics creates a room that both poet and "friend" inhabit: the "spoken space" of the Other World and *The Changing Light of Sandover* itself; the spaces of lyrics like "Clearing the Title" (for David Jackson) and "A Room at the Heart of Things" (for Peter Hooten). But the love between JM and DJ never returns, in *Sandover*, to the heat of its early days. And even in "An Upward Look," the final poem of his final book, Merrill could see himself as a man grown "colder and wiser" as he made his way back "Up from his quieted / quarry." Merrill places this old fear, however, at the *center* of his poem, not at its conclusion—which is to say, he is willing to pass through its shame to a deeper, more beautiful resolution. Like Maggie Verver in *The Golden Bowl*, he is willing to practice a necessary betrayal, to take up the work of love as a work of sacrifice, of loss, and only then of a "crucial recrystallizing / from inmost depths of clear dark blue."[93] A "rite /

distinct from both the blessing [of eros, of early rapture] and the blight [of irony, of regret]," Merrillian love does something that de Beauvoir found impossible, and that one strain of American lovers and poets have hoped for for some time.[94] It makes the "too pathetic, too pitiable world" of human interrelation turn out to be, transposed to art, a mode of salvation after all.

Notes

Introduction "If ever two were one"

1. Robert Creeley, *The Collected Essays of Robert Creeley* (Berkeley: University of California Press, 1989), p. 158.

2. Roy Harvey Pearce, *The Continuity of American Poetry* (Princeton: Princeton University Press, 1961), pp. 5–6.

3. Walt Whitman, *Complete Poetry and Collected Prose* (New York: Library of America, 1982), p. 312.

4. Emily Dickinson, *The Letters of Emily Dickinson*, ed. Thomas H. Johnson and Theodora Ward, 3 vols. (Cambridge: Belknap Press / Harvard University Press, 1958), 1:34.

5. I take the phrase "America of love" from Allen Ginsberg's "A Supermarket in California." See Allen Ginsberg, *Collected Poems, 1947–1980* (New York: Harper and Row, 1984), p. 136.

6. Anne Carson, *Eros the Bittersweet* (Princeton: Princeton University Press, 1986), p. 16.

7. I take this mordant phrase from J. V. Cunningham's "Ars Amoris." "Love's willful potion," he writes, "Veils the ensuing, / And brief, commotion." *Collected Poems and Epigrams* (Columbus: Ohio University Press, 1971), p. 65.

8. Quoted in Edmund Leites, *The Puritan Conscience and Modern Sexuality* (New Haven: Yale University Press, 1986), p. 132.

9. See Jean Hagstrum, *Esteem Enlivened by Desire: The Couple from Homer to Shakespeare* (Chicago: University of Chicago Press, 1991).

10. John Milton, "The Doctrine and Discipline of Divorce," in *Complete Poems and Major Prose*, ed. Merritt Y. Hughes (New York: Macmillan, 1957), p. 709.

11. Anthony Low, *The Reinvention of Love: Poetry, Politics, and Culture from Sidney to Milton* (Cambridge: Cambridge University Press, 1993), pp. 200–201.

12. May Swenson, "A History of Love," in *The Love Poems of May Swenson* (Boston: Houghton Mifflin, 1991), p. 37; Ortega y Gasset, *On Love*, trans. Toby Talbot (New York: Meridian Books, 1957), p. 20.

13. See, for example, Denis de Rougemont's justly famous *Love in the Western World*, trans. Montgomery Belgion (New York: Schocken, 1983). Also helpful, and indebted to de Rougemont, is David McWhirter, *Desire and Love in Henry James* (Cambridge: Cambridge University Press, 1989).

14. See Irving Singer, *The Nature of Love*, vol. 1, *Plato to Luther*; vol. 2, *Courtly and Romantic*; and vol. 3, *The Modern World* (Chicago: University of Chicago Press, 1984).

15. Plato, *The Collected Dialogues of Plato*, ed. Edith Hamilton and Huntington Cairns (Princeton: Princeton University Press, 1963), pp. 544–45.

16. According to Singer, Proust never rejects the idealist assumption that love should overcome our separateness through an act of imaginative sympathy and identification. He's a realist in the way he shows us why this act can't work. The American Proust, at least in this small way, is Emerson. Wallace Stevens, who is steeped in Emerson, and James Merrill, who loves both Proust and Stevens, treat the same sad case with very different tonal and aesthetic results.

17. Ralph Waldo Emerson, *The Collected Works of Ralph Waldo Emerson*, ed. Alfred R. Ferguson, 4 vols. to date (Cambridge: Belknap Press / Harvard University Press, 1971–), 3:81; hereafter cited as *CW*.

18. Jessica Benjamin, *The Bonds of Love: Psychoanalysis, Feminism, and the Problem of Domination* (New York: Pantheon, 1988), p. 47.

19. See Robert M. Polhemus, *Erotic Faith: Being in Love from Jane Austen to D. H. Lawrence* (Chicago: University of Chicago Press, 1990).

20. Emerson, "Experience," *CW*, 3:44.

21. I explore the meanings of "authentic" love at length in Chapter 3. I use the term here in two senses: first, for a love that is not a "mode of salvation" but merely a "human interrelation"; and second, for a love that is *eigentlich*, or willing to "own" its own desires, disappointments, and failures to fuse. For the first, see Simone de Beauvoir, *The Second Sex*, trans. H. M. Parshley (New York: Knopf, 1953), p. 654. For the second, see Stephen Kern, *The Culture of Love: Victorians to Moderns* (Cambridge: Harvard University Press, 1992), p. 5.

22. See Joseph Wood Krutch, *The Modern Temper: A Study and a Confession* (New York: Harcourt, Brace, 1929).

23. Benjamin, *Bonds of Love*, p. 36.

24. Creeley, *Collected Essays*, p. 40.

25. Julia Kristeva, *Tales of Love*, trans. Leon S. Roudiez (New York: Columbia University Press, 1987), p. 380.

26. Hugh Kenner, "The Making of the Modernist Canon," in *Mazes* (San Francisco: North Point Press, 1989), p. 42.

27. For Milton's importance in the "otherwise inexplicable historical myth" of the Puritan origins of American literature, and for the bracing suggestion that *Paradise Lost* is "a more American poem than, say, Bradstreet's 'Contemplations,'" see William C. Spengemann, *A New World of Words: Redefining Early American Literature* (New Haven: Yale University Press, 1994), pp. 96, 116. For a useful reading of Milton's *Doctrine and Discipline of Divorce* as a manifesto of federal love, see Stanley Cavell, "Two Cheers for Romance," in *Passionate Attachments*, ed. Williard Gaylin and Ethel Person (London: Macmillan, 1988), pp. 85–100.

28. For examples of Winthrop's "Modell" as a predictive text, see Douglas Anderson, *A House Undivided: Domesticity and Community in American Literature* (Cambridge: Cambridge University Press, 1990), pp. 2–18. Since the mid-1970s, claims for a "continuity" of American culture from the Puritans through the nineteenth century have come under increasing criticism. They entail, according to William Spengemann, "a kind of verbal shell game, in which the prestidigitator places his thematic pea under one shell labeled 'Puritan,' makes a lot of rapid movements on his typewriter, and then produces the pea from under another shell marked 'American literature.'" See his "Review Essay [of Emory Elliot's *Puritan Influences in American Literature*]," *Early American Literature* 16 (1981): 179–84. Nevertheless, in the case of idolatry, the historical work of Karen Lystra and others establishes a continuity of concern—one revealed in diaries and love letters, as well as in more literary texts. See Karen Lystra, *Searching the Heart: Women, Men, and Romantic Love in Nineteenth-Century America* (New York: Oxford University Press, 1989). For an excellent summary of the "continuities" controversy through the late 1980s, with extensive notes to the relevant parries and ripostes, see Philip Gura, "The Study of Colonial American Literature, 1966–1987: A Vade Mecum," *William and Mary Quarterly* 45 (April 1988): 305–41.

29. John Winthrop, "A Modell of Christian Charity," in *Winthrop Papers*, vol. 2 (Boston: Massachusetts Historical Society, 1931), pp. 282–95.

30. See Elizabeth Cady Stanton, "The Solitude of Self," in *Elizabeth Cady Stanton / Susan B. Anthony: Correspondence, Writings, Speeches*, ed. Ellen Carol DuBois (New York: Schocken, 1981).

31. I paraphrase, in part, Stanley Cavell: "In making the knowledge of others a metaphysical difficulty, philosophers deny how real the practical difficulty is of coming to know another person, and how little we can reveal of ourselves to another's gaze, or bear of it. Doubtless such denials are part of the motive which sustains metaphysical difficulties." *The Claim of Reason* (New York: Oxford University Press, 1979), p. 90. Cavell spots this undoing of the intimate relationship between knower and known in Lutheran theology, Cartesian philosophy, and the tragedies of Shakespeare. See *Claim*, p. 470, and *Disowning Knowledge in Six Plays of Shakespeare* (Cambridge: Cambridge University Press, 1987).

32. Cavell, "Two Cheers," p. 91; and *Disowning*, p. 10.

33. De Beauvoir, *Second Sex*, p. 654.

34. John Milton, "Doctrine and Discipline," p. 707. For a helpful, nuanced explana-

tion of this tension in Puritan love doctrine, see Robert Daly, *God's Altar: The World and the Flesh in Puritan Poetry* (Berkeley: University of California Press, 1978), p. 104.

35. See William Haller and Malleville Haller, "The Puritan Art of Love," *Huntington Library Quarterly* 5 (January 1942): 271, and Edmund Leites, "The Duty to Desire: Love, Friendship, and Sexuality in Some Puritan Theories of Marriage," *Comparative Civilizations Review* 10–11 (1983–84): 124.

36. Singer, *Nature of Love*, 2:6.

37. Winthrop, "Modell," pp. 290–91.

38. Singer, *Nature of Love*, 2:254.

39. John Saffin, *John Saffin His Book (1665–1708)*, intro. Caroline Hazard (New York: Harbor Press, 1928), p. 72.

40. Thomas Thatcher, "A Love Letter," in *Seventeenth-Century American Poetry*, ed. Harrison T. Meserole (New York: New York University Press, 1968), p. 406.

41. Quoted in Frederick Morgan, *The Puritan Family: Religion and Domestic Relations in Seventeenth-Century New England* (New York: Harper and Row, 1966), p. 52.

42. William Shakespeare, *Troilus and Cressida*, 3.2.80–83.

43. Walter Hughes, " 'Meat Out of the Eater': Panic and Desire in American Puritan Poetry," in *Engendering Men: The Question of Male Feminist Criticism*, ed. Joseph Allen Boone and Michael Cadden (New York: Routledge, 1990), p. 104. For the promise that God's caresses will be "full and uninterrupted," see Samuel Willard's *A Compleat Body of Divinity*, quoted in Kathleen Verduin, " 'Our Cursed Natures': Sexuality and the Puritan Conscience," *New England Quarterly* 56 (June 1983): 235.

44. *The Bay Psalm Book*, quoted in Jeffrey A. Hammond, *Sinful Self, Saintly Self: The Puritan Experience of Poetry* (Athens: University of Georgia Press, 1993), p. 4.

45. For Bradstreet's reaction against Petrarchan ideals of love, see Ann Stanford, *Anne Bradstreet: The Worldly Puritan* (New York: Burt Franklin, 1974), pp. 20–21. For a more general account of the Puritan response to Petrarchism, see Leites, *Puritan Conscience*, pp. 2–11.

46. I pick up an image from Daniel Rogers: "Put case," asks Rogers, that "thou hadst grounds of first love to thy companion: what then? Thinks thou that this edge will hold without dayly whetting?" Quoted in Leites, "Duty to Desire," p. 138.

47. Anne Bradstreet, *The Works of Anne Bradstreet*, ed. Jeannine Hensley (Cambridge: Harvard University Press, 1967), p. 225. Bradstreet also wrote several weaker, occasional verses for her husband. They focus on his illness and recovery, or on his departure for, absence in, and return from England. These later efforts are not up to the standard of the earlier suite. They're *private* work—more prayers than poems, really—and the "fainting soul" we find in them is less compelling than the brave one who risked idolatry through her skill with "seeming thine."

48. Quoted in Joseph Allen Boone, *Tradition Counter Tradition: Love and the Form of Fiction* (Chicago: University of Chicago Press, 1987), p. 51.

49. The Italian humanist Marsilio Ficino, for example, taught that lovers die in themselves to be reborn through each other in a "double resurrection," with each lover

now possessing a double self, his lover's and his own. Quoted in Singer, *Nature of Love*, 2:174–75.

50. See Stanford, *Anne Bradstreet*, pp. 139–41. Bradstreet's response to Sidney recalls Milton's dismissal of Petrarchan love in *Paradise Lost*. See Low, *Reinvention*, p. 200.

51. Edward Taylor, *The Poems of Edward Taylor*, ed. Donald E. Stanford (Chapel Hill: University of North Carolina Press, 1989), pp. 8–9, 5.

52. John Milton, *Paradise Lost*, 4.299, in *Complete Poems and Major Prose*, p. 285.

53. Adrienne Rich, "The Tensions of Anne Bradstreet," in *On Lies, Secrets, and Silence* (New York: Norton, 1979), p. 22.

54. Ivy Schweitzer, *The Work of Self-Representation: Lyric Poetry in Colonial New England* (Chapel Hill: University of North Carolina Press, 1991), p. 178, my emphasis.

55. I take the phrase "fictive design" from Rosamund Rosenmeier, *Anne Bradstreet Revisited* (Boston: Twayne, 1991), pp. xiii and 10–12. See also Daly, *God's Altar*, p. 88, Hammond, *Sinful Self*, pp. 83–84, and William J. Scheick, *Design in Puritan American Literature* (Lexington: University Press of Kentucky, 1992), pp. 32–45. Like Rosenmeier, I use the word "fictive" with an emphasis on its overtones of shaping and fashioning, rather than of feigning or deceit. As Hammond insists, "It would be wrong to describe Bradstreet's speaker . . . as a deliberately invented self. In poem after poem she forged what *she* saw as the very opposite of a fictive voice—an identity shaped not by human invention but divine truth." *Sinful Self*, p. 139.

56. Bradstreet, *Works*, p. 226.

57. Daly, *God's Altar*, pp. 106–7, 108.

58. Hammond, *Sinful Self*, p. 89.

59. Rosenmeier, *Anne Bradstreet*, p. 124.

60. Ibid.

61. Quoted in ibid., Rosenmeier, *Anne Bradstreet Revisited*, p. 102.

62. Bradstreet, *Works*, p. 225.

63. John Donne, *Selected Poetry and Prose*, ed. T. W. Craik and R. J. Craik (New York: Methuen, 1986), p. 86.

64. Singer, *Nature of Love*, 2:245.

65. Milton, *Paradise Lost*, 9.955–62, 965–71.

66. "Let this caution be minded," wrote Benjamin Wadsworth in *The Well-Ordered Family*, "that they don't love inordinately, because death will soon part them." Quoted in Morgan, *Puritan Family*, p. 49. When Cotton Mather linked this "inordinate" love to "Inexpressible Uncleannesses in the Married State," he had his reasons: idealist love and common lust are both exorbitant, both unwilling to remain within established bounds. Quoted in Verduin, "Our Cursed Natures," pp. 225–26.

67. Milton, *Paradise Lost*, 12.617–18, my emphasis.

68. In their own small way her allusions provide the "contagion of illicit love" that George Bataille insists we need to stir up the "rudimentary eroticism of marriage." See his *Erotism: Death and Sensuality* (New York: Ballantine Books, 1962), pp. 112–13.

69. I quote from Ellen K. Rothman, *Hands and Hearts: A History of Courtship in America* (New York: Basic Books, 1984), p. 19; and Lystra, *Searching*, p. 234.

70. See Martin F. Tupper, "Of Marriage" and "Of Love," in *Proverbial Philosophy* (London: Thomas Hatchard, Piccadilly, 1854), pp. 162, 159. The Rod McKuen of his day, Tupper eventually sold over 300,000 copies of *Proverbial Philosophy*, one of them to Whitman, who filled it with underlinings and marginalia. See David Reynolds, *Walt Whitman's America: A Cultural Biography* (New York: Knopf, 1995), p. 315.

71. You can see the change in a tasty paraphrase of Canticles 5 by Jane Coleman (later Turrell): a passage Bradstreet invoked in "To My Dear and Loving Husband." "*Who is thy love?*" the "*scornful Maids*" that surround Coleman's Shulamite-bride demand. "For what Form waste you your Bloom in sighs? / Let's know the *Man*, if he be worth your Care." In response the poet dwells on his manly attractiveness: his "well turn'd Legs" that "like stately Pillars stand / Of Marble, polished by a curious Hand." She sees no need to read him as a figure for Christ. Quoted in Emily Stipes Watts, *The Poetry of American Women from 1632 to 1945* (Austin: University of Texas Press, 1977), p. 32.

72. William Horne, *Making a Heaven of Hell: The Problem of the Companionate Ideal in English Marriage Poetry, 1650–1800* (Athens: University of Georgia Press, 1993), pp. 279, 295. In her amatory acrostic "Oh, may propitious Heaven . . . ," published in the mid-1750s, Martha Brewster thus begs God to "Love us up to Heaven," implying that the couple will be carried up as such, a proposition that Bradstreet, though tempted, scrupled to suggest. *Poems on Divers Subjects* (Boston, 1757), p. 33.

73. Richard Henry Dana Sr., "The Husband and Wife's Grave," in *Poems* (Boston: Bowles and Dearborn, 1827), p. 79; my emphasis.

74. Quoted in Lystra, *Searching*, p. 246.

75. Erotic faith, writes Polhemus, is "an emotional conviction, ultimately religious in nature, that meaning, value, hope, and even transcendence can be found through love—erotically focused love, the kind of love we mean when we say that people are in love." *Erotic Faith*, p. 1.

76. Lystra, *Searching*, pp. 256–58.

77. Ibid., p. 42.

78. Mary E. Hewitt, "He Loves Me," in *Poems: Sacred, Passionate, and Legendary* (New York, 1854), p. 87.

79. For a demographic account of this shift in marriage patterns, see Lee Chambers-Schiller, *Liberty, a Better Husband: Single Women in America; the Generations of 1780–1840* (New Haven: Yale University Press, 1984), p. 5.

80. Margaret Fuller, "The Great Lawsuit," in *The Harper American Literature, Vol. 1*, ed. Donald McQuade et al. (New York: Harper and Row, 1987), pp. 1210, 1203, 1210. "I whose name is Unit," Emerson called himself in a letter to Fuller. His published work is full of such pronouncements. "No man is fit for society who is not fit to stand alone," he told the Second Church congregation in 1829. "The condition which high friendship demands is ability to do without it," he attests in his essay "Friendship." "There must be

two, before there can be very one." *The Letters of Ralph Waldo Emerson*, ed. Ralph L. Rusk, 6 vols. (New York: Columbia University Press, 1939), 2:258; *The Complete Sermons of Ralph Waldo Emerson*, ed. Albert J. von Frank, 4 vols. (Columbia: University of Missouri Press, 1989–92), 2:84; and *CW*, 2:123.

81. For Duffy's claim, see Bernard Duffy, *Poetry in America: Expression and Its Values in the Times of Bryant, Whitman, and Pound* (Durham, N.C.: Duke University Press, 1978), p. xiii. See Gertrude Reif Hughes, " 'Imagining the Existence of Something Uncreated': Elements of Emerson in Adrienne Rich's *The Dream of a Common Language*," in *Reading Adrienne Rich*, ed. Jane Roberta Cooper (Ann Arbor: University of Michigan Press, 1984), pp. 152–53; and Virginia M. Kouidis, "Prison into Prism: Emerson's 'Many-Colored Lenses' and the Woman Writer of Early Modernism," in *The Green American Tradition: Essays and Poems for Sherman Paul*, ed. H. Daniel Peck (Baton Rouge: Louisiana State University Press, 1989), pp. 115–34.

82. Emerson, "Historic Notes of Life and Letters in New England," in *The Complete Works of Ralph Waldo Emerson*, ed. Edward Waldo Emerson, 12 vols. (Boston: Houghton-Mifflin, 1903–4), 10:325, 329; hereafter cited as *W*.

83. Emerson, "The Uses of Great Men," in *CW*, 4:15, and "The Initial, Daemonic, and Celestial Love," in *W*, 9:96–97, 104.

84. Emerson, *CW*, 2:164.

85. Robert D. Richardson Jr., *Emerson: The Mind on Fire* (Berkeley: University of California Press, 1995), p. 92.

86. Recall the Puritan admonishment: "Let this caution be minded, that they don't love inordinately, because death will soon part them." Quoted in Morgan, *Puritan Family*, p. 49.

87. Emerson, *Collected Poems and Translations*, ed. Harold Bloom and Paul Kane (New York: Library of America, 1994), pp. 326, 331, 326.

88. Lystra, *Searching*, pp. 241–42.

89. Emerson, *The Early Lectures of Ralph Waldo Emerson*, ed. Stephen E. Whicher, Robert E. Spiller, and Wallace E. Williams, 3 vols. (Cambridge: Belknap Press / Harvard University Press, 1959–72), 1:278–79, hereafter cited as *EL*; and "The Oversoul," in *CW*, 2:164.

90. See *W*, 9:92; *EL*, 2:279; and *CW*, 2:164.

91. Emerson, *Collected Poems*, p. 75.

92. For typical responses to Emerson's account of love, see John McCormick, " 'The Heyday of the Blood': Ralph Waldo Emerson," in *American Declarations of Love*, ed. Ann Massa (London: Macmillan, 1990), and Erik Ingvar Thurin, *Emerson as Priest of Pan* (Lawrence: Regents Press of Kansas, 1981).

93. See, respectively, Emerson, *Letters*, 4:33; "Philosopher," in *W*, 9:314; and "Love," in *CW*, 2:105–6, 108.

94. Emerson, *The Journals and Miscellaneous Notebooks of Ralph Waldo Emerson*, ed. William H. Gilman et al., 16 vols. (Cambridge: Belknap Press / Harvard University Press, 1960–82), 7:368; hereafter cited as *JMN*.

194

95. Emerson, *CW,* 2:109, 3:43–44.

96. Emerson, "The Heart," in *EL,* 2:278–79; "Love," in *EL,* 3:56; "Nominalist and Realist," in *CW,* 3:135; and "Love," in *CW,* 2:126, 117.

97. Emerson, "Experience," in *CW,* 3:44.

98. Creeley, *Collected Essays,* p. 158.

99. Emerson, "Love," in *CW,* 2:109. When Emerson infamously declares that "love is temporary and ends with marriage," he has this enjoyment in mind. "Marriage is the perfection love aimed at," this passage continues, "ignorant of what it sought. Marriage is a good known only to the parties. A relation of perfect understanding, aid, content-ment, possession of themselves and of the world—which dwarfs love to green fruit." See *JMN,* 11:199.

100. I give a full-scale reading of them in my essay " 'Too Pathetic, Too Pitiable': Emerson's Lessons in Love's Philosophy," *ESQ: A Journal of the American Renaissance* 40, no. 2 (1994): 139–82.

101. Emerson, *CW,* 2:115, 119, 121; 4:72; and 2:121.

102. Ibid., 2:127.

103. Emerson, "Experience," ibid., 3:35; "Illusions," in *W,* 6:319.

104. Whitman, "To You," in *Complete Poetry,* pp. 376–77.

105. Cavell, *Disowning,* p. 10.

106. Emerson, *CW,* 2:190.

Chapter 1   An Example to Lovers

1. In the *Lysis* Socrates skewers the lovestruck young poet Hippothales for his un-conscious self-aggrandizement. For the quotation about lusciousness, see Whitman, *Complete Poetry,* p. 212.

2. Leslie Fiedler, *No! in Thunder* (Boston: Beacon Press, 1960), p. 70. For examples of these critical opinions, see Anderson, *House Undivided,* pp. 137–38, and Kerry C. Lar-son, *Whitman's Drama of Consensus* (Chicago: University of Chicago Press, 1988), pp. 98–99. I take the contrast between children's and prosody's feet from James Merrill's "Up and Down," in *Selected Poems: 1946–1985* (New York: Knopf, 1992), p. 230. As Fiedler's remarks make clear, "successful" love affairs should be both heterosexual and fertile. For an elaborate attack on such invidious assumptions, see Michael Moon, "Rereading Whitman under Pressure of AIDS," in *The Continuing Presence of Walt Whitman: The Life after the Life,* ed. Robert K. Martin (Iowa City: University of Iowa Press, 1992), pp. 53–66.

3. Moon, "Rereading," p. 66.

4. Whitman, "Starting from Paumanok" and "Letter to Ralph Waldo Emerson," in *Complete Poetry,* pp. 179, 1334–35. For an example of such historical-cum-erotic-political readings, see M. Jimmie Killingsworth, *Whitman's Poetry of the Body: Sexuality, Politics, and the Text* (Chapel Hill: University of North Carolina Press, 1989). David Reynolds's sprawling *Walt Whitman's America* gives an encompassing introduction to

the poet and his times—one that challenges intuitive notions of Whitman's daring and sexual prophecy, especially when it comes to same-sex love.

5. Whitman, *Complete Poetry*, p. 1010.

6. Alicia Ostriker, "Loving Walt Whitman and the Problem of America," in *Continuing Presence of Walt Whitman*, pp. 222, 227.

7. I quote from "Scented Herbage of My Breast," Whitman, *Collected Poetry*, p. 269; and *Notebooks and Unpublished Prose Manuscripts*, ed. Edward F. Grier, 6 vols. (New York: New York University Press, 1984), 1:96, hereafter cited as *NUPM*. "I do not believe the people of these days are happy," Whitman declares in a notebook (*NUPM*, 1:216). With economic dislocations, the threat of war, and rising rates of divorce and infidelity marking the antebellum decades, they had reasons. See M. Wynn Thomas, *The Lunar Light of Whitman's Poetry* (Cambridge: Harvard University Press, 1987), pp. 10–35.

8. Readers' responses to this address range from the naive to the embarrassed to the analytic-resistant to the touched and grateful. See, respectively, Justin Kaplan, *Walt Whitman: A Life* (New York: Simon and Schuster, 1980), pp. 329–34; David Leverenz, *Manhood and the American Renaissance* (Ithaca: Cornell University Press, 1989), pp. 29–32; Larson, *Whitman's Drama*, pp. 46–47 and 50–51; Terry Nathanson, *Whitman's Presence: Body, Voice, and Writing in Leaves of Grass* (New York: New York University Press, 1992), pp. 352–59; and Hart Crane's line "My hand / in yours, / Walt Whitman— / so—," in *The Complete Poems and Selected Letters and Prose of Hart Crane*, ed. Brom Weber (Garden City, N.Y.: Doubleday, 1966), p. 95.

9. Cavell, *Disowning*, p. 37.

10. Whitman, *Complete Poetry*, pp. 11–12, 1010.

11. See Kaplan, *Walt Whitman*, pp. 327–34.

12. The "language of love . . . is literature," Kristeva thus writes, and the "imagination is a discourse of transference—of love." *Tales*, pp. 1, 381.

13. Emerson, *CW*, 3:44.

14. Ibid., 2:190.

15. Ibid., 3:29. For a reading of the "handsome" and "manipular" wordplay in "Experience," see Cavell, "Founding as Finding," in *This New Yet Unapproachable America* (Albuquerque: Living Batch Press, 1989), p. 87.

16. See Singer, *Nature of Love*, 1:3–22.

17. Whitman, "A Song for Occupations," in *Complete Poetry*, p. 357.

18. See Singer, *Nature of Love*, 1:13.

19. Whitman, *Complete Poetry*, p. 9.

20. Ibid., p. 370.

21. Singer, *Nature of Love*, 1:9.

22. Ibid., 1:18.

23. Ibid., 1:15–16.

24. "Love supplements the human search for value with a capacity for bestowing it gratuitously," Singer writes. "To one who has succeeded in cultivating this attitude,

anything may become an object of love." Ibid., 1:14. His example is "the saint," but in Whitman, this lover of all is the Poet.

25. Whitman, *NUPM*, 1:74.

26. Whitman, *Complete Poetry*, p. 91.

27. Whitman, "I Sing the Body Electric," in ibid., p. 123.

28. Whitman, ibid., p. 57.

29. Frank O'Hara, *Selected Poems*, ed. Donald Allen (New York: Vintage, 1974), p. 175.

30. Singer, *Nature of Love*, 1:16.

31. Whitman, *Complete Poetry*, pp. 27, 38.

32. Winthrop, "Modell," p. 292.

33. Whitman, "These I Singing in Spring" and "Song of Myself," in *Complete Poetry*, pp. 273, 76.

34. Ezra Pound will speak of these as moments "when a man feels his immortality upon him." *The Spirit of Romance* (New York: New Directions, 1968), p. 94.

35. Whitman, *Complete Poetry*, pp. 299–300.

36. Kristeva, *Tales*, pp. 6, 33.

37. Whitman, *Complete Poetry*, pp. 51–52.

38. Martha C. Nussbaum, *Love's Knowledge: Essays on Philosophy and Literature* (Oxford: Oxford University Press, 1990), p. 282.

39. Whitman, "Song of Myself," in *Complete Poetry*, p. 29.

40. Whitman, *Complete Poetry*, pp. 177, 179. Whitman certainly understood the appeal of Emerson's "noble doubt" about the reality of the phenomenal world. In "There Was a Child Went Forth" his representative boy-poet suffers "The doubts of daytime and the doubts of nighttime. . . . the curious whether and how, / Whether that which appears so is so. . . . Or is it all flashes and specks?" But Whitman connects these epistemological twinges to the boy's father, with his bargaining, craftiness, and self-sufficiency. He contrasts them to the mother's "affection" and "mild words" in their quiet, detailed distinctiveness. Compare the reductive "is it all flashes and specks" with the loving specificity of "light falling on roofs and gables of white or brown, three miles off" and the water's "quickbroken crests and slapping." If the first is not quite "the quick loud word" of the father, it's heading in that direction, driving too hard a bargain with language and perception. *Complete Poetry*, pp. 138–39.

41. Cavell, *Disowning*, pp. 5–6.

42. Ibid., p. 95. "There is no life without satisfaction," the poet declares in "To Think of Time"; "What is the earth? what are body and soul without satisfaction?" See Whitman, *Complete Poems*, p. 105. For discussions of satisfaction and skepticism, see Cavell, *Disowning*, pp. 95–97 and 108–9; elsewhere Cavell applauds Blake's "brave acceptance of the sufficiency of human finitude, an achievement of the complete disappearance of its disappointment, in oneself and in others, an acknowledgment of satisfaction and of reciprocity." *Claim*, p. 471.

43. Whitman, *Complete Poetry*, pp. 53, 275.

44. Ibid., p. 192.

45. Ibid., pp. 192, 193, 204; my emphasis. In an early draft of "Song of Myself," Whitman insists on the ordinariness of his knowledge even more explicitly. "I am the poet of reality," he announces; "I say that the earth is not an echo, / Nor man," whatever Emerson may say, "an apparition."

> I have split the earth and the hard coal and rocks and the solid bed of the sea
> And went down to reconnoiter there a long time,
> And bring back a report,
> And I understand that those are positive and dense every one
> And that what they seem to the child they are.

These lines display the romantic hope for an innocence after experience, a childlike pleasure and confidence in the world that is regained not by ignoring "the doubts of daytime and the doubts of nighttime" which mark the end of childhood but by passing through these doubts into a new assurance and faith in the local, the commonly known. *Uncollected Poetry and Prose of Walt Whitman*, vol. 2, ed. Emory Holloway (New York: Doubleday, 1921), p. 64; for "the doubts," see "There was a child went forth," in *Complete Poetry*, p. 139.

46. Whitman, *Complete Poetry*, pp. 250–51.

47. Singer, *Nature of Love*, 1:9.

48. See Theodore Van de Velde, *Ideal Marriage: Its Physiology and Technique* (New York: Random House, 1941), p. 157. For other late-century claims about the innocent, soulful potential of sex, see Peter Gardella, *Innocent Ecstasy* (New York: Oxford University Press, 1985), pp. 69–75.

49. William James, *The Principles of Psychology* (selections), in *William James: The Essential Writings*, ed. Bruce W. Wilshire (Albany: State University of New York Press, 1984), p. 83.

50. Adrienne Rich, *The Fact of a Doorframe: Poems Selected and New, 1950–84* (New York: Norton, 1984), p. 241. I quote Rich advisedly. Philosophical skepticism, including Emerson's "noble doubt," has been seen as a masculine "flight from the feminine," a revolt against the entanglements and claims of the domestic, the body, and the everyday, all identified with women. See Cavell, *Disowning*, pp. 16–17, and Susan R. Bordo, *The Flight to Objectivity: Essays on Cartesianism and Culture* (Albany: SUNY Press, 1987), pp. 97–112. Whitman calls a halt to that retreat. Hence, no doubt, the link between him and the "Imperative of Intimacy" that Ostriker spots at the heart of contemporary women's love poetry in "Loving Walt Whitman."

51. D. H. Lawrence, *Studies in Classic American Literature* (New York: Viking, 1961), pp. 165, 169.

52. Whitman, *Complete Poetry*, p. 269; Lawrence, *Studies*, pp. 173–74.

53. Kern, *Culture*, pp. 289, 286, 290.

54. Whitman, *Complete Poetry*, pp. 269, 271.

55. Ibid., p. 55.

56. Bataille, *Erotism*, p. 55.

57. Whitman, *Complete Poetry*, p. 55.

58. Lawrence, *Studies*, pp. 174, 176.

59. Whitman, *Complete Poetry*, p. 9.

60. Benjamin, *Bonds of Love*, p. 192.

61. Whitman, *Complete Poetry*, pp. 251–52.

62. Camille Paglia, *Sexual Personae* (New Haven: Yale University Press, 1990), p. 607.

63. See Nathanson, *Whitman's Presence*, p. 92.

64. This vision of other-reliance is shared by William James and his philosophical sparring partner Josiah Royce. "I am not first self-conscious and then secondarily conscious of my fellow," writes Royce. "On the contrary, I am conscious of myself . . . as in relation to some real or ideal fellow, and apart from my consciousness of my fellow, I have only secondary and derived states and habits of self-consciousness." *Studies of Good and Evil* (New York: Appleton, 1898), p. 201. It is a hallmark of continental phenomenologies of love during this period as well. See Kern, *Culture*, p. 43.

65. Whitman, *Complete Poetry*, p. 280.

66. Kristeva, *Tales*, pp. 4, 11.

67. Ibid., pp. 15, 7, 11.

68. Reynolds, *Whitman's America*, pp. 326, 332; Whitman quoted on 331.

69. As Jay Grossman explains, in the years before the war Whitman "remains deeply committed to resolving the crisis of the republic, even and especially when he appears to us to be 'only' profoundly sexual." See Jay Grossman, " 'The Evangel-Poem of Comrades and of Love': Revising Whitman's Republicanism." *ATQ* 4, n.s. (September 1990): 215.

70. Whitman, "These I Singing in Spring," in *Complete Poetry*, p. 273.

71. Emerson, *W,* 6:319.

72. Whitman, *Complete Poetry*, pp. 376–77.

73. Ibid., pp. 72, 47, 90.

74. Thomas, *Lunar Light*, pp. 22, 10, 14, 35.

75. Whitman, *Complete Poetry*, pp. 93–94.

76. Ibid., p. 306.

77. Ibid., p. 376.

78. Quoted in Helen Vendler, *The Music of What Happens* (Cambridge: Harvard University Press, 1988), p. 372.

79. I have equated Whitman's bestowals with God's free grace, his agape. Kristeva equates agape with the crucial "primary identification" that brings the infant subject into being. *Tales*, p. 50.

80. Julia Kristeva, "Joyce 'The Gracehoper' or the Return of Orpheus," in *James Joyce: The Augmented Ninth*, ed. Bernard Benstock (Syracuse, N.Y.: Syracuse University Press, 1988), p. 169.

81. Whitman, *Complete Poetry*, pp. 114–16.

82. Harold Bloom, Introduction to *Walt Whitman* (New York: Chelsea House, 1985), pp. 3–4.

83. Quoted in Paul Zweig, *Walt Whitman: The Making of the Poet* (New York: Basic Books, 1984), pp. 19–20.

84. See Larson, *Whitman's Drama*, pp. 48, 251.

85. Whitman, *Complete Poetry*, p. 375.

86. Larson, *Whitman's Drama*, pp. 47, 51.

87. Nathanson, *Whitman's Presence*, p. 359.

88. Ibid., pp. 13, 15.

89. Jacques Derrida, *Of Grammatology*, trans. Gayatri Chakravorty Spivak (Baltimore: Johns Hopkins University Press, 1974), p. 141. The poet is prepared to claim for writing what the French phenomenologist Maurice Merleau-Ponty claims for spoken language. "In speech," Merleau-Ponty explains, "we realize the impossible agreement between two rival totalities [that is, two speaking subjects] not because speech forces us back upon ourselves to discover some unique spirit in which we participate but because speech concerns us, catches us indirectly, seduces us, trails us along, transforms us into the other and him into us, abolishes the limit between mine and not-mine, and ends the alternative between what has sense for me and what is non-sense for me, between me as subject and the other as object." *The Prose of the World* (Evanston, Ill.: Northwestern University Press, 1973), p. 145.

90. W. H. Auden, *The Dyer's Hand* (New York: Vintage International, 1989), p. 23.

91. Emerson, *CS*, 2:66.

92. Whitman, *Complete Poetry*, pp. 310, 312.

93. Mark Bauerlein, *Whitman and the American Idiom* (Baton Rouge: Louisiana State University Press, 1991), pp. 120–57. A quote from Melville's *Pierre* illuminates his hopes and failures: "If to affirm, be to expand one's isolated self; and to deny, be to contract one's isolated self, then to respond is a suspension of all isolation." *Pierre; Israel Potter; The Piazza Tales; The Confidence Man; Uncollected Prose; Billy Budd, Sailor* (New York: Library of America, 1984), p. 341. Emerson, we may well say, denies. Whitman invites response. But by the 1860s his disappointment in the response he actually *received* leads him to affirm and expand, expand and affirm, as the close of "Brooklyn Ferry" will show. See Nathanson, *Whitman's Presence*, pp. 259–64.

94. For an explanation of such "lyric moments" in love poetry, particularly as distinguished from epistolary love poems, see Maeera Yaffa Shreiber, "The Discourse of Love in the Lyric and the Letter," Ph. D. diss., Brandeis University, 1991 (Ann Arbor: UMI, no. 9129754), pp. 1–57.

95. Whitman, *Complete Poetry*, p. 389.

96. Several "arrogant poems" can, in fact, be seen peeping between the new lines. When Whitman confesses that "I have not really understood any thing . . . / Nature here . . . taking advantage of me to dart upon me and sting me," we hear a parenthetical comment from "Of the Terrible Doubt of Appearances," where the world's apparitions "dart out of themselves as if to confound me and mock me!" Likewise, and more touch-

ingly, when the echoes of his earlier "blab" of poetry recoil upon him, Whitman exclaims that he is "baffled, balk'd, bent to the very earth"—a line that borrows a term from the climax of "Crossing Brooklyn Ferry": "Throb, baffled and curious brain! throw out questions and answers!" Clearly those answers no longer suffice. *Complete Poetry*, pp. 274, 312.

97. Ibid., p. 395.

98. Thomas B. Byers, *What I Cannot Say: Self, Word, and World in Whitman, Stevens, and Merwin* (Chicago: University of Illinois Press, 1989), p. 41.

99. Roland Barthes, *A Lover's Discourse: Fragments*, trans. Richard Howard (New York: Farrar, Straus and Giroux, 1978), p. 100.

100. For Anderson, this redemption from loneliness does not occur. *"Leaves of Grass* is, finally, a marriage that fails," he writes, because of the poet's "inability to locate a lover, outside himself, who could sustain the immense weight of significance and expectation that Whitman attached to 'adhesiveness.'" *House Undivided*, p. 137. I disagree. The book is a courtship, not a marriage. It tests us, and entreats us to *be* that lover as we read.

101. Whitman, *Complete Poetry*, pp. 671, 275, 287, 308, 270, 286, 671.

102. Ibid., pp. 285, 271.

103. Ibid., pp. 270, 277, 270, 275 (my emphasis), 277.

104. See Nathanson, *Whitman's Presence*, p. 442.

105. Whitman, *Complete Poetry*, pp. 287, 289.

106. "When the object that I incorporate is the speech of the other," writes Kristeva—restating the "Crossing Brooklyn Ferry" project from the reader's perspective — "I bind myself to him in a primary fusion, communion, unification. An identification. . . . In being able to receive the other's words, to assimilate, repeat, and reproduce them, I become like him: One. A subject of enunciation. Through psychic osmosis / identification. Through love." *Tales*, p. 26.

107. Although I cannot prove direct influence—indeed, Whitman's letters are comparatively artless—Whitman's therapeutic poetry of love recalls the patterns of test and reassurance observed by Karen Lystra in nineteenth-century American epistolary courtships. In these exchanges, Lystra observes, "a prospective mate's emotional commitment was assessed repeatedly through negative self-images, presented to test the reaction of the potential partner." In a rhythm of self-disclosure or self-criticism and positive response, "the partners reassured each other that they were indeed capable, attractive, intelligent, and worthy," each hastening to "hold up a roseate mirror to the loved one." *Searching*, pp. 38–39.

This mirror did not exclude or deny each partner's shortcomings. Rather, to use Singer's terms, it set those appraisals in a context of bestowal, so that one might be loved in spite of or in part *because* of one's faults and fears. A lover might confess that he had "Blabb'd, blush'd, resented, lied, stole, grudg'd," and so on, as Whitman does in "Crossing Brooklyn Ferry" (*Complete Poetry*, p. 311). And his reader and correspondent, like the critic M. Wynn Thomas, would probably note the "glib ecstasy of self-accusation" in his lines (*Lunar Light*, p. 104). He or she would, then, respond to this overstated weakness as the poet has treated our own earlier confessions, with a pooh-poohing forgiveness.

Again, let me stress, Whitman's own love letters show few of these features. By and large, he's simply sweet and paternal, refusing to enter into cycles of confession and embrace.

I cite Thomas here in part because Lystra's description of epistolary courtships so closely resembles his reading of Whitman's "poetry of praise." The "strong dose of reassurance" they administered from lover to lover "had public as well as private implications," Lystra observes. American culture "increasingly emphasized individual motivation and achievement"; and "the fostering of self-esteem and nurturing of individual ego strength" assured lovers of an identity outside and above their public roles, while giving them greater strength to take part in an increasingly competitive and alienating economy. *Searching*, p. 40.

108. Shreiber, *Discourse of Love*, pp. 41, 43–47.

109. Lystra, *Searching*, p. 24.

110. Whitman, *Complete Poetry*, p. 611.

111. Emerson, "Gifts," in *CW*, 3:94; for an example of such resistance, see Larson, *Whitman's Drama*, pp. 48–49.

112. John Ashbery, *Self-Portrait in a Convex Mirror* (New York: Penguin, 1976), p. 57.

113. Stephen Railton, "'As If I Were With You'—The Performance of Whitman's Poetry," in *The Cambridge Companion to Walt Whitman*, ed. Ezra Greenspan (Cambridge: Cambridge University Press, 1995), p. 21.

114. Whitman, "Democratic Vistas," *Complete Poetry*, p. 960.

115. Emily Dickinson, poem 1, in *The Complete Poems of Emily Dickinson*, ed. Thomas H. Johnson (Boston: Little, Brown, 1960), pp. 3–4; hereafter cited parenthetically in the text as "P" and the Thomas Johnson poem number.

116. Dickinson, *Letters*, 1:34; hereafter cited parenthetically in the text as "L" and the number.

Chapter 2 "Bondage as Play"

1. For information about Austin's mutilations, see R. W. Franklin, *The Editing of Emily Dickinson: A Reconsideration* (Madison: University of Wisconsin Press, 1967), pp. 78–81; Betsy Erkkila, *The Wicked Sisters: Women Poets, Literary History, and Discord* (Oxford: Oxford University Press, 1992), p. 28; and especially Martha Nell Smith's splendid *Rowing in Eden: Rereading Emily Dickinson* (Austin: University of Texas Press, 1992), pp. 21–30.

2. See Lillian Faderman, "Emily Dickinson's Letters to Sue Gilbert," *Massachusetts Review* 18 (Summer 1977): 197–225.

3. See the introduction to Dickinson's *Love Poems* (White Plains, N.Y.: Peter Pauper Press, n.d.), p. i. Such overheated speculations can be found in scholarly accounts, too. As recently as 1984 Barton Levi St. Armand could weigh down his useful *Emily Dickinson*

and Her Culture: The Soul's Society (Cambridge: Cambridge University Press, 1984) with the following: "As the South withdrew from the Union, so did Master leave for parts unknown, probably not without a sense of relief that he was escaping such an all-devouring passion. But Dickinson was still a slave to her religion of romance; only death could emancipate her" (p. 101).

4. Quoted in Smith, *Rowing*, p. 98. The scrupulous John Evangelist Walsh states this biographical case in its logical extreme. "Any attempt to get at the secret of Emily's broken heart," Walsh declares, "must begin by sweeping to one side her entire body of verse, wholly removing it from consideration. After surer ground has been attained through other avenues, *if some of the poems demand attention*, they may be permitted to offer their cautious corroboration." See, *The Hidden Life of Emily Dickinson* (New York: Simon and Schuster, 1971), p. 178.

5. For treatments of Dickinson's "joy in the drama of pleading," see Susan Howe, *My Emily Dickinson* (Berkeley: North Atlantic Books, 1985), pp. 26–27; Smith, *Rowing*, pp. 112–16, and, more broadly, Judith Farr, *The Passion of Emily Dickinson* (Cambridge: Harvard University Press, 1992), pp. 100–244.

6. Adrienne Rich, *What Is Found There: Notebooks on Poetry and Politics* (New York: Norton, 1993), p. 94.

7. "Cherish Power—dear," the poet wrote in a letter to Susan Gilbert. It "stands in the Bible between the Kingdom and the Glory, because it is wilder than either of them" (L 583). This note, writes Gary Lee Stonum, "epitomizes the commitments shaping Dickinson's entire body of work," since to "cherish" rather than seek or wield or submit to power suggests "a sort of jujitsu on the poetics of mastery, drawing much of its strength from the resources of domination, submission, and the intersubjective rivalry underlying them while at the same time seeking to turn those resources toward different ends." *The Dickinson Sublime* (Madison: University of Wisconsin Press, 1990), pp. 53–54.

8. Rainer Maria Rilke, *Letters to a Young Poet*, trans. Stephen Mitchell (Boston: Shambhala, 1993), p. 89.

9. Here, as elsewhere in this book, I take the phrase "erotic faith" from Robert Polhemus. See Polhemus, *Erotic Faith*, p. 1.

10. My sense of Dickinson as a poet in whom "the epistemological drama of a subject / object relation" is transformed into a "contest for supremacy between two subjectivities" is indebted to Benjamin's work and to that of Gary Lee Stonum. See Stonum, *Dickinson Sublime*, p. 20. I have also profited from Allen Grossman and Mark Halliday, *The Sighted Singer: Two Works on Poetry for Readers and Writers* (Baltimore: Johns Hopkins University Press, 1992), pp. 160–81.

11. Quoted in Karl Keller, *The Only Kangaroo among the Beauty: Emily Dickinson and America* (Baltimore: Johns Hopkins University Press, 1979), p. 302.

12. Sewall notes that it is "difficult to isolate and define" the "Puritan qualities in her heritage," and so speaks in broad terms of the virtues of discipline, simplicity, and self-denial for the Glory of God, of a "fierce introspection" and inner dialogue, of "sublime

self-reliance" and the loneliness of being chosen. See Richard B. Sewall, *The Life of Emily Dickinson* (New York: Farrar, Straus, Giroux, 1974), pp. 19–26. See also St. Armand, *Emily Dickinson*, p. 87.

13. Cynthia Griffin Wolff, *Emily Dickinson* (New York: Knopf, 1986), p. 255.

14. See, for example, poem 1601, "Of God we ask one favor."

15. In poem 721, Dickinson thus images God's "long Paradise" as an uninviting kingdom of masculine reflections, marked by a conspicuous absence of both human intercourse and linguistic variety. See also the more epigrammatic poem 1719.

16. Friedrich Nietzsche, *The Birth of Tragedy and The Case of Wagner*, trans. Walter Kaufman (New York: Vintage, 1967), p. 40; see also p. 74.

17. Bataille, *Erotism*, p. 276.

18. See Emerson, *JMN*, 7:532.

19. Henry Wadsworth Longfellow, *Selected Poems* (New York: Viking Penguin, 1988), pp. 92–147.

20. See Mikhail Mikhailovich Bakhtin, *The Dialogic Imagination*, ed. Michael Holquist, trans. Caryl Emerson and Michael Holquist (Austin: University of Texas Press, 1981), pp. 5–9.

21. Polhemus, *Erotic Faith*, pp. 4, 82.

22. Bataille, *Erotism*, pp. 11, 23, 24.

23. De Rougemont, *Love in the Western World*, pp. 15, 42, 41.

24. Ibid., p. 74.

25. For Abelard and Heloise in Victorian America, see St. Armand, *Emily Dickinson*, p. 95; for his account of Dickinson's broader education in erotic faith, see pp. 79–151.

26. Emily Brontë, *Wuthering Heights: An Authoritative Text with Essays in Criticism*, ed. William M. Sale Jr. (New York: Norton, 1963), pp. 126, 134.

27. Emerson's antisocial, self-reliant faith—learned in part from his unmarried aunt Mary Moody—thus plays itself out in Dickinson as a "Lover-reliance." She is as resistant as Emerson to being socially responsible, and far more aristocratic in her responses. See Erkkila, *Wicked Sisters*, pp. 58–60.

28. Polhemus, *Erotic Faith*, p. 80.

29. De Beauvoir, *Second Sex*, p. 646.

30. In poems where Dickinson's speaker names herself as masculine directly—say "The Malay—took the Pearl—/Not—I—the Earl" (P 452)—the poet's "he" seems a hapless character, afraid of the erotic Sea that the speaker of "How sick—to wait—" will brave. See Vivian R. Pollak, *Dickinson: The Anxiety of Gender* (Ithaca: Cornell University Press, 1984), p. 156.

31. Stonum, *Dickinson Sublime*, p. 155.

32. Margaret Homans, " 'Oh, Vision of Language!': Dickinson's Poems of Love and Death," in *Feminist Critics Read Emily Dickinson*, ed. Suzanne Juhasz (Bloomington: Indiana University Press, 1983), p. 114.

33. Benjamin, *Bonds of Love*, p. 60.

34. See Paglia, *Sexual Personae*, pp. 623–73.

35. Benjamin, *Bonds of Love*, p. 73.

36. Emerson, *CW,* 3:44, 46.

37. "In all men and women there lurks an atavistic dread of insolvency," writes Singer, "whenever we generate more emotion than something has a right to demand of us." *Nature of Love*, 1:15. But that dread suggests a possible pleasure, too, for there are times when, as Bataille reminds his readers, "we want to feel as remote from the world where thrift is the rule as we can," and enter into the extravagant world of the erotic. *Erotism*, p. 170.

38. Benjamin, *Bonds of Love*, p. 72.

39. I quote, respectively, Stonum, *Dickinson Sublime*, p. 20, and Dickinson, P 107.

40. De Beauvoir, *Second Sex*, p. 399.

41. For Adelaide Morris, the poems and letters addressed to Master "offer the spectacle of a self willing itself to be an inessential other," a reading indebted, as mine is, to De Beauvoir. " 'The Love of Thee—A Prism Be': Men and Women in the Love Poetry of Emily Dickinson," in *Feminist Critics Read Emily Dickinson*, p. 106. I find the element of *will* in these poems rather more important than Morris does, and connect it to their playful tone. And we must be sure to read the poems in their largest possible context. "Over the course of her career," as Stonum explains, "Dickinson speaks from every position within the hierarchy of master and minion, and she adopts every possible attitude toward the relation," from "resentment and awe" of the idolized master to "tones of haughty imperiousness" of her own. *Dickinson Sublime*, p. 18.

42. Paglia, *Sexual Personae*, p. 669.

43. Paula Bennett, *Emily Dickinson: Woman Poet* (Iowa City: University of Iowa Press, 1990), p. 171.

44. Karl Keller, "Notes on Sleeping with Emily Dickinson," in *Feminist Critics Read Emily Dickinson,* p. 67.

45. De Beauvoir, *Second Sex*, p. 416.

46. Morris, "Love of Thee," pp. 100, 106.

47. Bennett, *Emily Dickinson*, pp. 160–63.

48. Homans, "O Vision," pp. 120, 122, 124.

49. Michael Warner's outraged questions about the psychoanalytic construction of homosexuality are quite relevant here. "Can it actually be imagined," he demands, "that people in homosexual relations have no other way of distinguishing between self and not-self? That no other marker of difference, such as race, could intervene; or that the pragmatics of dialogue would not make alterity meaningful ... ? Why is gender assumed to be our only access to alterity?" "Homo-Narcissism: or, Heterosexuality," in *Engendering Men: The Question of Male Feminist Criticism*, ed. Joseph Allen Boone and Michael Cadden (New York: Routledge, 1990), p. 200. Jean Hagstrum echoes his puzzlement. "Surely the spice of *human* difference ... is not confined to *sexual* difference. The tension between personal autonomy and benevolent regard for the other must certainly arise whenever two individuals embark on the project of making lasting love." *Esteem Enlivened*, pp. 17–18. See also Erkkila, *Wicked Sisters*, p. 33.

50. Morris, "Love of Thee," pp. 110–11.

51. Bennett, *Emily Dickinson*, p. 165.

52. Erkkila, *Wicked Sisters*, p. 28.

53. Sewall, *Life*, p. 202.

54. See Farr, *Passion*, p. 141; my quotation is from Dickinson, P 299.

55. Farr, *Passion*, p. 142.

56. Morris, "Love of Thee," p. 101.

57. If the "sublime" insolvency of masochism involves being "ravished" by an other greater than herself—a ravishment central to the Emersonian sublime—as a woman poet Dickinson might have found it hard to see herself reflected in or nourished by that ravishing, powerful, masculine figure. Yet when a woman poet "experiences this external power as feminine, as the mother" explains Joanne Feit Diehl, "her 'inspiration' does not impart the gift of tradition," as it does when nature enraptures her male counterpart. *Women Poets and the American Sublime* (Bloomington: Indiana University Press, 1990), p. 3. Dickinson's poems to Susan bring her the best of both poetic worlds.

58. See, for example, poem 815.

59. Keller, "Sleeping," pp. 71–72.

60. Wolff, *Emily Dickinson*, pp. 409–10, 96–97, 54, 416.

61. William Wordsworth, *Selected Poems and Prefaces*, ed. Jack Stillinger (Boston: Houghton Mifflin, 1965), pp. 237, 268.

62. Kristeva, *Revolution in Poetic Language*, trans. Margaret Waller (New York: Columbia University Press, 1984), p. 150.

63. I borrow this tonal and prosodic path into the poem from Stonum, *Dickinson Sublime*, p. 105.

64. Cavell, *Claim*, p. 440.

65. Grossman, "The Evangel-Poem," p. 160.

Chapter 3 Liberation and Its Discontents

1. Krutch, *Modern Temper*, pp. 73, 77, 73, 59, 66 (my emphasis). For an account of American religious-cum-medical advice texts that exemplify Krutch's argument, see Gardella, *Innocent Ecstasy*, pp. 69–73. For a discussion of later, secular sex reformers, see Steven Seidman, *Romantic Longings: Love in America, 1830–1980* (New York: Routledge, 1991), pp. 65–91.

2. Seidman, *Romantic Longings*, pp. 4, 73.

3. Krutch, *Modern Temper*, p. 71.

4. I adapt this helpful list of qualities from Kern, *Culture of Love*, p. 404.

5. A. S. Byatt, *Possession: A Romance* (New York: Random House, 1990), p. 290.

6. Krutch anticipates the evisceration of meaning and selfhood in the "loveless" modern world. See *Modern Temper*, p. 78. For a psychoanalytic account of the links between single, separate selfhood, feeling one's life has meaning, and loving or being loved, see Kristeva, *Tales*.

7. Kristeva, *Tales*, p. 7.

8. Julia Kristeva, *Black Sun* (New York: Columbia University Press, 1989), p. 216.

9. Kern, *Culture of Love*, p. 9. Kern takes his use of "authentic" from Heidegger, whose use of the word *eigentlich* in *Being and Time* attends to its root in the word *eigen*, to own. Since it resists the loss of self in amorous merger, and is instead a human relationship, Kern's "authentic" love largely corresponds to the one described by De Beauvoir.

10. Loy is not an American by birth, but in 1916, a year after the then-notorious *Love Songs* were published in Alfred Kreymbourg's little magazine *Others*, she became an integral part of the Greenwich Village–New York City avant-garde. See Carolyn Burke, *Becoming Modern: The Life of Mina Loy* (New York: Farrar, Straus, and Giroux, 1996).

11. I take this phrase from Ezra Pound, "Of Jacopo del Sellaio," in *Collected Early Poems of Ezra Pound*, ed. Michael John King (New York: New Directions, 1976), p. 197.

12. Cheryl Walker, *The Nightingale's Burden: Women Poets and American Culture before 1900* (Bloomington: Indiana University Press, 1982), pp. 91–141.

13. Edna St. Vincent Millay, *Collected Sonnets* (New York: Harper and Row, 1988), p. 41.

14. Elizabeth Perlmutter Frank, "A Doll's Heart: The Girl in the Poetry of Edna St. Vincent Millay and Louise Bogan," in *Critical Essays on Edna St. Vincent Millay*, ed. William B. Thesing (New York: G. K. Hall, 1993), p. 184.

15. Krutch, *Modern Temper*, pp. 73, 77.

16. Quoted by Carolyn Burke, "The New Poetry and the New Woman: Mina Loy," in *Coming to Light: American Women Poets in the Twentieth Century*, ed. Diane Wood Middlebrook and Marilyn Yalom (Ann Arbor: University of Michigan Press, 1985), p. 36.

17. Mina Loy, *The Lost Lunar Baedeker: Poems of Mina Loy*, ed. Roger L. Conover (New York: Farrar, Straus, Giroux, 1996), p. 22.

18. Emma Goldman, "Marriage and Love," in *The Philosophy of (Erotic) Love*, ed. Robert C. Solomon and Kathleen M. Higgins (Lawrence: University Press of Kansas, 1991), p. 212. In the end, notes one critic, "Goldman had been party to the dismantling of sentimental power ... but the critique turned into a denigration of the lover's discourse so pervasive she feared it would extend to her own revelations." Suzanne Clark, *Sentimental Modernism: Women Writers and the Revolution of the Word* (Bloomington: Indiana University Press, 1991), p. 63.

19. Loy, *Lost Lunar Baedeker*, p. 154. These corrosive gestures echo Sanger and Goldman far less than avant-gardists such as the Italian Futurists, for whom not just marriage but *amore* itself was to be debunked, replaced with "Futurist mating." See Virginia M. Kouidis, *Mina Loy: American Modernist Poet* (Baton Rouge: Louisiana State University Press, 1980), p. 61. For Loy's biographical and literary relationships with the Futurists, see Burke, *Becoming Modern* and Elizabeth Arnold, "Mina Loy and the Futurists," *Sagetrieb* 8 (Spring/Fall, 1989): 83–117.

20. Loy, *Lost Lunar Baedeker*, p. 156.

21. Wallace Stevens, "Romance for a Demoiselle Lying in the Grass," *Opus Posthumous*, ed. Milton J. Bates (New York: Vintage Books, 1990), p. 44.

22. Kristeva, *Black Sun*, p. 6, and *Tales*, p. 372.

23. Loy, *Lost Lunar Baedeker*, p. 53.

24. Kouidis has argued that this reference to "coloured glass" looks back to the "colored and distorting lenses which we are" in Emerson's essay "Experience," an essay that insists on every subject's distance from every object, including one's beloved. See "From Prison to Prism." From such an ever-"virginal" remove one might well mock love and sex, with their panting, repetitive promise to cross this great epistemological divide.

25. The image of "Pig Cupid" aroused considerable anxiety, and no little amusement, in the *Songs'* first conservative readers. "Readers accustomed to the conventions of romantic poetry were totally unprepared for her frank exploration of love from a woman's perspective," Burke writes. "Even the ostensibly modern Amy Lowell was so shocked by Loy's poems that she threatened to withdraw her support from *Others*. As Alfred Kreymbourg observed in *Our Singing Strength* a dozen years later, 'To reduce eroticism to the sty was an outrage, and to do so without verbs, sentence structure, punctuation, even more offensive.'" Burke, "New Poetry," p. 45.

26. Whitman, *Complete Poetry*, pp. 1334–35.

27. Loy, *Lost Lunar Baedeker*, p. 63.

28. Kouidis, *Mina Loy*, p. 70. The *Love Songs* are not the only modernist poem to embody a failure of love in a failure of language. In Stevens's "Le Monocle de Mon Oncle" one finds a similar split between a language of ironic "pinched gestures" and the "odious chords" that would boom forth "If sex were all." Wallace Stevens, *The Collected Poems* (New York: Vintage Books, 1982), p. 17. But even Stevens's most brutal ironies, usually directed against himself, are finally eased by the aesthetic resolution of well-wrought, accomplished verse. Stevens may push his poems to the point of failure, that is to say, but he will not push them past it, *make* them fail, in order to see what comes next. Loy takes that risk, and her speaker, unlike Stevens's, pays the price.

29. Kouidis, "Prison into Prism," pp. 130–31.

30. Loy, *Lost Lunar Baedeker*, p. 57.

31. Ibid., p. 155.

32. Ibid., p. 59.

33. Ibid., p. 62.

34. Ibid., p. 60.

35. Gertrude Stein, *The Yale Gertrude Stein*, ed. Richard Kostelanetz (New Haven: Yale University Press, 1980), p. 36.

36. Loy, *Lost Lunar Baedeker*, p. 58.

37. Ibid., pp. 57–58.

38. Ibid., p. 59.

39. For an elegant use of such allusions, see the penultimate scene of Byatt's *Possession*. After Maud and Roland sleep together at last, the world has a "strange new smell . . . which bore some relation to the smell of bitten apples. It was the smell of death and destruction and it smelled fresh and lively and hopeful" (p. 551).

40. Kristeva, *Black Sun*, p. 23; see also pp. 206–16.

41. Kouidis gives a valiant effort to read the sequence in the terms suggested by this myth, where the "I" is Psyche in search of a fleeing Pig Cupid. *Mina Loy*, p. 77. The fact that Kouidis must read the sequence backwards, leaving out several poems en route, hardly invalidates her master narrative. But there are so many loose ends—the transformation of the speaker into a weed, the multiple attributions given Joannes, the juxtaposition of this symbolic structure and several biblical ones—that it seems safer to refer to this as a deliberately awkward gesture *toward* an organizing schema than a closely woven subtext in the manner of H.D.'s "Winter Love."

42. Carol Thomas Neely, "The Structure of English Renaissance Sonnet Sequences," *ELH* 45 (1978): 376, 384.

43. Kristeva, *Black Sun*, p. 216; see also p. 5.

44. Ibid., p. 206.

45. T. S. Eliot, "Baudelaire," in *Selected Essays* (New York: Harcourt, Brace and World, 1960), p. 379.

46. Quoted in Calvin Bedient, *He Do the Police in Different Voices: "The Waste Land" and Its Protagonist* (Chicago: University of Chicago Press, 1986), p. 81.

47. See Lyndall Gordon, *Eliot's Early Years* (New York: Oxford University Press, 1977), pp. 34–35, 51, 123.

48. Eliot, "Dante," in *Selected Essays*, p. 235.

49. Bedient, *Police*, p. 32.

50. Eliot, "A Dedication to My Wife," in *The Complete Poems and Plays: 1909–1962* (New York: Harcourt, Brace and World, 1962), p. 221. See Gordon, *Eliot's New Life* (New York: Farrar, Straus, Giroux, 1988), pp. 255–56.

51. De Rougemont, *Love*, p. 314. I may be glossing over shifts in Eliot's spiritual vision in this quick account. In *The Waste Land*, as Bedient notes, the failure of human and sexual love may be *required* by spiritual success, the poet's Plotinian flight of the Alone to the Alone. *He Do the Police*, p. 32. William Arrowsmith, who reads a Neoplatonic Christianity in the bulk of Eliot's mature works, including *The Waste Land*, seems to disagree. "Eros in Terre Haute: T. S. Eliot's 'Lune de Miel,'" *New Criterion* 1 (October 1982): 22–41.

52. Eliot, *Selected Essays*, pp. 323, 380, 234–35.

53. Sigmund Freud, "The Most Prevalent Form of Degradation in Erotic Life," in *Sexuality and the Psychology of Love* (New York: Collier Books, 1963), p. 67.

54. Eliot, *Collected Poems*, 119; see Arrowsmith, "Eros," pp. 24, 34.

55. T. S. Eliot, *The Waste Land: Facsimile and Transcript of the Original Drafts*, ed. Valerie Eliot (New York: Harcourt Brace Jovanovich, 1971), p. 23.

56. Arrowsmith, "Eros," pp. 28, 32.

57. Quoted in ibid., p. 32.

58. Eliot, *Selected Essays*, p. 379.

59. See Humphrey Carpenter, *A Serious Character: The Life of Ezra Pound* (Boston: Houghton Mifflin, 1988), p. 62.

60. Kevin Oderman, *Ezra Pound and the Erotic Medium* (Durham, N. C.: Duke University Press, 1986), p. xi.

61. Carpenter, *Serious Character*, p. 67. See Hilda Doolittle [H.D.], *End to Torment* (New York: New Directions, 1979), pp. 11, 22–23; and William French and Timothy Materer, "Far Flung Vortices: Ezra's 'Hindoo' Yogi," *Paideuma* 11 (1982): 39–53.

62. Pound, *Collected Early Poems*, p. 171.

63. Ibid., p. 173.

64. Pound, *Spirit of Romance*, pp. 94, 97.

65. For an account of Gourmont's reaction against naturalism, see Richard Sieburth, *Instigations: Ezra Pound and Remy de Gourmont* (Cambridge: Harvard University Press, 1978), p. 40. For more on Pound's link between glands and glory, see Oderman, *Ezra Pound*, pp. 25, 39–47, and Ian F. A. Bell, *Critic as Scientist: The Modernist Poetics of Ezra Pound* (New York: Methuen, 1981), p. 138.

66. Pound, *Spirit of Romance*, p. 99; see Oderman, *Ezra Pound*, pp. 115–16, and Akiko Miyake, *Ezra Pound and the Mysteries of Love: A Plan for "The Cantos"* (Durham, N.C.: Duke University Press, 1991), p. 19. Pound was fascinated by a secret European tradition of the "mystic cult of love," proposing at one point to write a history of sexual mysteries, "the Dionysian rites, and so on—from earlier days to the present." Carpenter, *Serious Character*, p. 136. As Dorothy Shakespear, H.D., and others attest, he believed that a "mystical marriage had taken place in his own person": a "marriage to the goddess" that caused his rebirth "into the mystical being, Dionysus, the god of pristine energy and motion." Miyake, *Ezra Pound*, p. 11; Robert Casillo, *The Genealogy of Demons: Anti-Semitism, Fascism, and the Myths of Ezra Pound* (Evanston, Ill.: Northwestern University Press, 1988), p. 290; see Massimo Bacigalupo, *The Formed Trace: The Later Poetry of Ezra Pound* (New York: Columbia University Press, 1980), pp. 33–36. It is too easy to dismiss such claims. As the poet attests, "There are in the 'normal course of things' certain times, a certain sort of moment . . . when a man feels his immortality upon him." If the cultural context to explain these feelings includes theophanic marriage, such interpretations will be made. Pound, *Spirit of Romance*, p. 94.

67. Pound, *Collected Early Poems*, p. 197.

68. For the poem's use of Swinburne, see Christine Froula, *A Guide to Ezra Pound's Selected Poems* (New York: New Directions, 1983), p. 42. For an extensive and expertly written account of Pound, Yeats, and the occult elitism they shared, see James Longenbach, *Stone Cottage: Pound, Yeats, and Modernism* (New York: Oxford University Press, 1988), pp. 18–19. For more examples of Pound's commitment to an "aristocracy of emotion," see Pound, *Spirit of Romance*, p. 90 and passim.

69. Pound, "Praise of Ysolt," in *Collected Early Poems*, p. 80.

70. Pound, "Na Audiart," in ibid., p. 13.

71. Ezra Pound, *The Cantos of Ezra Pound* (New York: New Directions, 1970), pp. 92–93.

72. Ibid., p. 180.

73. Rachel Blau DuPlessis, *The Pink Guitar: Writing as Feminist Practice* (New York: Routledge, 1990), p. 43.

74. Thomas Simmons, *Erotic Reckonings: Mastery and Apprenticeship in the Work of Poets and Lovers* (Chicago: University of Illinois Press, 1994), pp. 28, 26.

75. De Rougemont, *Love*, p. 312.

76. See, for example, Lillian Feder, "Pound and Ovid," in *Ezra Pound Among the Poets*, ed. George Bornstein (Chicago: University of Chicago Press, 1985), pp. 27, 93.

77. Pound, *Cantos*, Canto 76, pp. 459–60.

78. Ibid., pp. 457, 802.

79. Hammond, *Sinful Self,* p. 90.

80. See, for example, H.D.'s novel *Bid Me to Live* (Redding Ridge, Conn.: Black Swan Books, 1983), where the poet's stand-in, Julia Ashton, tucks a passionate love letter from Rico (D. H. Lawrence) into a Victorian jewel box, lined with red plush and a portrait of her mother, "old-fashioned" even in 1880. There, at least, it will be safe from the prying eyes and, more, the mockery of her husband Rafe (Richard Aldington).

81. H.D., *Collected Poems, 1912–1944* (New York: New Directions, 1983), p. 172. For more on H.D.'s interest in such amatory esoterica, see Adelaide Morris, "A Relay of Power and of Peace: H.D. and the Spirit of the Gift," in *Signets: Reading H.D.*, ed. Susan Stanford Friedman and Rachel Blau DuPlessis (Madison: University of Wisconsin Press, 1990), pp. 52–82; and Susan Stanford Friedman, *Psyche Reborn: The Emergence of H.D.* (Bloomington: Indiana University Press, 1981), pp. 157–207. Although she does not go so far as to speak, like Pound, of "glands," the poet also found the visionary grounded in extraordinary but still physical experience As she puts it in *Notes on Thought and Vision,* "we cannot have spirit without body, the body of nature, or the body of individual men and women." *Notes on Thought and Vision and The Wise Sappho* (San Francisco: City Lights Books, 1982), p. 48.

82. Morris, "Relay," p. 68.

83. H.D., *Collected Poems*, p. 179. For a useful discussion of H.D.'s relationship with Pound, and her deliberate if risky exploration of idolatrous love, see Simmons, *Erotic Reckonings*, pp. 54–55, 69–72. See also Friedman, *Psyche Reborn*, pp. 40–43, and DuPlessis, *Pink Guitar*, pp. 20–40.

84. Morris, "Relay," p. 68.

85. H.D., *Collected Poems*, "Epigrams," p. 172.

86. See Barbara Guest, *Herself Defined: The Poet H.D. and Her World* (New York: Doubleday, 1984), p. 329, and Friedman, *Psyche Reborn*, p. 101.

87. De Rougemont, *Love*, pp. 10, 121–22.

88. See Carpenter, *Serious Character*, p. 61.

89. H.D., *End to Torment*, pp. 18–19.

90. H.D., *Collected Poems*, p. 446.

91. H.D., *Hermetic Definition* (New York: New Directions, 1972), p. 91.

92. See, for example, Carpenter, *Serious Character*, p. 167.

93. Kern, *Culture of Love*, p. 289.

94. See Barbara M. Fisher, *Wallace Stevens: The Intensest Rendezvous* (Charlottesville: University Press of Virginia, 1990), p. 3.

95. Milton J. Bates, *Wallace Stevens: A Mythology of Self* (University of California Press, 1985), pp. 81–82, 83.

96. Stevens, *Collected Poems*, p. 161.

97. Mark Halliday, *Stevens and the Interpersonal* (Princeton: Princeton University Press, 1991), p. 77.

98. Stevens, "Arrival at the Waldorf," in *Collected Poems*, pp. 240–41.

99. Stevens, "Two Figures in Dense Violet Light," in ibid., p. 86.

100. Ibid., p. 524.

101. Halliday, *Stevens*, p. 110.

102. Stevens, "Re-statement of Romance," in *Collected Poems*, p. 146.

103. Halliday, *Stevens*, p. 145.

104. Stevens, "An Ordinary Evening," in *Collected Poems*, p. 468.

105. Halliday, *Stevens*, pp. 94, 5, 43, 56, 72.

106. See, for example, Martha Banta's discussion of Josiah Royce and love in *Imaging American Women: Idea and Ideals in Cultural History* (New York: Columbia University Press, 1987), pp. 18–20.

107. Singer, *Nature of Love*, 1:26–27.

108. McWhirter, *Desire and Love*, pp. 6–7.

109. A similar resignation of the beloved person, in favor of the beloved poem, marks Hart Crane's "Voyages." See my essay "When I'm Calling You: Reading, Romance, and Rhetoric In and Around Hart Crane's 'Voyages,'" *Arizona Quarterly* 47 (Winter 1991): 85–118.

110. Stevens, *Collected Poems*, pp. 231–32.

111. William Carlos Williams, *The Collected Poems of William Carlos Williams, Volume 1:1909–1939*, ed. A. Walton Litz and Christopher MacGowan (New York: New Directions, 1986), p. 200.

112. William Carlos Williams, *Imaginations* (New York: New Directions, 1970), p. 166.

113. See, for example, *A Novelette*, where Williams tells his wife, "In this ["borrowed" literature] you have no existence." In *Imaginations*, p. 293.

114. Williams, *A Dream of Love*, in *Many Loves and Other Plays* (New York: New Directions, 1961), p. 200.

115. Williams, *Novelette*, pp. 166–67. "The fusion of marriage and writing that Williams proclaims in *A Novelette*," Terence Diggory explains, "is not merely an equation of the two institutions." Rather, "the writing simultaneously sustains and undoes the marriage," forming as it does the " 'hard work' of the imagination by which the writer 'unmarries' husband and wife." The text is thus a mosaic of questions, explanations, and more-or-less benign misunderstandings. *William Carlos Williams and the Ethics of Painting* (Princeton: Princeton University Press, 1991), pp. 82, 110.

116. William Carlos Williams, *Selected Letters*, ed. John C. Thirlwall (New York: McDowell, Obolensky, 1957), pp. 11–12.

117. Williams, *Imaginations*, p. 22.

118. Ibid.

119. Williams, *Collected Poems*, 1:94, 216.

120. Benjamin, *Bonds of Love*, p. 38.

121. Williams, *Many Loves*, p. 200.

122. Benjamin, *Bonds of Love*, pp. 38, 36.

123. Williams, *Imaginations*, p. 22.

124. Williams, *Collected Poems*, 1:164.

125. He had reason to beg forgiveness of Floss, having confessed his "tortured constancy" to clear his conscience, at a terrible cost to her. See Paul Mariani, *William Carlos Williams: A New World Naked* (New York: McGraw Hill, 1981), pp. 661–62.

126. Williams, "The Ivy Crown," in *The Collected Poems of William Carlos Williams, Volume 2: 1939–1962*, ed. Chistopher MacGowan (New York: New Directions, 1988), p. 290.

127. Kristeva, *Black Sun*, pp. 206–7.

128. For this use of the term "design" in Williams, see "The Orchestra," in *Collected Poems*, 2:252.

129. Williams, "Asphodel," in ibid. 2:326, 332–33.

130. Ibid., 2:331; my emphasis.

131. Williams, *Collected Poems*, 1:343–46.

132. Stevens, "Gallant Château," in *Collected Poems*, p. 161.

133. Early in *Paterson* the poet declares that "divorce" is "the sign of knowledge in our time." William Carlos Williams, *Paterson* (New York: New Directions, 1963), p. 18. Many metaphorical divorces and marriages follow, leading up to the—to my ear—unconvincing resolution of book 5. I focus here on book 2 because of its influence on Lowell's *The Dolphin*. For readings of the rest of the poem informed by Jessica Benjamin's ideas, see Brian A. Bremen, *William Carlos Williams and the Diagnostics of Culture* (Oxford: Oxford University Press, 1993). For a sympathetic, Kristevan account of book 5, see Diggory, *Williams*.

134. Williams's treatment of Nardi, in life and in verse, has prompted a good deal of debate. The most balanced and insightful treatments I have encountered are Theodora R. Graham's " 'Her Heigh Compleynte': The Cress Letters of William Carlos Williams' Paterson," in *Ezra Pound and William Carlos Williams: The University of Pennsylvania Conference Papers*, ed. Daniel Hoffman (Philadelphia: University of Pennsylvania Press, 1983), pp. 164–93, and Bremen's discussion in *Williams*, pp. 174–79. Bremen's application of Jessica Benjamin to Williams's work has been extremely helpful to my readings of both Williams and Creeley.

135. Benjamin, *Bonds of Love*, p. 38.

136. Williams, *Paterson*, p. 44.

137. Stein, *Yale*, p. 287. For admiring accounts of Stein's love poems, see Harriet

Scott Chessman, *The Public Is Invited to Dance: Representation, the Body, and Dialogue in Gertrude Stein* (Stanford, Calif.: Stanford University Press, 1989), and Peter Quartermain, *Disjunctive Poetics: From Gertrude Stein and Louis Zukofsky to Susan Howe* (Cambridge: Cambridge University Press, 1992). For a more skeptical treatment, see Catherine R. Stimpson, "Gertrude Stein and the Transposition of Gender," in *The Poetics of Gender*, ed. Nancy K. Miller (New York: Columbia University Press, 1986), pp. 1–18.

138. Williams, *Paterson*, p. 87.

139. Williams, *Collected Poems*, 2:147.

140. See ibid., 1:195, and *Imaginations*, p. 293.

Chapter 4 Real Crises in Real Homes

1. Allan Bloom, *Love and Friendship* (New York: Simon and Schuster, 1993), pp. 24–25.

2. De Beauvoir, *Second Sex*, p. 654. I call upon Simone de Beauvoir to define this ideology of love. In doing so I suggest three things: that it is international; that it is modern; and that it is feminist. All are partly true, since, as Jessica Benjamin explains, "the conception of equal subjects has begun to seem intellectually plausible only because women's demand for equality has achieved real social force." *Bonds of Love*, p. 221. This ideal of love between powerful equals has deep American roots, however, in Emerson and Fuller.

The scope and force of this companionate ideal can best be seen when those within it look back on the writings of those outside its pale. When poet-critic Mark Halliday tells readers of Stevens, for example, that the poet consistently fails to "describe the female other as a fully human individual, as a separate subjectivity, an independent actor and perceiver outside his own mind"—that he refuses "to consider romantic love as a relationship between two distinct, separately subjective human beings"—we hear de Beauvoir's key terms. *Stevens*, pp. 54, 44. Halliday clearly expects that his readers will agree with him, at least about the nature of true love.

3. Bloom, *Love and Friendship*, pp. 27, 29.

4. Creeley, *Collected Essays*, p. 170.

5. Swenson, *Love Poems*, p. 37. Alicia Ostriker sees this "imperative of intimacy" in love poems by women as a gendered cultural norm. *Stealing the Language: The Emergence of Women's Poetry in America* (Boston: Beacon Press, 1986), pp. 165–209. Elsewhere, however, she notes that this imperative takes many cues from Whitman (see "Loving Walt Whitman"); and male poets like Mark Halliday, Stephen Dunn, and Albert Goldbarth write poems as "intimate," I think, as anything in Swenson or Van Duyn.

6. Creeley, *Collected Essays*, p. 173.

7. Quoted in Cynthia Dubin Edelberg, *Robert Creeley's Poetry: A Critical Introduction* (Albuquerque: University of New Mexico Press, 1978), p. 4.

8. Creeley, *Collected Essays*, p. 40.

9. Williams, "The Orchestra" and "To Daphne and Virginia," in *Collected Poems*, 2:282, 317, 248.

10. Robert Creeley, letters of July 4, 1950, and June 26, 1950, in *Charles Olson and Robert Creeley: The Complete Correspondence*, ed. George Butterick (Santa Barbara: Black Sparrow, 1980), 2:47, 20–21.

11. Robert Creeley, *Tales Out of School: Selected Interviews* (Ann Arbor: University of Michigan Press, 1993), p. 81.

12. *For Love* also brought Creeley a wide audience—a nice irony, given the anxious isolation of his usual "I," and perhaps a testimony to how common the "real crises" he sketched turned out to be. Robert von Hallberg notes that it sold 39,000 copies in its first decade in print. *American Poetry and Culture, 1945–1980* (Cambridge: Harvard University Press, 1985), p. 13.

13. Creeley, "A Song," in *The Collected Poems of Robert Creeley* (Berkeley: University of California Press, 1982), p. 112.

14. Ibid., p. 113.

15. Creeley, *Collected Essays*, p. 159.

16. Creeley, *Collected Poems*, p. 137.

17. Ibid., p. 236.

18. De Beauvoir, *Second Sex*, p. 655.

19. Creeley, *Collected Essays*, pp. 474–75.

20. For a corresponding scene in *The Island*, where John hopes for a fight in order to gain recognition, and finally forgiveness, see Creeley, *The Collected Prose of Robert Creeley* (Berkeley: University of California Press, 1988), pp. 150–151.

21. See Benjamin, *Bonds of Love*, pp. 36–37.

22. Creeley, *Collected Poems*, p. 140.

23. Charles Bernstein, "Hearing 'Here': Robert Creeley's Poetics of Duration," in *Robert Creeley: The Poet's Workshop*, ed. Carroll F. Terrell (Orono, Me.: National Poetry Foundation, 1984), p. 92.

24. Creeley, *Collected Essays*, p. 48; Williams, "The Ivy Crown," in *Collected Poems*, 2:288.

25. Benjamin, *Bonds of Love*, pp. 55, 50.

26. Quoted in Edelberg, *Creeley's Poetry*, p. 167.

27. Creeley, *Collected Essays*, pp. 220–21.

28. See Robert Graves, *The White Goddess* (New York: Farrar, Straus and Giroux, 1966), p. 5.

29. Robert Duncan, "After *For Love*," in *Robert Creeley's Life and Work: A Sense of Increment*, ed. John Wilson (Ann Arbor: University of Michigan Press, 1987), pp. 98–99.

30. Creeley, *Collected Essays*, p. 222.

31. Ibid., Creeley, *Collected Essays*, p. 241.

32. For Graves, this distinction between muse and wife was utterly necessary. "The White Goddess is anti-domestic; she is the perpetual 'other woman,'" he declares. When "the woman whom he [the poet] took to be a Muse, or who was a Muse, turns into a domestic woman and would have him turn similarly into a domesticated man," something in both of them dies. *White Goddess*, p. 449.

33. For a discussion of Creeley's interest in and debt to Stevens, see Edelberg, *Creeley's Poetry*, p. 16. With the suspicion of the "erring brain" announced in *Bottom: On Shakespeare* and implied in many of his verses, Louis Zukofsky, too, may have shaped Creeley's response to the "secret ways of love." See, for example, Creeley, *Collected Essays*, pp. 67, 148, 161.

34. Creeley, *Collected Essays*, p. 172.

35. Creeley, *Collected Poems*, p. 146.

36. Margaret Homans, *Bearing the Word: Language and Experience in Nineteenth Century Women's Writing* (Chicago: University of Chicago Press, 1986), p. 18.

37. Creeley, *Collected Poems*, pp. 168, 164, 252.

38. Creeley, *Tales Out of School*, p. 81; "For Love," *Collected Poems*, p. 258. Because it bears on his self-critical project from *For Love* to *A Day Book*, this passage from a 1967 interview is worth quoting at length. "Growing up with five women in the house, man," Creeley sighs, "I knew all the signs and gestures and contents, or at least I knew a lot of them that were manifest in women's conduct. Ways of saying things, ways of reacting, making the world daily. But I didn't have a clue as to what men did, except literally I was a man. It's like growing up in the forest attended by wolves or something. It took me a curiously long time to come into man's estate. . . . So that for me to get to be a man was extremely awkward at times, and I learned it from my contemporaries and from one or two older men who somehow sensed my dilemma and were able to make forms that would give me articulation or show me how articulation might be possible." *Tales Out of School*, pp. 81–82.

39. Homans, *Bearing*, pp. 30–31.

40. Creeley, *Collected Poems*, p. 207.

41. Cavell, *Disowning*, p. 35.

42. Creeley, *Collected Poems*, p. 267.

43. Ibid., p. 281.

44. Ibid., p. 270.

45. This unforced, mindful inquiry would go on well into the 1970s. See, for example, "Erotica," in Creeley's collection *Later* (New York: New Directions, 1979), where the speaker joins some young boys hungry to glimpse " 'what they look like / underneath' "—but as the use of quotes suggests, "they" means "boys' or men's imaginations" as much as women's bodies.

46. Creeley, *Collected Poems*, pp. 291, 340.

47. Ibid., pp. 344–45; see also the second entry in *Day Book*, in *Collected Prose*, p. 273.

48. Creeley, *Collected Poems*, pp. 334–35.

49. Ibid., p. 347.

50. For an excellent treatment of "the obscenity of the sentimental" in modernism—the way the modernist revolution "inaugurated a reversal of values which emphasized erotic desire, not love" and "rupture and innovation rather than the conventional appeals of sentimental language," see Clark, *Sentimental Modernism*, pp. 1–2.

51. Creeley, *Collected Poems*, p. 375.

52. Ibid., p. 382; Harold Mesch, "Robert Creeley's Epistemopathic Path," in Terrell, *Robert Creeley*, pp. 64, 70.

53. For comments from Creeley on this felt need "to find some way whereby to have a life with others," especially as enacted in his work from *The Island* onward, see *Tales Out of School*, pp. 92–100, 122.

54. Creeley, *Collected Poems*, pp. 283, 379, 411.

55. Ibid., pp. 445–46, 442.

56. Creeley, *Collected Prose*, p. 281.

57. Ibid., p. 290.

58. Creeley, *Later*, p. 79.

59. "Some concerns have been persistent," Creeley has said, "e.g. the terms of marriage, relations of men and women, senses of isolation, senses of place in the intimate measure. But I have never to my own knowledge begun with any sense of 'subject,'" since "the point I wish to make is that I am writing." *Tales Out of School*, p. 46.

60. See, for example, "Love Comes Quietly," from *For Love*, or the previously uncollected poem "But," which Creeley uses to close his *Collected Poems*.

61. Mona Van Duyn, *Merciful Disguises: Published and Unpublished Poems* (New York: Atheneum, 1973), p. 32.

62. See Vereen M. Bell, *Robert Lowell: Nihilist as Hero* (Cambridge: Harvard University Press, 1983), p. 135.

63. Creeley, *Collected Essays*, p. 41.

64. Alan Williamson, *Pity the Monsters: The Political Vision of Robert Lowell* (New Haven: Yale University Press, 1974), pp. 208–9.

65. See Benjamin, *Bonds of Love*, p. 37.

66. Robert Lowell, *Life Studies and For the Union Dead* (New York: Farrar, Straus, Giroux, 1964), p. 86.

67. See Stephen Yenser, *Circle to Circle: The Poetry of Robert Lowell* (Berkeley: University of California Press, 1975), p. 159.

68. Lowell, *Life Studies*, p. 87.

69. See Yenser, *Circle to Circle*, pp. 234–37, and Steven Gould Axelrod, *Robert Lowell: Life and Art* (Princeton: Princeton University Press, 1978), p. 143.

70. For a judicious account of *The Dolphin*'s reception, by friends and critics, see Mariani, *Lost Puritan*, pp. 421–23.

71. Adrienne Rich, "Caryatid: A Column," *American Poetry Review* 2 (September/October 1973): 10–11.

72. As Williamson would argue somewhat later, the letter-poems signal Lowell's "transcendence of a false appearance of control" and his effort to "undermine the authorial prestige of his own voice" by making his ex-wife seem "a presence who cannot be answered, whose point of view will not fade into the customarily inclusive authorial one." Like Creeley, almost twenty years before, Lowell is now determined to "prevent his mind from saying more than his whole consciousness apprehends"; in case he falters in this determination, as Creeley never seems to fear he will, Lowell adds a second co

sciousness to remind him of his limits, to help him escape the world in which "no subject is an object." Alan Williamson, *Introspection and Contemporary Poetry* (Cambridge: Harvard University Press, 1984), pp. 20, 23.

73. Robert Lowell, *The Dolphin* (New York: Farrar, Straus, Giroux, 1973), p. 48.

74. Robert Lowell, *For Lizzie and Harriet* (New York: Farrar, Straus, Giroux, 1973), p. 14.

75. See Gabriel Pearson, "*For Lizzie and Harriet*: Robert Lowell's Domestic Apocalypse," in *Modern American Poetry*, ed. R. W. Butterfield (London: Barnes and Noble, 1984), p. 189.

76. Robert Lowell, *Notebook* (New York: Farrar, Straus, Giroux, 1970), p. 97.

77. Robert Lowell, *Notebook 1967-68* (New York: Farrar, Straus, Giroux, 1969), p. 56.

78. Pearson, "*For Lizzie and Harriet*," p. 189; see Lowell, *Notebook*, p. 79.

79. "Où vais-je sans Euridice?" an aria wonders as the poet, an adulterous Orpheus, finds himself in "undergrowth, dense beyond reward." See "Through the Night," Sonnet 2, in Lowell, *For Lizzie and Harriet*, p. 17.

80. Lowell, *For Lizzie and Harriet*, p. 43.

81. Williams, *Collected Poems*, 2:290, 333.

82. Creeley, *Collected Essays*, p. 241.

83. Lowell, *Dolphin*, p. 59.

84. George Santayana, "Platonic Love in Some Italian Poets," in *Essays in Literary Criticism by George Santayana*, ed. Irving Singer (New York: Scribners, 1956), pp. 44-45.

85. Lowell, *Notebook*, p. 160.

86. Lowell, *Dolphin*, pp. 59, 47, 48, 22.

87. Bell, *Robert Lowell*, p. 195.

88. Lowell, *Dolphin*, p. 54.

89. Ibid., p. 34.

90. Bell, *Robert Lowell*, pp. 198-99.

91. Bedient, "Illegible Lowell (The Late Volumes)," in *Robert Lowell: Essays on the Poetry*, ed. Steven Gould Axelrod and Helen Deese (Cambridge: Cambridge University Press, 1986), pp. 150-51. Bedient's quote is from Lowell, *Dolphin*, p. 35.

92. Lowell, *Dolphin*, p. 28.

93. Ibid., pp. 23, 47.

94. See, for one example, the way she quotes him in the sonnet "Marriage?" and then uses an automotive metaphor that he picks up a sonnet later. She even suggests he use a phrase of hers in his *Notebook*—and he quotes her suggestion. Ibid., p. 52.

95. Reading *The Dolphin* without knowing how it all came out "in real life," you might well see the poet's return to New York as a permanent one: the result of some late tinkering with sonnet order by the poet. The final tribute to the Dolphin-Muse thus slips into the past tense, with a valedictory tone. (And, as fate had it, the poet *did* return to Hardwick, dying as he took a taxi to her apartment.)

96. Anatole Broyard, "Parents and Purple Prose: Let's Give Them a Break," *New York Times Book Review*, November 30, 1986, p. 14.

97. Lowell, *Day by Day* (New York: Farrar, Straus, Giroux, 1977), p. 127.

98. Lowell, *Dolphin*, p. 50.

Chapter 5 Solitude Shared

1. Stanton, "Solitude of Self," pp. 247–48. "For the treatment of the treatment of the universal, in politics, metaphysics, or anything," writes Whitman in "Democratic Vistas," "sooner or later we come down to one single, solitary soul." This radical individualism finds an answer for him, as it does not seem to for Stanton in this speech, in democracy's aspect of "adhesiveness or love." *Complete Poetry*, pp. 960, 946.

2. Rich, "Splittings," "When We Dead Awaken," and "Transcendental Etude," in *Fact*, pp. 229, 151, 268–69.

3. For more on Rich's ethical, "relational subjectivity," see Kevin McGuirk, "Philoctetes Radicalized: 'Twenty-one Love Poems' and the Lyric Career of Adrienne Rich," *Contemporary Literature* 34 (Spring 1993): 61–87.

4. Creeley, *Collected Essays*, p. 158.

5. Emerson, *CW,* 2:121.

6. Rich, "Twenty-One Love Poems," in *Fact*, p. 261.

7. Cavell, "Two Cheers," p. 91.

8. Rich, *Fact*, pp. 3, 5, and *On Lies*, p. 43.

9. Rich, "Novella," in *Fact*, p. 51.

10. "Stepping Backward" echoes all of these, in roughly this order. See Rich, *Fact*, pp. 6–7.

11. Ibid., p. 7.

12. Emerson, *CW,* 3:29.

13. See Cavell, "Founding," p. 87. As I have argued elsewhere, one poet of this "handsome" Emersonianism is Rich's contemporary John Ashbery. See my essay "When I'm Calling You."

14. Kern, *Culture of Love*, p. 285.

15. Rich, *Fact*, p. 7.

16. Rich, "Ideal Landscape," *Fact*, p. 13. This early hope is quite Whitmanian. "Whitman is able," writes M. Wynn Thomas, "to turn . . . disturbing feelings of inadequacy and isolation into common ground between human beings. They become the inevitable corollary of social involvement, a reflex of social activity, and are therefore accepted as an immutable aspect of social experience. The historically specific problems Whitman experienced in participating in mid-nineteenth-century American life are in the process subtly translated into existential problems that are an eternal part of the human condition. . . . Self-consciousness is seen as an unavoidable consequence of human consciousness; isolation becomes an inescapable aspect of individuated being; and so those experiences that threatened to be divisive . . . are themselves turned against the odds into strong social adhesives." *Lunar Light*, pp. 112–13. As I will show, Rich finds the

"social adhesives" of shared separateness inadequate, at least until they are returned to their ground in historical being. For extended reflections on Whitman by Rich, see her *What Is Found There*, pp. 90–96, and "The Genesis of 'Yom Kippur 1984' " in *Adrienne Rich's Poetry*, ed. Barbara Charlesworth Gelppi (New York: Norton, 1991), pp. 255–56.

17. Rich, *Fact*, p. 8.

18. Ibid., p. 130.

19. Rich, "A Marriage in the 'Sixties," in ibid., p. 45.

20. Rich, *Fact*, p. 131.

21. See Michael Fischer, *Stanley Cavell and Literary Skepticism* (Chicago: University of Chicago Press, 1989), p. 65.

22. Creeley, *Collected Essays*, pp. 170–73.

23. Ibid., p. 173.

24. Rich, *Fact*, p. 50.

25. David Kalstone, *Five Temperaments* (New York: Oxford University Press, 1977), p. 154.

26. Rich, *Fact*, p. 76; Dickinson, P 872.

27. Rich, *Fact*, p. 45.

28. Ibid., p. 205.

29. Kalstone, *Five Temperaments*, p. 154.

30. "The oppressive forces," Charles Altieri explains, are "not ontological features . . . but political factors that prevent language from fulfilling functions inherent in its potential nature." *Self and Sensibility in Contemporary American Poetry* (Cambridge: Cambridge University Press, 1984), p. 179.

31. Rich, *Fact*, p. 103.

32. Whitman, *Complete Poetry*, pp. 947, 960.

33. Rich, *Fact*, pp. 193–94.

34. Stanton, "Solitude of Self," p. 254.

35. Ibid., pp. 253–54, 247; my emphasis.

36. For a useful summary of such thought in the context of women's love poetry, see Ostriker, *Stealing the Language*, pp. 166–68.

37. Robin West, "Jurisprudence and Gender," *University of Chicago Law Review* 55 (Winter 1988): 2–3.

38. Rich, *Fact*, p. 193.

39. West, "Jurisprudence," p. 40.

40. Rich, "Amnesia," *Fact*, p. 208; Rich quoted in Gelpi, *Adrienne Rich's Poetry*, p. 118.

41. Rich, "Natural Resources," in *Fact*, pp. 258, 261.

42. Whitman, *Complete Poetry*, pp. 564–65.

43. Rich, *Fact*, p. 463.

44. Matthew Arnold, "Culture and Anarchy," in *Poetry and Criticism of Matthew Arnold*, ed. A. Dwight Culler (Boston: Houghton Mifflin, 1961), p. 467.

45. Altieri, *Self*, p. 174.

46. Erkkila, *Wicked Sisters*, pp. 171–72.

47. Kristeva, *Tales*, pp. 254–45; Louise Glück, *Ararat* (New York: Ecco, 1990), p. 56.

48. Rich, *Fact*, p. 222.

49. Stanton, "Solitude of Self," p. 248.

50. See Rich, *On Lies*, pp. 306–7.

51. Erkkila, *Wicked Sisters*, p. 175.

52. Adrienne Rich, *Blood, Bread, and Poetry* (New York: Norton, 1986), p. x.

53. Rich, *On Lies*, p. 307.

54. Adrienne Rich, *Time's Power* (New York: Norton, 1989), p. 19.

55. Rich, *Fact*, pp. 151, 229. The persistence of separateness appears on a purely formal level, too, inscribed in Rich's lineation. See Helena Michie, *Sororophobia: Differences among Women in Literature and Culture* (New York: Oxford University Press, 1992), pp. 124, 126.

56. Rich, *Fact*, pp. 267, 263.

57. Stanton, "Solitude of Self," p. 253.

58. Rich, *Fact*, p. 232.

59. Ibid., p. 242.

60. Adrian Oktenberg, " 'Disloyal to Civilization': The Twenty-One Love Poems of Adrienne Rich," in *Reading Adrienne Rich: Reviews and Re-Visions, 1951–81*, ed. Jane Roberta Cooper (Ann Arbor: University of Michigan Press, 1984), p. 80.

61. De Rougemont, *Love*, p. 42.

62. Rich, *Fact*, pp. 235–36.

63. Stanton, "Solitude of Self," p. 253.

64. Rich, *Fact*, p. 237.

65. See ibid., pp. 6, 13.

66. Ibid., p. 239. For a useful discussion of Rich's wrestling with the tradition of sonnet sequences, see Jane Hedley, " 'Old Songs with New Words': The Achievement of Adrienne Rich's 'Twenty-One Love Poems,' " *Genre* 23 (Winter 1990): 325–54.

67. Rich, *Fact*, p. 242.

68. Ibid., p. 241.

69. Ibid., 241–42.

70. See Jan Montefiore, *Feminism and Poetry* (New York: Pandora, 1987), p. 164.

71. Rich, *Fact*, p. 245.

72. Cavell, *Claim*, p. 90.

73. Rich, *Fact*, p. 245; see McGuirk, "Philoctetes," p. 81.

74. Michie, *Sororophobia*, p. 129.

75. Fuller, "Great Lawsuit," p. 1210.

76. West, "Jurisprudence," p. 19.

77. Rich, *Fact*, p. 246.

78. Ibid., p. 246; Emerson, *CW*, 2:190.

79. Rich, "Transcendental Etude," in *Fact*, p. 268.

80. Whitman, *Complete Poetry*, pp. 1010–11; for a discussion of the effect of Rich's *Dream* on readers, see Michie, *Sororophobia*, p. 123.

221

81. See Michie, *Sororophobia*, p. 125.

82. Benjamin, *Bonds of Love*, pp. 174, 177.

83. Emerson, "Friendship," in *CW*, 2:121.

84. Erkkila, *Wicked Sisters*, p. 177.

85. Rich, *Fact*, p. 300.

86. See Erkkila, *Wicked Sisters*, p. 181.

87. Rich, *Fact*, pp. 275, 278.

88. Fuller, "Great Lawsuit," pp. 1198–99.

89. Emerson, *CW*, 2:109.

90. Rich, "Contradictions: Tracking Poems," in *Your Native Land, Your Life* (New York: Norton, 1986), p. 83. These images look back to the house and garden of "Culture and Anarchy," as well as to more immediate references in this particular sequence.

91. Ibid., pp. 103, 84–85.

92. I paraphrase a passage from *In Quest of the Ordinary*, in which Cavell hazards that the Ancient Mariner "may have wanted at once to silence the bird's claim upon him and to establish a connection with it closer, as it were, than his caring for it: a connection beyond the force of his human responsibilities, whether conventional or personal, either of which can seem arbitrary." *In Quest of the Ordinary: Lines of Skepticism and Romanticism* (Chicago: University of Chicago Press, 1990), p. 197.

93. Rich, *Your Native Land*, p. 76.

94. Rich, "On the Genesis of 'Yom Kippur 1984,' " p. 257, and *Your Native Land*, p. 77.

95. Benjamin, *Bonds of Love*, p. 47.

96. Rich, *Fact*, p. 7.

97. Rich, *Time's Power*, pp. 53–54.

98. Ibid., p. 54.

99. Quoted in Morgan, *Puritan Family*, p. 52.

100. Such love may lead one to value and enjoy the other's autonomy. In it, as Irving Singer says, "the lover takes an interest in the beloved as a person, and not merely as a commodity," so that "he bestows importance upon her needs and her desires, even when they do not further the satisfaction of his own." *Nature of Love*, 1:6. But unlike the love that Rich espouses, it does not *depend* on such interest in the other as autonomous, even resistant to the self.

101. Rich, *On Lies*, p. 43.

102. Rich, "Yom Kippur 1984," in *Your Native Land*, p. 77.

103. Auden, *Dyer's Hand*, p. 338.

104. James Merrill, "An Upward Look," *A Scattering of Salts* (New York: Knopf, 1995), p. 96.

Chapter 6 Soliloquy or Kiss

1. Van Duyn, *Merciful Disguises*, p. 33.

2. Cavell, *Quest*, p. 60.

3. Van Duyn, *Merciful Disguises*, p. 33.

4. Stevens, *Collected Poems*, pp. 241, 231–32.

5. My sense of the shape of Merrill's career, as well as my reading of several key poems, is indebted to the work of Caroline Anne Fraser, "A Perfect Contempt: The Poetry of James Merrill" (Ph. D. diss., Harvard University, 1987; Ann Arbor: UMI, 1988).

6. James Merrill, *From the First Nine: Poems 1946–1976* (New York: Atheneum, 1984), p. 361; see Stephen Yenser, *The Consuming Myth: The Work of James Merrill* (Cambridge: Harvard University Press, 1987), pp. 33–35.

7. James Merrill, *The Black Swan* (Athens: Icaros, 1946), p. 9.

8. Merrill "teethed" on Brooks and Warren, he confesses in an interview. See his *Recitative*, ed. J. D. McClatchy (San Francisco: North Point, 1986), p. 54. Surely Cleanth Brooks's "The Language of Paradox" was part of that early learning, with its praise for a poet who "has actually before our eyes built within the song the 'pretty room' with which he says the lovers can be content." *The Well Wrought Urn: Studies in the Structure of Poetry* (New York: Harcourt Brace Jovanovich, 1947), p. 17.

9. Helen Vendler, *The Odes of John Keats* (Cambridge: Harvard University Press, 1983), p. 49.

10. "Nor marble, nor the gilded monuments / Of princes shall outlive this powerful rhyme," Shakespeare swore in Sonnet 55. *Shakespeare's Sonnets*, ed. Stanley Wells (New York: Oxford University Press, 1985), p. 69. Here, though, any promise that anything will "live in this, and dwell in lovers' eyes" rings hollow.

11. John Keats, *The Poems*, ed. Gerald Bullett (New York: Knopf, Everyman's Library, 1992), pp. 203, 206.

12. James Merrill, *A Different Person* (New York: Knopf, 1993), pp. 53, 46, 113.

13. Stevens, *Collected Poems*, p. 161.

14. Merrill, *Selected Poems*, p. 85.

15. Ibid., p. 91.

16. Von Hallberg, *American Poetry*, p. 98.

17. Merrill, *Different Person*, p. 53.

18. Merrill, *Selected Poems*, p. 97; see Fraser, "Perfect Contempt," pp. 23–26.

19. Loy, *Lost Lunar Baedeker*, p. 68; Lowell, *Dolphin*, p. 20.

20. Quoted in McWhirter, *Desire and Love*, p. 1.

21. Hugh Kenner, *A Homemade World* (New York: Morrow, 1975), p. 75; Halliday, *Stevens*, p. 44.

22. Merrill, *Recitative*, p. 119. Merrill offers one other road not taken. "To use people as Frost did was something else again," he explains, since "a young poet could easily have been cowed by the sheer human experience needed in order to render 'real life' with even minimal authority. Thanks to the example of Stevens, this pressure could be postponed until the time came" (pp. 118–19). As I hope this chapter suggests, Merrill has managed to incorporate a good deal of "sheer human experience" into his work without sacrificing his Stevensian training.

23. Merrill, *Selected Poems*, p. 125.

24. Yenser, *Consuming Myth*, p. 149.

25. Merrill, *Selected Poems*, p. 131.

26. Kristeva, *Tales*, p. 4; see Fraser, "Perfect Contempt," pp. 60, 68–71.

27. Merrill, *Selected Poems*, p. 133.

28. Emerson, *CW,* 6:316; 3:44.

29. Lynn Keller, *Re-making It New: Contemporary American Poetry and the Modernist Tradition* (Cambridge: Cambridge University Press, 1987), p. 211.

30. Singer, *Nature of Love*, 1:21.

31. Krutch, *Modern Temper,* pp. 73, 77.

32. Merrill, *Selected Poems*, p. 132.

33. Keller, *Re-making,* pp. 207, 213.

34. Singer, *Nature of Love* 1:17, 19.

35. Merrill, *Selected Poems*, p. 133.

36. Plato, *Collected Dialogues*, pp. 492, 491; my emphasis.

37. Merrill, *Selected Poems*, p. 134.

38. Barthes, *Lover's Discourse*, p. 30.

39. Merrill, "To My Greek," in *Selected Poems*, p. 152.

40. Roland Barthes, *Roland Barthes*, trans. Richard Howard (New York: Farrar, Straus and Giroux, 1977), p. 91.

41. Merrill, *Selected Poems*, p. 163.

42. Stevens, *Collected Poems*, p. 524; Merrill, *Selected Poems*, p. 151. It may be objected that a poet with Merrill's love for wordplay would hardly mind the sort of loose pun we find in "common sense" and "common scenes." "A Freudian slip is taken seriously," he complains in "Object Lessons," because "it betrays its maker's hidden wish. The pun (or the rhyme, for that matter) 'merely' betrays the hidden wish of words." *Recitative*, p. 111. The date of this interview, though, is 1972, coinciding to my mind with the reconciliation with the muse we find in that year's collection of poems, *Braving the Elements*, and not with the tone of *The Fire Screen*.

43. See Fraser, "Perfect Contempt," pp. 89–90, 93.

44. Stevens, *Opus Posthumous*, p. 195; Merrill, *First Nine*, p. 189.

45. Emerson, "Nominalist and Realist," *CW,* 3:135; Whitman, "To You," in *Complete Poetry*, p. 376.

46. Merrill, *Scattering*, p. 96.

47. Merrill, *First Nine*, p. 193.

48. Lowell, *Dolphin*, pp. 78, 49.

49. William Butler Yeats, *The Collected Poems*, ed. Richard J. Finneran (New York: MacMillan, 1989), p. 347.

50. Merrill, *Selected Poems*, p. 156.

51. Gertrude Stein, *Selected Writings of Gertrude Stein*, ed. Carl Van Vechten (New York: Vintage, 1962), p. 270.

52. Merrill, *Selected Poems*, p.160; Friedrich Nietzsche, selections from *Daybreak: Thoughts on the Prejudices of Morality*, in *The Philosophy of (Erotic) Love*, ed. Robert. C. Solomon and Kathleen M. Higgins (Lawrence: University of Kansas Press, 1991), p. 142.

53. Kristeva, *Tales*, p. 380.

54. Ibid., p. 77.

55. Merrill, *First Nine*, p. 200.

56. How badly? As if in resistance or as an example, he goes so far as to urge the very embodiment of his craft to "speak freely, without art": an insulting, impossible demand. Merrill, *Selected Poems*, p. 200.

57. Henry James, *Literary Criticism: French Writers, Other European Writers, The Prefaces to the New York Edition* (New York: Library of America, 1984), p. 1063.

58. Henry James, "The Art of Fiction," in *The Art of Criticism: Henry James on the Theory and the Practice of Fiction*, ed. William Veedar and Susan M. Griffin (Chicago: University of Chicago Press, 1986), p. 172.

59. Merrill, *First Nine*, p. 201.

60. Yenser, *Consuming Myth*, pp. 163–64.

61. Kalstone, *Five Temperaments*, p. 109.

62. Merrill, *Selected Poems*, pp. 161–62.

63. Kalstone, *Five Temperaments*, p. 110; Yenser, *Consuming Myth*, p. 164.

64. "Mornings" and "Matinees" are linked by more than etymology. It's as though the "flue choking with the shock" of anger in "Mornings" caused the "coughing fit" the boy declares himself "so sorry" for in the later poem. Merrill, *Selected Poems*, p. 166.

65. Ibid., pp. 169, 170, 171.

66. Stendhal, selections from *On Love*, in *Philosophy of (Erotic) Love*, p. 135.

67. Merrill, *Selected Poems*, pp. 177, 220–21.

68. Yenser, *Consuming Myth*, p. 176.

69. Quoted in James Merrill, "The Book of Ephraim," in *Divine Comedies* (New York: Atheneum, 1983), p. 106.

70. Merrill, "The Summer People," in *Selected Poems*, pp. 175–76; "Mandala," in *First Nine*, p. 252. For more on Merrill's changing stance toward artifice during this period, see Fraser, "Perfect Comtempt," pp. 152–53.

71. Merrill, "Log," in *Selected*, p. 189.

72. Merrill, *Selected Poems*, p. 191; my emphasis.

73. Ibid., pp. 192–93.

74. Merrill, "Days of 1971," in ibid., p. 235.

75. Merrill, "Strato in Plaster," in ibid., p. 224.

76. Kristeva, *Tales*, p. 46.

77. Merrill, *Selected Poems*, pp. 195, 198.

78. Kalstone, *Five Temperaments*, p. 79.

79. Merrill, *Selected Poems*, pp. 202–3.

80. Ibid., p. 197.

81. Ibid., p. 229.

82. Ibid., p. 228. For a fuller reading of this poem, see Fraser, "Perfect Comtempt," p. 215.

83. Merrill, "In Nine Sleep Valley," in *Selected Poems*, p. 215.

84. Kristeva, *Black Sun*, pp. 206–7.

85. His tutor is probably neither Stevens nor Williams, of course, but W. H. Auden, who advises us in the "New Year's Letter" that "'To set in order'" is "the task / Both Eros and Apollo ask." *Collected Poems*, ed. Edward Mendelson (New York: Random House, 1976), p. 161.

86. Merrill, *Selected Poems*, p. 216.

87. Auden, *Dyer's Hand*, p. 338.

88. Merrill, *Selected Poems*, pp. 217, 225.

89. David Perkins, *A History of Modern Poetry: Modernism and After* (Cambridge: Harvard University Press, 1987), p. 652.

90. Merrill, *Divine Comedies*, p. 103.

91. Merrill, *Selected Poems*, p. 291.

92. Emerson, *W*, 6:316.

93. Merrill, *Scattering*, p. 96.

94. Merrill, "The House Fly," in *Late Settings* (New York: Atheneum, 1985), p. 34.

Bibliography

Altieri, Charles. *Self and Sensibility in Contemporary American Poetry*. Cambridge: Cambridge University Press, 1984.

Anderson, Douglas. *A House Undivided: Domesticity and Community in American Literature*. Cambridge: Cambridge University Press, 1990.

Arnold, Elizabeth. "Mina Loy and the Futurists." *Sagetrieb* 8 (Spring/Fall 1989): 83–117.

Arnold, Matthew. "Culture and Anarchy." In *Poetry and Criticism of Matthew Arnold*, ed. A. Dwight Culler. Boston: Houghton Mifflin, 1961.

Arrowsmith, William. "Eros in Terre Haute: T. S. Eliot's 'Lune de Miel.'" *New Criterion* 1 (October 1982): 22–41.

Ashbery, John. *Self-Portrait in a Convex Mirror*. New York: Penguin, 1976.

Auden, W. H. *Collected Poems*. Ed. Edward Mendelson. New York: Random House, 1976.

——. *The Dyer's Hand*. New York: Vintage International, 1989.

Axelrod, Steven Gould. *Robert Lowell: Life and Art*. Princeton: Princeton University Press, 1978.

Bacigalupo, Massimo. *The Formèd Trace: The Later Poetry of Ezra Pound*. New York: Columbia University Press, 1980.

Bakhtin, Mikhail Mikhailovich. *The Dialogic Imagination*. Ed. Michael Holquist. Trans. Caryl Emerson and Michael Holquist. Austin: University of Texas Press, 1981.

Banta, Martha. *Imaging American Women: Idea and Ideals in Cultural History*. New York: Columbia University Press, 1987.

Barthes, Roland. *A Lover's Discourse: Fragments*. Trans. Richard Howard. New York: Farrar, Straus and Giroux, 1978.

——. *Roland Barthes*. Trans. Richard Howard. New York: Farrar, Straus and Giroux, 1977.

Bataille, George. *Erotism: Death and Sensuality*. New York: Ballantine Books, 1962.

Bates, Milton J. *Wallace Stevens: A Mythology of Self*. Berkeley: University of California Press, 1985.

Bauerlein, Mark. *Whitman and the American Idiom*. Baton Rouge: Louisiana State University Press, 1991.

Beauvoir, Simone de. *The Second Sex*. Trans. H. M. Parshley. New York: Knopf, 1953.

Bedient, Calvin. *He Do the Police in Different Voices: The Waste Land and Its Protagonist*. Chicago: University of Chicago Press, 1986.

———. "Illegible Lowell (The Late Volumes)." In *Robert Lowell: Essays on the Poetry*, ed. Steven Gould Axelrod and Helen Deese. Cambridge: Cambridge University Press, 1986.

Bell, Ian F. A. *Critic as Scientist: The Modernist Poetics of Ezra Pound*. New York: Methuen, 1981.

Bell, Vereen M. *Robert Lowell: Nihilist as Hero*. Cambridge: Harvard University Press, 1983.

Benjamin, Jessica. *The Bonds of Love: Psychoanalysis, Feminism, and the Problem of Domination*. New York: Pantheon, 1988.

Bennett, Paula. *Emily Dickinson: Woman Poet*. Iowa City: University of Iowa Press, 1990.

Bernstein, Charles. "Hearing 'Here': Robert Creeley's Poetics of Duration." In *Robert Creeley: The Poet's Workshop*, ed. Carroll F. Terrell, pp. 87–96. Orono, Me.: National Poetry Foundation, 1984.

Bloom, Allan. *Love and Friendship*. New York: Simon and Schuster, 1993.

Bloom, Harold. Introduction. *Walt Whitman*. New York: Chelsea House, 1985.

Boone, Joseph Allen. *Tradition Counter Tradition: Love and the Form of Fiction*. Chicago: University of Chicago Press, 1987.

Bordo, Susan R. *The Flight to Objectivity: Essays on Cartesianism and Culture*. Albany: SUNY Press, 1987.

Bradstreet, Anne. *The Works of Anne Bradstreet*. Ed. Jeannine Hensley. Cambridge: Harvard University Press, 1967.

Bremen, Brian A. *William Carlos Williams and the Diagnostics of Culture*. New York: Oxford University Press, 1993.

Brewster, Martha. *Poems on Divers Subjects*. Boston, 1757.

Brontë, Emily. *Wuthering Heights: An Authoritative Text with Essays in Criticism*. Ed. William M. Sale Jr. New York: Norton, 1963.

Brooks, Cleanth. *The Well Wrought Urn: Studies in the Structure of Poetry*. New York: Harcourt Brace Jovanovich, 1947.

Broyard, Anatole. "Parents and Purple Prose: Let's Give Them a Break." *New York Times Book Review*, November 30, 1986, p. 14.

Burke, Carolyn. *Becoming Modern: The Life of Mina Loy*. New York: Farrar, Straus and Giroux, 1996.

———. "The New Poetry and the New Woman: Mina Loy." In *Coming to Light: American*

Women Poets in the Twentieth Century, ed. Diane Wood Middlebrook and Marilyn Yalom, pp. 37–57. Ann Arbor: University of Michigan Press, 1985.

Byatt, A. S. *Possession: A Romance*. New York: Random House, 1990.

Byers, Thomas B. *What I Cannot Say: Self, Word, and World in Whitman, Stevens, and Merwin*. Chicago: University of Illinois Press, 1989.

Carpenter, Humphrey. *A Serious Character: The Life of Ezra Pound*. Boston: Houghton Mifflin, 1988.

Carson, Anne. *Eros the Bittersweet*. Princeton: Princeton University Press, 1986.

Casillo, Robert. *The Genealogy of Demons: Anti-Semitism, Fascism, and the Myths of Ezra Pound*. Evanston, Ill.: Northwestern University Press, 1988.

Cavell, Stanley. *The Claim of Reason*. New York: Oxford University Press, 1979.

——. *Disowning Knowledge in Six Plays of Shakespeare*. Cambridge University Press, 1987.

——. "Founding as Finding." In *This New Yet Unapproachable America*, pp. 77–119. Albuquerque: Living Batch Press, 1989.

——. *In Quest of the Ordinary: Lines of Skepticism and Romanticism*. Chicago: University of Chicago Press, 1990.

——. "Two Cheers for Romance." In *Passionate Attachments*, ed. Williard Gaylin and Ethel Person, pp. 85–100. London: Macmillan, 1988.

Chambers-Schiller, Lee. *Liberty, a Better Husband: Single Women in America; the Generations of 1780–1840*. New Haven: Yale University Press, 1984.

Chessman, Harriet Scott. *The Public Is Invited to Dance: Representation, the Body, and Dialogue in Gertrude Stein*. Stanford, Calif.: Stanford University Press, 1989.

Clark, Suzanne. *Sentimental Modernism: Women Writers and the Revolution of the Word*. Bloomington: Indiana University Press, 1991.

Crane, Hart. *The Complete Poems and Selected Letters and Prose of Hart Crane*. Ed. Brom Weber. Garden City, N.Y.: Doubleday, 1966.

Creeley, Robert. *The Collected Essays of Robert Creeley*. Berkeley: University of California Press, 1989.

——. *The Collected Poems of Robert Creeley*. Berkeley: University of California Press, 1982.

——. *The Collected Prose of Robert Creeley*. Berkeley: University of California Press, 1988.

——. *Later*. New York: New Directions, 1979.

——. *Tales Out of School: Selected Interviews*. Ann Arbor: University of Michigan Press, 1993.

Cunningham, J. V. *Collected Poems and Epigrams*. Columbus: Ohio University Press, 1971.

Daly, Robert. *God's Altar: The World and the Flesh in Puritan Poetry*. Berkeley: University of California Press, 1978.

Dana, Richard Henry, Sr. *Poems*. Boston: Bowles and Dearborn, 1827.

Derrida, Jacques. *Of Grammatology*. Trans. Gayatri Chakravorty Spivak. Baltimore: Johns Hopkins University Press, 1974.

Dickinson, Emily. *The Complete Poems of Emily Dickinson*. Ed. Thomas H. Johnson. Boston: Little, Brown, 1960.

———. *The Letters of Emily Dickinson*. 3 vols. Ed. Thomas H. Johnson and Theodora Ward. Cambridge: Belknap Press / Harvard University Press, 1958.

———. *Love Poems*. White Plains, N.Y.: Peter Pauper Press. Undated.

Diehl, Joanne Feit. *Women Poets and the American Sublime*. Bloomington: Indiana University Press, 1990.

Diggory, Terence. *William Carlos Williams and the Ethics of Painting*. Princeton: Princeton University Press, 1991.

Donne, John. *Selected Poetry and Prose*. Ed. T. W. Craik and R. J. Craik. New York: Methuen, 1986.

Doolittle, Hilda [H.D.]. *Bid Me to Live*. Redding Ridge, Conn.: Black Swan Books, 1983.

———. *Collected Poems 1912–1944*. New York: New Directions, 1983.

———. *End to Torment*. New York: New Directions, 1979.

———. *Hermetic Definition*. New York: New Directions, 1972.

———. *HERmione*. New York: New Directions, 1981.

———. *Notes on Thought and Vision and The Wise Sappho*. San Francisco: City Lights Books, 1982.

Duffy, Bernard. *Poetry in America: Expression and its Values in the Times of Bryant, Whitman, and Pound*. Durham, N. C.: Duke University Press, 1978.

Duncan, Robert. "After *For Love*." In *Robert Creeley's Life and Work: A Sense of Increment*, ed. John Wilson, pp. 95–102. Ann Arbor: University of Michigan Press, 1987.

DuPlessis, Rachel Blau. *The Pink Guitar: Writing as Feminist Practice*. New York: Routledge, 1990.

Edelberg, Cynthia Dubin. *Robert Creeley's Poetry: A Critical Introduction*. Albuquerque: University of New Mexico Press, 1978.

Eliot, Thomas Stearns. *The Complete Poems and Plays, 1909–1962*. New York: Harcourt, Brace and World, 1962.

———. *Selected Essays*. New York: Harcourt, Brace and World, 1960.

———. *The Waste Land: Facsimile and Transcript of the Original Drafts*. Ed. Valerie Eliot. New York: Harcourt Brace Jovanovich, 1971.

Emerson, Ralph Waldo. *Collected Poems and Translations*. Ed. Harold Bloom and Paul Kane. New York: Library of America, 1994.

———. *The Collected Works of Ralph Waldo Emerson*. 4 vols. to date. Ed. Alfred R. Ferguson et al. Cambridge: Belknap Press/Harvard University Press, 1971–.

———. *The Complete Sermons of Ralph Waldo Emerson*. 4 vols. Ed. Albert J. von Frank. Columbia: University of Missouri Press, 1989–92.

———. *The Early Lectures of Ralph Waldo Emerson*. 3 vols. Ed. Stephen E. Whicher, Robert

E. Spiller, and Wallace E. Williams, Cambridge: Belknap Press/Harvard University Press, 1959–72.

———. "Historic Notes of Life and Letters in New England." In *The Complete Works of Ralph Waldo Emerson*, ed. Edward Waldo Emerson. Vol. 10. Boston: Houghton Mifflin, 1903–4.

———. *The Journals and Miscellaneous Notebooks of Ralph Waldo Emerson*. 16 vols. Ed. William H. Gilman et al. Cambridge: Belknap Press/Harvard University Press, 1960–82.

———. *The Letters of Ralph Waldo Emerson*. 6 vols. Ed. Ralph L. Rusk. New York: Columbia University Press, 1939.

———. *Poems*. Vol. 10 of *The Complete Works of Ralph Waldo Emerson*. Ed. Edward Waldo Emerson. Boston: Houghton Mifflin, 1903–4.

Erkkila, Besty. *The Wicked Sisters: Women Poets, Literary History, and Discord.* New York: Oxford University Press, 1992.

Faderman, Lillian. "Emily Dickinson's Letters to Sue Gilbert." *Massachusetts Review* 18 (Summer 1977): 197–225.

Farr, Judith. *The Passion of Emily Dickinson.* Cambridge: Harvard University Press, 1992.

Feder, Lillian. "Pound and Ovid." In *Ezra Pound Among the Poets*, ed. George Bornstein, pp. 13–34. Chicago: University of Chicago Press, 1985.

Fiedler, Leslie. *No! in Thunder.* Boston: Beacon Press, 1960.

Fischer, Michael. *Stanley Cavell and Literary Skepticism.* Chicago: University of Chicago Press, 1989.

Fisher, Barbara M. *Wallace Stevens: The Intensest Rendezvous.* Charlottesville: University Press of Virginia, 1990.

Frank, Elizabeth Perlmutter. "A Doll's Heart: The Girl in the Poetry of Edna St. Vincent Millay and Louise Bogan." In *Critical Essays on Edna St. Vincent Millay*, ed. William B. Thesing, pp. 179–199. New York: G. K. Hall, 1993.

Franklin, R. W. *The Editing of Emily Dickinson: A Reconsideration.* Madison: University of Wisconsin Press, 1967.

Fraser, Caroline Anne. "A Perfect Contempt: The Poetry of James Merrill." Ph.D. diss, Harvard University 1987. Ann Arbor: UMI, 1988.

French, William, and Timothy Materer. "Far Flung Vortices: Ezra's 'Hindoo' Yogi." *Paideuma* 11 (Spring 1982): 39–53.

Freud, Sigmund. *Sexuality and the Psychology of Love.* New York: Collier Books, 1963.

Friedman, Susan Stanford. *Psyche Reborn: The Emergence of H.D.* Bloomington: Indiana University Press, 1981.

Froula, Christine. *A Guide to Ezra Pound's Selected Poems.* New York: New Directions, 1983.

Fuller, Margaret. "The Great Lawsuit." In *The Harper American Literature*, ed. Donald McQuade et al., pp. 1178–212. Vol. 1. New York: Harper and Row, 1987.

Gardella, Peter. *Innocent Ecstasy*. New York: Oxford University Press, 1985.

Gelpi, Barbara Charlesworth, and Albert Gelpi. *Adrienne Rich's Poetry*. New York: Norton, 1975.

Ginsberg, Allen. *Collected Poems 1947–1980*. New York: Harper and Row, 1984.

Glück, Louise. *Ararat*. New York: Ecco, 1990.

Goldman, Emma. "Marriage and Love." In *The Philosophy of (Erotic) Love*. Ed. Robert C. Solomon and Kathleen M. Higgins, pp. 208–13. Lawrence: University Press of Kansas, 1991.

Gordon, Lyndall. *Eliot's Early Years*. New York: Oxford University Press, 1977.

——. *Eliot's New Life*. New York: Farrar, Straus, Giroux, 1988.

Graham, Theodora R. " 'Her Heigh Compleynte': The Cress Letters of William Carlos Williams' Paterson." In *Ezra Pound and William Carlos Williams: The University of Pennsylvania Conference Papers*, ed. Daniel Hoffman, pp. 164–93. Philadelphia: University of Pennsylvania Press, 1983.

Graves, Robert. *The White Goddess*. New York: Farrar, Straus and Giroux, 1966.

Grossman, Allen, and Mark Halliday. *The Sighted Singer: Two Works on Poetry for Readers and Writers*. Baltimore: Johns Hopkins University Press, 1992.

Grossman, Jay. " 'The Evangel-Poem of Comrades and of Love': Revising Whitman's Republicanism." *ATQ* 4, n.s. (September 1990): 201–18.

Guest, Barbara. *Herself Defined: The Poet H.D. and Her World*. New York: Doubleday, 1984.

Gura, Philip. F. "The Study of Colonial American Literature, 1966–1987: A Vade Mecum." *William and Mary Quarterly* 45 (April 1988): 305–41.

Hagstrum, Jean. *Esteem Enlivened by Desire: The Couple from Homer to Shakespeare*. Chicago: University of Chicago Press, 1991.

Haller, William, and Malleville Haller. "The Puritan Art of Love." *Huntington Library Quarterly* 5 (January 1942): 235–72.

Halliday, Mark. *Stevens and the Interpersonal*. Princeton: Princeton University Press, 1991.

Hammond, Jeffrey A. *Sinful Self, Saintly Self: The Puritan Experience of Poetry*. Athens: University of Georgia Press, 1993.

Hedley, Jane. " 'Old Songs with New Words': The Achievement of Adrienne Rich's 'Twenty-One Love Poems.' " *Genre* 23 (Winter 1990): 325–54.

Hewitt, Mary E. *Poems: Sacred, Passionate, and Legendary*. New York: Lamport, Blakeman, 1854.

Homans, Margaret. *Bearing the Word: Language and Experience in Nineteenth Century Women's Writing*. Chicago: University of Chicago Press, 1986.

——. " 'Oh, Vision of Language!': Dickinson's Poems of Love and Death." In *Feminist Critics Read Emily Dickinson*, ed. Suzanne Juhasz, pp. 114–33. Bloomington: Indiana University Press, 1983.

Horne, William. *Making a Heaven of Hell: The Problem of the Companionate Ideal in English Marriage Poetry, 1650–1800*. Athens: University of Georgia Press, 1993.

Howe, Susan. *My Emily Dickinson.* Berkeley: North Atlantic Books, 1985.

Hughes, Gertrude Reif. " 'Imagining the Existence of Something Uncreated': Elements of Emerson in Adrienne Rich's *The Dream of a Common Language.*" In *Reading Adrienne Rich,* ed. Jane Roberta Cooper, pp. 151–70. Ann Arbor: University of Michigan Press, 1984.

Hughes, Walter. " 'Meat Out of the Eater': Panic and Desire in American Puritan Poetry." In *Engendering Men: The Question of Male Feminist Criticism,* ed. Joseph Allen Boone and Michael Cadden, pp. 102–21. New York: Routledge, 1990.

James, Henry. "The Art of Fiction." In *The Art of Criticism: Henry James on the Theory and the Practice of Fiction,* ed. William Veeder and Susan M. Griffin, pp. 165–96. Chicago: University of Chicago Press, 1986.

———. *Prefaces to the New York Edition.* In *Literary Criticism: French Writers, Other European Writers, The Prefaces to the New York Edition,* pp. 1035–342. New York: Library of America, 1984.

James, William. *The Principles of Psychology,* selections. In *William James: The Essential Writings.* Ed. Bruce W. Wilshire. Albany: SUNY Press, 1984.

Kalstone, David. *Five Temperaments.* New York: Oxford University Press, 1977.

Kaplan, Justin. *Walt Whitman: A Life.* New York: Simon and Schuster, 1980.

Keats, John. *The Poems.* Ed. Gerald Bullett. New York: Knopf/Everyman's Library, 1992.

Keller, Karl. "Notes on Sleeping with Emily Dickinson." In *Feminist Critics Read Emily Dickinson,* ed. Suzanne Juhasz, pp. 67–79. Bloomington: Indiana University Press, 1983.

———. *The Only Kangaroo among the Beauty: Emily Dickinson and America.* Baltimore: Johns Hopkins University Press, 1979.

Keller, Lynn. *Re-making It New: Contemporary American Poetry and the Modernist Tradition.* Cambridge: Cambridge University Press, 1987.

Kenner, Hugh. *A Homemade World.* New York: Morrow, 1975.

———. "The Making of the Modernist Canon." In *Mazes,* pp. 28–42. San Francisco: North Point Press, 1989.

Kern, Stephen. *The Culture of Love: Victorians to Moderns.* Cambridge: Harvard University Press, 1992.

Killingsworth, M. Jimmie. *Whitman's Poetry of the Body: Sexuality, Politics, and the Text.* Chapel Hill: University of North Carolina Press, 1989.

Kouidis, Virginia M. *Mina Loy: American Modernist Poet.* Baton Rouge: Louisiana State University Press, 1980.

———. "Prison into Prism: Emerson's 'Many-Colored Lenses' and the Woman Writer of Early Modernism." In *The Green American Tradition: Essays and Poems for Sherman Paul,* ed. H. Daniel Peck, pp. 115–34. Baton Rouge: Louisiana State University Press, 1989.

Kristeva, Julia. *Black Sun.* New York: Columbia University Press, 1989.

———. "Joyce 'The Gracehoper' or the Return of Orpheus." In *James Joyce: The Augmented Ninth,* ed. Bernard Benstock, pp. 167–80. Syracuse University Press, 1988.

——. *Revolution in Poetic Language*. Trans. Margaret Waller. New York: Columbia University Press, 1984.

——. *Tales of Love*. Trans. Leon S. Roudiez. New York: Columbia University Press, 1987.

Krutch, Joseph Wood. *The Modern Temper: A Study and a Confession*. New York: Harcourt, Brace, 1929.

Larson, Kerry C. *Whitman's Drama of Consensus*. Chicago: University of Chicago Press, 1988.

Lawrence, D. H. *Studies in Classic American Literature*. New York: Viking, 1961.

Leites, Edmund. "The Duty to Desire: Love, Friendship, and Sexuality in Some Puritan Theories of Marriage." *Comparative Civilizations Review* 10–11 (1983–84): 117–49.

——. *The Puritan Conscience and Modern Sexuality*. New Haven, Yale University Press, 1986.

Leverenz, David. *Manhood and the American Renaissance*. Ithaca: Cornell University Press, 1989.

Longenbach, James. *Stone Cottage: Pound, Yeats, and Modernism*. New York: Oxford University Press, 1988.

Longfellow, Henry Wadsworth. *Selected Poems*. New York: Viking Penguin, 1988.

Low, Anthony. *The Reinvention of Love: Poetry, Politics and Culture from Sidney to Milton*. Cambridge: Cambridge University Press, 1993.

Lowell, Robert. *Day by Day*. New York: Farrar, Straus, Giroux, 1977.

——. *The Dolphin*. New York: Farrar, Straus, Giroux, 1973.

——. *For Lizzie and Harriet*. New York: Farrar, Straus, Giroux, 1973.

——. *Life Studies and For the Union Dead*. New York: Farrar, Straus, Giroux, 1964.

——. *Notebook*. New York: Farrar, Straus, Giroux, 1970.

——. *Notebook 1967–68*. New York: Farrar, Straus, Giroux, 1969.

Loy, Mina. *The Lost Lunar Baedeker*. Ed. Roger L. Conover. New York: Farrar, Straus, Giroux, 1996.

Lystra, Karen. *Searching the Heart: Women, Men, and Romantic Love in Nineteenth-Century America*. New York: Oxford University Press, 1989.

Mariani, Paul. *Lost Puritan: A Life of Robert Lowell*. New York: Norton, 1994.

——. *William Carlos Williams: A New World Naked*. New York: McGraw Hill, 1981.

McCormick, John. " 'The Heyday of the Blood': Ralph Waldo Emerson." In *American Declarations of Love*, ed. Ann Massa. London: Macmillan, 1990.

McGuirk, Kevin. "Philoctetes Radicalized: 'Twenty-One Love Poems' and the Lyric Career of Adrienne Rich." *Contemporary Literature* 34 (Spring 1993): 61–87.

McWhirter, David. *Desire and Love in Henry James*. Cambridge: Cambridge University Press, 1989.

Melville, Herman. *Pierre*. In *Pierre; Israel Potter; The Piazza Tales; The Confidence Man; Uncollected Prose; Billy Budd, Sailor*. New York: Library of America, 1984.

Merleau-Ponty, Maurice. *The Prose of the World.* Evanston, Ill.: Northwestern University Press, 1973.

Merrill, James. *The Black Swan.* Athens: Icaros, 1946.

——. *A Different Person.* New York: Knopf, 1993.

——. *Divine Comedies.* New York: Atheneum, 1983.

——. *From the First Nine: Poems 1946–1976.* New York: Atheneum, 1984.

——. *Late Settings.* New York: Atheneum, 1985.

——. *Recitative.* Ed. J. D. McClatchy. San Francisco: North Point Press, 1986.

——. *A Scattering of Salts.* New York: Knopf, 1995.

——. *Selected Poems: 1946–1985.* New York: Knopf, 1992.

Mesch, Harold. "Robert Creeley's Epistemopathic Path." In *Robert Creeley: The Poet's Workshop,* ed. Carroll F. Terrell, pp. 57–86. Orono, Me.: National Poetry Foundation, University of Maine at Orono, 1984.

Michie, Helena. *Sororophobia: Differences among Women in Literature and Culture.* New York: Oxford University Press, 1992.

Millay, Edna St. Vincent. *Collected Sonnets.* Revised and expanded edition. New York: Harper and Row, 1988.

Milton, John. "The Doctrine and Discipline of Divorce." In *Complete Poems and Major Prose,* ed. Merritt Y. Hughes, pp. 696–715. New York: Macmillan, 1957.

——. *Paradise Lost.* In *Complete Poems and Major Prose,* ed. Merritt Y. Hughes, pp. 211–469. New York: Macmillan, 1957.

Miyake, Akiko. *Ezra Pound and the Mysteries of Love: A Plan for The Cantos.* Durham, N. C.: Duke University Press, 1991.

Montefiore, Jan. *Feminism and Poetry.* New York: Pandora, 1987.

Moon, Michael. "Rereading Whitman under Pressure of AIDS." In *The Continuing Presence of Walt Whitman: The Life after the Life,* ed. Robert K. Martin. Iowa City: University of Iowa Press, 1992.

Morgan, Frederick. *The Puritan Family: Religion and Domestic Relations in Seventeenth-Century New England.* New York: Harper and Row, 1966.

Morris, Adelaide. " 'The Love of Thee—A Prism Be': Men and Women in the Love Poetry of Emily Dickinson." In *Feminist Critics Read Emily Dickinson,* ed. Suzanne Juhasz, pp. 98–113. Bloomington: Indiana University Press, 1983.

——. "A Relay of Power and of Peace: H.D. and the Spirit of the Gift." In *Signets: Reading H.D.,* ed. Susan Stanford Friendman and Rachel Blau DuPlessis, pp. 52–82. Madison: University of Wisconsin Press, 1990.

Nathanson, Terry. *Whitman's Presence: Body, Voice, and Writing in* Leaves of Grass. New York: New York University Press, 1992.

Neely, Carol Thomas. "The Structure of English Renaissance Sonnet Sequences." *ELH* 45 (1978): 359–89.

Nietzsche, Friedrich. *The Birth of Tragedy and The Case of Wagner.* Trans. Walter Kaufman. New York: Vintage, 1967.

———. Selections from *Daybreak: Thoughts on the Prejudices of Morality.* In *The Philosophy of (Erotic) Love*, ed. Robert C. Solomon and Kathleen M. Higgins, pp. 140–43. Lawrence: University of Kansas Press, 1991.

Nussbaum, Martha C. *Love's Knowledge: Essays on Philosophy and Literature.* New York: Oxford University Press, 1990.

Oderman, Kevin. *Ezra Pound and the Erotic Medium.* Durham, N. C.: Duke University Press, 1986.

O'Hara, Frank. *Selected Poems.* Ed. Donald Allen. New York: Vintage, 1974.

Oktenberg, Adrian. " 'Disloyal to Civilization': The *Twenty-One Love Poems* of Adrienne Rich." In *Reading Adrienne Rich*, ed. Jane Roberta Cooper, pp. 72–90. Ann Arbor: University of Michigan Press, 1984.

Olson, Charles, and Robert Creeley. *The Complete Correspondence.* Ed. George Butterick. Vol. 2. Santa Barbara: Black Sparrow Press, 1980.

Ortega y Gasset, José. *On Love.* Trans. Talbot. New York: Meridian Books, 1957.

Ostriker, Alicia. "Loving Walt Whitman and the Problem of America." In *The Continuing Presence of Walt Whitman: The Life after the Life*, ed. Robert K. Martin, pp. 217–231. Iowa City: University of Iowa Press, 1992.

———. *Stealing the Language: The Emergence of Women's Poetry in America.* Boston: Beacon Press, 1986.

Paglia, Camille. *Sexual Personae.* New Haven: Yale University Press, 1990.

Pearce, Roy Harvey. *The Continuity of American Poetry.* Princeton: Princeton University Press, 1961.

Pearson, Gabriel. "For Lizzie and Harriet: Robert Lowell's Domestic Apocalypse." In *Modern American Poetry*, ed. R. W. Butterfield, pp. 187–203. Totowa, N.J.: Barnes and Noble, 1984.

Perkins, David. *A History of Modern Poetry: Modernism and After.* Cambridge: Harvard University Press, 1987.

Plato. *Lysis, Phaedrus*, and *The Symposium.* In *The Collected Dialogues of Plato*, ed. Edith Hamilton and Huntington Cairns. Princeton: Princeton University Press, 1963.

Polhemus, Robert M. *Erotic Faith: Being in Love from Jane Austen to D. H. Lawrence.* Chicago: University of Chicago Press, 1990.

Pollak, Vivian R. *Dickinson: The Anxiety of Gender.* Ithaca: Cornell University Press, 1984.

Pound, Ezra. *The Cantos of Ezra Pound.* New York: New Directions, 1970.

———. *Collected Early Poems of Ezra Pound.* Ed. Michael John King. New York: New Directions, 1976.

———. *The Spirit of Romance.* New York: New Directions, 1968.

Quartermain, Peter. *Disjunctive Poetics: From Gertrude Stein and Louis Zukofsky to Susan Howe.* Cambridge: Cambridge University Press, 1992.

Railton, Stephen. " 'As If I Were With You'—The Performance of Whitman's Poetry." In *The Cambridge Companion to Walt Whitman*, ed. Ezra Greenspan. pp. 7–26. Cambridge: Cambridge University Press, 1995.

Reynolds, David S. *Walt Whitman's America: A Cultural Biography.* New York: Knopf, 1995.

Rich, Adrienne. *An Atlas of the Difficult World.* New York: Norton, 1991.

———. *Blood, Bread, and Poetry.* New York, Norton, 1986.

———. "Caryatid: A Column." *American Poetry Review* 2 (September/October 1973) 10–11.

———. *Collected Early Poems: 1950–1970.* New York: Norton, 1993.

———. *Dark Fields of the Republic.* New York: Norton, 1995.

———. *The Fact of a Doorframe: Poems Selected and New, 1950–84.* New York: Norton, 1984.

———. "The Genesis of 'Yom Kippur 1984.'" In *Adrienne Rich's Poetry and Prose,* ed. Barbara Charlesworth Gelpi, pp. 252–57. New York: Norton, 1993.

———. *On Lies, Secrets, and Silence.* New York: Norton, 1979.

———. *Time's Power.* New York: Norton, 1989.

———. *What Is Found There: Notebooks on Poetry and Politics.* New York: Norton, 1993.

———. *Your Native Land, Your Life.* New York: Norton, 1986.

Richardson, Robert D., Jr. *Emerson: The Mind on Fire.* Berkeley: University of California Press, 1995.

Rilke, Rainer Maria. *Letters to a Young Poet.* Trans. with a foreword by Stephen Mitchell. Boston: Shambhala, 1993.

Rosenmeier, Rosamund. *Anne Bradstreet Revisited.* Boston: Twayne, 1991.

Rothman, Ellen K. *Hands and Hearts: A History of Courtship in America.* New York: Basic Books, 1984.

Rougemont, Denis de. *Love in the Western World.* Trans. Montgomery Belgion. New York: Schocken, 1983.

Royce, Josiah. *Studies of Good and Evil.* New York: Appleton, 1898.

Saffin, John. *John Saffin His Book (1665–1708).* Introduction by Caroline Hazard. New York: Harbor Press, 1928.

Santayana, George. "Platonic Love in Some Italian Poets." In *Essays in Literary Criticism by George Santayana,* ed. Irving Singer, pp. 40–102. New York: Scribners, 1956.

Scheick, William J. *Design in Puritan American Literature.* Lexington: University Press of Kentucky, 1992.

Schweitzer, Ivy. *The Work of Self-Representation: Lyric Poetry in Colonial New England.* Chapel Hill: University of North Carolina Press, 1991.

Seidman, Steven. *Romantic Longings: Love in America, 1830–1980.* New York: Routledge, 1991.

Selinger, Eric. "'Too Pathetic, Too Pitiable': Emerson's Lessons in Love's Philosophy." *ESQ: A Journal of the American Renaissance* 40, no. 2 (1994): 139–82.

———. "When I'm Calling You: Reading, Romance, and Rhetoric in and around Hart Crane's 'Voyages.'" *Arizona Quarterly* 47 (Winter 1991): 85–118.

Sewall, Richard B. *The Life of Emily Dickinson.* New York: Farrar, Straus, Giroux, 1974.

Shakespeare, William. *Shakespeare's Sonnets*. Ed. Stanley Wells. New York: Oxford University Press, 1985.

Shreiber, Maeera Yaffa. "The Discourse of Love in the Lyric and the Letter." Ph.D. diss., Brandeis University, 1991. Ann Arbor: UMI, 1992.

Sieburth, Richard. *Instigations: Ezra Pound and Remy de Gourmont*. Cambridge: Harvard University Press, 1978.

Simmons, Thomas. *Erotic Reckonings: Mastery and Apprenticeship in the Work of Poets and Lovers*. Chicago: University of Illinois Press, 1994.

Singer, Irving. *The Nature of Love, Volume 1: Plato to Luther*. University of Chicago Press, 1984.

———. *The Nature of Love, Volume 2: Courtly and Romantic*. University of Chicago Press, 1984.

———. *The Nature of Love, Volume 3: The Modern World*. University of Chicago Press, 1984.

Smith, Martha Nell. *Rowing in Eden: Rereading Emily Dickinson*. Austin: University of Texas Press, 1992.

Spengemann, William C. *A New World of Words: Redefining Early American Literature*. New Haven: Yale University Press, 1994.

———. "Review Essay [of Emory Elliot's *Puritan Influences in American Literature*]." *Early American Literature* 16 (1981): 179–84.

Stanford, Ann. *Anne Bradstreet: The Worldly Puritan*. New York: Burt Franklin, 1974.

Stanton, Elizabeth Cady. "The Solitude of Self." In *Elizabeth Cady Stanton / Susan B. Anthony: Correspondence, Writings, Speeches*. Ed. Ellen Carol DuBois. New York: Schocken Books, 1981.

St. Armand, Barton Levi. *Emily Dickinson and Her Culture: The Soul's Society*. Cambridge: Cambridge University Press, 1984.

Stein, Gertrude. *Selected Writings of Gertrude Stein*. Ed. Carl Van Vechten. New York: Vintage, 1962.

———. *The Yale Gertrude Stein*. Ed. Richard Kostelanetz. New Haven: Yale University Press, 1980.

Stendhal. Selections from *On Love*. In *The Philosophy of (Erotic) Love*, ed. Robert C. Solomon and Kathleen M. Higgins. Lawrence: University of Kansas Press, 1991.

Stevens, Wallace. *The Collected Poems*. New York: Vintage Books, 1982.

———. *Opus Posthumous*. Ed. Milton J. Bates. New York: Vintage Books, 1990.

Stimpson, Catherine R. "Gertrude Stein and the Transposition of Gender." In *The Poetics of Gender*, ed. Nancy K. Miller, pp. 1–18. New York: Columbia University Press, 1986.

Stonum, Gray Lee. *The Dickinson Sublime*. Madison: University of Wisconsin Press, 1990.

Swenson, May. *The Love Poems of May Swenson*. Boston: Houghton Mifflin, 1991.

Taylor, Edward. *The Poems of Edward Taylor*. Ed. Donald E. Stanford. Chapel Hill: University of North Carolina Press, 1989.

Thatcher, Thomas. "A Love Letter." In *Seventeenth-Century American Poetry*, ed. Harrison T. Meserole, p. 406. New York: New York University Press, 1968.

Thomas, M. Wynn. *The Lunar Light of Whitman's Poetry*. Cambridge: Harvard University Press, 1987.

Thurin, Erik Ingvar. *Emerson as Priest of Pan*. Lawrence: Regents Press of Kansas, 1981.

Tupper, Martin F. *Proverbial Philosophy*. London: Thomas Hatchard, Piccadilly. 1854.

Van de Velde, M.D., Th. H. *Ideal Marriage: Its Physiology and Technique*. New York: Random House, 1941.

Van Duyn, Mona. *Merciful Disguises: Published and Unpublished Poems*. New York: Atheneum, 1973.

Vendler, Helen. *The Music of What Happens*. Cambridge: Harvard University Press, 1988.

——. *The Odes of John Keats*. Cambridge: Harvard University Press, 1983.

Verduin, Kathleen. " 'Our Cursed Natures': Sexuality and the Puritan Conscience." *New England Quarterly* 56 (June 1983): 220–37.

Von Hallberg, Robert. *American Poetry and Culture, 1945–1980*. Cambridge: Harvard University Press, 1985.

Walker, Cheryl. *The Nightingale's Burden: Women Poets and American Culture before 1900*. Bloomington: Indiana University Press, 1982.

Walsh, John Evangelist. *The Hidden Life of Emily Dickinson*. New York: Simon and Schuster, 1971.

Warner, Michael. "Homo-Narcissism: or, Heterosexuality." In *Engendering Men: The Question of Male Feminist Criticism*, ed. Joseph Allen Boone and Michael Cadden, pp. 190–206. New York: Routledge, 1990.

Watts, Emily Stipes. *The Poetry of American Women from 1632 to 1945*. Austin: University of Texas Press, 1977.

West, Robin. "Jurisprudence and Gender." *University of Chicago Law Review* 55 (Winter 1988): 1–72.

Whitman, Walt. *Complete Poetry and Collected Prose*. New York: Library of America, 1982.

——. *Notebooks and Unpublished Prose Manuscripts*. Ed. Edward F. Grier. New York: New York University Press, 1984.

——. *Uncollected Poetry and Prose of Walt Whitman*, Vol. 2. Ed. Emory Holloway. New York: Doubleday, 1921.

Williams, William Carlos. *The Collected Poems of William Carlos Williams, Volume 1: 1909–1939*. Ed. A. Walton Litz and Christopher MacGowan. New York: New Directions, 1986.

——. *The Collected Poems of William Carlos Williams, Volume 2: 1939–1962*. Ed. Christopher MacGowan, New York: New Directions, 1988.

——. *Imaginations*. New York: New Directions, 1970.

——. *Many Loves and Other Plays*. New York: New Directions, 1961.

———. *Paterson*. New York: New Directions. 1963.

———. *Selected Letters*. Ed. John C. Thirlwall. New York: McDowell, Obolensky, 1957.

Williamson, Alan. *Introspection and Contemporary Poetry*. Cambridge: Harvard University Press, 1984.

———. *Pity the Monsters: The Political Vision of Robert Lowell*. New Haven: Yale University Press, 1974.

Winthrop, John. "A Modell of Christian Charity." In *Winthrop Papers*. Vol. 2, pp. 282–95. Boston: Massachusetts Historical Society, 1931.

Wolff, Cynthia Griffin. *Emily Dickinson*. New York: Knopf, 1986.

Wordsworth, William. *Selected Poems and Prefaces*. Ed. Jack Stillinger. Boston: Houghton Mifflin, 1965.

Yeats, William Butler. *The Collected Poems*. Ed. Richard J. Finneran. New York: Macmillan/Collier Books, 1989.

Yenser, Stephen. *Circle to Circle: The Poetry of Robert Lowell*. Berkeley: University of California Press, 1975.

———. *The Consuming Myth: The Work of James Merrill*. Cambridge: Harvard University Press, 1987.

Zukofsky, Louis. *Bottom; On Shakespeare*. Berkeley: University of California Press, 1986.

Zweig, Paul. *Walt Whitman: The Making of the Poet*. New York: Basic Books, 1984.

Index